Performance Practice and Process

d
10.9.08

Also by Elaine Aston and Geraldine Harris
FEMINIST FUTURES? Theatre, Performance, Theory

By Elaine Aston and Sue-Ellen Case
STAGING INTERNATIONAL FEMINISMS

This book is dedicated to the artists and participants of the Women's Writing for Performance Project (AHRC), 2003–6

Contents

List of Illustrations

Cover: 'Meringues' by Bobby Baker. Photograph © Andrew Whittuck
November 2006

Acknowledgements

The research for this book comes out of the 'Women's Writing for Performance' Project (2003–6), and we acknowledge our debt to the Arts and Humanities Research Council for funding this programme. It would also not have been possible without the support, generosity and inspiration of the practitioners, scholars and scholar-practitioners who participated in project workshops and events. A special thank you to all of the artists in this volume and also to project artists Gilly Adams, Geddy Aniksdal, Marisa Carnesky, Anna Furse, and Jackie Kay for their exciting and illuminating workshops. We are extremely grateful to have worked 'beside' an administrator of the quality of Susie Wood, whose wide ranging abilities are as extraordinary as her good humour. Our heartfelt thanks also go to Mike Bowen, Dave Blacow, Andy Sellers and Janan Yakula of Lancaster University Television Unit for their hard work and their patience with our technical hitches. Our gratitude also to Kerstin Bueschges, Sarah O'Brien and Lena Šimić, all of whom were vital members of the Lancaster team, and to all our other colleagues in Theatre Studies and the Nuffield Theatre. For Gerry – as always – thank heavens for Colin Knapp. For Elaine – a thank you to Maggie, Daniel and June, and to summer friends at Theritas and Tassos in Acharavi, Corfu, all of whom, one way or another, help to keep me going.

1
Performance Practice and Process

Contemporary [Women] Practitioners

Making a difference

This is a practice-based study that focuses on a selection of contemporary [women] practitioners. It arises out of a three-year project backed by the Arts and Humanities Research Council (AHRC), who funded us to research the performance-making strategies of a number of artists for whom a resistant gender practice is in some way important to their creativity. The main methodology of the project centred on a series of twelve practitioner-led workshops lasting between three and five days and supported by interviews with the artists. These events presented us with a unique opportunity to explore these artists' work from the *inside*: to be with them *at* work rather than, as is more customary, to comment from a position of post-performance analysis and reflection. Although we entitled our AHRC project 'Women's Writing for Performance', in our framing we explained 'writing' as always more than, and beyond 'text', and following the lead of such feminist thinkers as Gayatari Spivak and Judith Butler, we defined 'women' as an expansive and contingent category.[1] As a result, our focus on a resistant gender practice was to include consideration of the intersections between the discourses of gender, 'race', ethnicity and sexualities, amongst others, just as we aimed to cover a number of different fields of 'making' across theatre and performance traditions.

This study selects eight of the artists/companies with whom we worked during the course of the three years to detail their performance stories, processes and practice. Bobby Baker, Curious (Leslie Hill and Helen Paris), SuAndi, Sarah Daniels, Split Britches (Peggy Shaw and Lois Weaver), Rebecca Prichard, Vayu Naidu and Jenny Eclair are all seminal to their respective fields of performance.[2] Between them they cover a

1

range of performance genres that include performance art, live art, performance poetry, playwriting, performance storytelling, radio drama, stand-up comedy, and site-specific performance. Although very different in terms of genre, style and approach to 'gender matters', all of these practitioners can be said to operate artistically and politically on the principle that, to quote Lois Weaver: '*If you can imagine it you can make it. If you can make it then you can* change *it.*'[3]

Although all of these artists are women, we should make one thing clear from the outset: there is no attempt on our part to homogenise or to ghettoise them into some kind of specialist, women-only category. In the title of this book we have placed the word women in square brackets, again to signal the contingent nature of the term. Inevitably, the social experience of being gendered has played a significant, often major, role in the careers and in the work of all these artists, in terms of what they make and the social, cultural and theatrical conditions of their making. As such we can and do make connections and comparisons between them, artistically and politically, on the basis of this experience. Nevertheless, throughout the project our concern was also to explore the differences between the artists in terms of their own distinctive identities and their particular approaches to the genres of performance in which they practice.

Within these various genres, all of these practitioners are 'ground breaking' *regardless* of gender and in these terms the use of square brackets is also intended to signal a delicate balancing act. On the one hand, to omit the term 'women' altogether might support the 'postfeminist' fantasy that sometimes seems to circulate within the academy that gender and its attendant inequalities have been abolished by deconstruction and are no longer worth our attention. On the other hand, owing to the popularity of this fantasy and contemporary disconnections to feminism, it is again the case, as it was in the 1970s and 1980s, that to use this term in a title is to risk having the ideas, and more importantly the practice under discussion, being categorised as of interest only to a minority, and as marginal to 'more important' developments in the field. The square brackets therefore are intended to foreground the status of these women *as* practitioners whose work has had a significant impact and influence on the fields of theatre and performance as a whole. As such, a consideration of their practice and making processes is potentially of interest to *anyone* concerned with the practicalities and creative possibilities of artistically innovative and/or politically resistant performance-making.

Resisting the temptation, then, to 'write' these [women] artists back into some kind of narrativised 'whole', instead our aim is to share these quite different artists' stories, their processes and practices to stimulate and support 'making' in others. Our assumption is that many of the readers who read this book, like the majority of those who participated in the workshops, will be practitioners or practitioner-scholars, emergent and established, wanting to make performance work, looking for practical ideas and inspiration.[4] At the last public event of our project, an Artists' Forum hosted in London's Covent Garden,[5] Helen Paris (Curious) responded to a question about influences and role models by talking about the need to *'feed'* work. While who or what influences work can change over time, Helen explained, there is a constant need to be inspired by others: to engage with work by other artists as a way of *'putting stuff back in the bank'*. These different artists' stories are not therefore offered as a way of inviting others to make work like 'x' or 'y', but as a way of *'feeding'* and encouraging new, quite different kinds of performance, in others.

Conditions of making work

Between them, the artists featured in this study span approximately 40 years of performance making, from the 1970s through to the present day. This means that the conditions of making work have changed over the years, from the 'alternative', feminist and queer theatre opportunities in the 1970s at the time that Bobby Baker and Split Britches began making work, through the Thatcherite backlash against publicly funded arts in the 1980s Britain as experienced by Sarah Daniels and Jenny Eclair, the various funding (policy driven) initiatives around Black and Asian arts that SuAndi and Vayu Naidu have encountered (for better and for worse), to the attention to masculinities in the 1990s that Rebecca Prichard ran up against, and the current climate of postfeminism and a funding squeeze on the arts that means artists increasingly have to think imaginatively about how to 'place' their work, as Curious have done. Gender, 'race', sexualities, age – all of these figure variously in our artists' chapters not just as factors in the work but also in the material, social and cultural conditions of its making.

Nevertheless, there is not a single artist in this study who would advise a would-be practitioner to give up or to wait for 'better' times. They all agree that there is nothing else for it but to get out there and *make it happen*. 'Top tips' from the artists repeatedly stress the need to have confidence in the work, to refuse to take 'no' for an answer, to find ways and means to create it anyway, and to actively seek out spaces for it to be seen and audiences to see it. If money is a problem, Peggy Shaw advises, '*rob a bank*' – although perhaps a safer (stay-out-of-jail) option might be, as several other artists suggested, to create the work in your bedroom if necessary and show it somewhere else other than a theatre. Several of the practitioners in this study have performed in domestic spaces, outside in public spaces or in pubs, clubs, museums and other multi-functioning community venues. While our two contributing playwrights, Sarah Daniels and Rebecca Prichard, each have their own stories to tell about the difficulties of getting work on in theatres, the opportunities that radio offers as a medium for the first-time writer is, as Sarah advises, not to be overlooked. Also, Rebecca's reminder that '*there is a real hunger for new work and new voices*' is to be kept in mind: theatre and performance traditions *need* new makers to innovate and to revitalise. In other words, new makers need to understand themselves as essential to performance, even while the obstacles to making work may, at times, feel overwhelmingly stacked against them.

One obstacle mentioned not just by the workshop artists but also by many of the other practitioners we encountered throughout the project can be the lack of a support system, both practical and creative, and a consequent sense of isolation. This is particularly true for the amount of solo-making that we encountered over the last three years, both in professional practice and in 'practice as research' (PaR) projects within Higher Education, not just in Britain but also in the US and Australia. In the light of this apparent trend, what needs to be attended to more than our experience suggests is happening are the different kinds of artistic collaborations that can take place, most especially in terms of 'directorial' or 'editorial' input occurring at different points in the production process. Even practitioners primarily known as solo artists such as SuAndi, Vayu Naidu and Bobby Baker often collaborate with other performers, musicians, dancers, and so forth, while Jenny Eclair frequently works closely with another writer, Julie Balloo. Although the nature of these collaborations vary, they are achieved in ways that allow for a high level of 'authorial' control, and the same applies to 'directorial' or 'editorial' input. Obviously for playwrights like Sarah and Rebecca mutually supportive relationships with the theatre directors who realise their scripts in production are crucial, and Vayu has Chris Banfield as a director for her larger-scale shows. Curious and Split Britches each find different ways to collaborate within their respective partnerships: for their solo pieces, Leslie and Helen work as each other's 'outside eye'; Lois and Peggy always work closely together, with Lois functioning sometimes as co-devisor/co-performer/director/editor, sometimes just in the latter two roles. Bobby has evolved a making relationship with Pol Baloh-Brown, who comes to the process later on, after ideas have taken shape, but before they have been fully realised as a performance.

For us, it seems vital to recognise and explore the possibilities of all these very different models of collaboration, as they emerge in the chapters that follow, not least because they are informative and instructive about the processes of collaboration that are already occurring, but especially because they point to new and more expansive understandings about the role of those who 'direct' and/or 'facilitate' theatre and performance work. Moreover, several of the workshop artists stressed the enormous difference administrative support can make and how encouragement from arts workers such as Lois Keidan, a key figure in the development of Live and Performance Art in Britain, has been crucial and much appreciated by them at various moments in their careers.

Practice and process as open, passionate and labour intensive

As much as reading the individual artists' chapters will confirm the diversity of their processes and performance work, there are various points that we would like to cite as common to their personal and creative conditions for making work. First and foremost, every artist was adamant about being open to all creative possibilities, rather than closing down any options in advance. As well as seeking out 'alternative' spaces for performing, the majority of them have worked across and between numerous different forms and media and taken on various sorts of projects aimed at different types of 'communities'. In part this reflects the material hardships that artists generally face when trying to earn a living, and why, as SuAndi advocates, it may be a good idea to '*say yes to everything*' and only afterwards negotiate or reflect on what may be viable or desirable. Yet this also frequently points to a broader canvas of creativity than in the field in which an artist is best known. Although it is impossible for us to cover all of this in the different chapters, we do signal it to varying degrees, whether this is the detailed account of Sarah's work for radio, to which far less attention has been paid than to her theatre career, or noting that Jenny is also a published novelist, or that in addition to performance poetry SuAndi now also works on 'high culture' projects including opera.

Second, in making their work, all the artists tend to question and disrupt not just the orthodoxies of theatre and performance practice, but all kinds of other 'orthodoxies', often including those of feminism, academic or otherwise. Speaking at our London forum, for example,[6] Marisa

Carnesky, known for her work in 'burlesque', recollected her early years when she worried if it was possible to mix up her desire to explore her Jewish heritage and her concerns as a feminist with her interest in the fetish club scene and, in particular, an image which she could only describe as a 'gothic prostitute'. Could she be a (Jewish) feminist in a corset? Ultimately, Marisa argued that it is no good being puritanical about such desires since taking on and working through the kinds of contradictions and paradoxes they produce can be a dynamic driving force in creativity.

Related to both of these points above, we observed that all of the artists have a real passion for their work, or rather are passionate about whatever it is they want to, *have to* say through their performances. These are 'burning issues' that take root at deeply personal and or political depths and map with a commitment to exploring the best possible ways and means of giving them expression and communicating them to audiences. It might sound clichéd to say so, but for all of the artists there is a life-long commitment to the work they make, and it is hard to cite their passion without, at the same time, observing that what goes hand in hand with this is the hard labour that goes into making work. As any one involved in theatre-making knows, even in the most favourable of conditions, there is considerable labour involved in conceiving, devising and/or writing a show and bringing it to production. More than that, however, are the years that go into acquiring skills and the creative know-how for performance-making, alongside the gestation of ideas that are not necessarily the inspiration of a moment, but often the product of long periods of consideration and experimentation on the artist's part. The painstaking and, at times, painful process of finding out what does and does not 'work' demands a high degree of self-reflexivity and self-criticism. Many of the workshops artists were very open and generous in discussing or presenting to us examples of their own work that they judged in some way 'unsuccessful' to enable us to learn from their experience.

Allied to the sense of passion and the very real hard labour of making and production is the artists' belief in theatre and performance as inclusive practices. Personal experiences and stories underpin this belief, from Lois Weaver's joy at the very diverse communities of the Blue Ridge Mountains brought together by their first Split Britches show, to Sarah Daniels' damascene conversion from her experience of the (unimaginative uses) of drama in the school classroom to her (self) discoveries as a writer of what is achievable, creatively and politically, through theatre. More than this, however, for all of the practitioners, it is not just a question of keeping faith with one's own creativity, but of believing in theatre and performance as potentially enabling the creativity of others. This point especially surfaces in the artists' stories and experiences of working with socially disadvantaged communities – such as those we heard from Rebecca, Sarah, Lois and Peggy, who sometimes work in/for women's prisons. It also obtains as a general principle for all the project workshops, as all of the practitioners always operated on the principle that each and every one of us is capable of being creative. It is just a question of how to bring that creativity out. As project investigators we enjoyed the opportunities for exploring our own creativity, but we were especially inspired by the generosity of the artists in making their skills and knowledge available to others to adapt, use and make their 'own'.

Theory and 'practice as research'

Given the labour intensiveness of theatre and performance-making, in no sense could we argue our workshops with the artists as offering a comprehensive understanding and experience of their process and practice. As noted above, the initial motivation for undertaking this project was to investigate and to celebrate a body of gender-aware performance work in a 'postfeminist' climate, where we argue that there is a danger of a lack of attention being paid to [women's] performance practice. Nevertheless, more particularly, we also wanted to get back to, closer to, professional practice *on its own terms*.

In a majority of theatre departments in Higher Education in the UK, it has always been considered desirable, if not essential, for theatre staff to be able to 'perform' both critically and practically, to both theorise and to *do*, not as separate endeavours but as connecting up and complementing each other. The interdisciplinary theory explosion of the 1980s, and for us, given our research interests, specifically the explosion of feminist, queer and postcolonial theories, fuelled our thinking about [women's] performance practice. This growth in theory, whilst important and essential to philosophical and critical feminist thinking, as indeed it has been to the development of the field of performance studies as a whole, has nevertheless, tended to 'globalise' practice. By this we mean that practice has sometimes been used to *exemplify* or to explore interdisciplinary theories in ways that do not always take account of the specificity of the work itself and the creative, as well as social and political, contexts through which it is produced. In short, it could be argued that the attention to certain types of theory have sometimes made the theoretical apparatus itself, rather than the practice, the most important object of academic enquiry.

In the UK, attempts to counter these tendencies have come from the institutional definition and recognition of the term 'practice as research' (PaR). This mainly occurred as a result of the third Research Assessment Exercise in 1992[7] and was subsequently consolidated by the development of PhD programmes with PaR elements and later by funding initiatives from the AHRC. Yet as debates around PaR indicate and our various experiences of PaR projects (in Britain and elsewhere) suggest, in the final analysis, there is still sometimes a drive in such research to privilege knowledges drawn from interdisciplinary theories, rather than that which derives from the work of ground-breaking, professional practitioners.

One thing the workshops on this project dramatically (in all senses of the term) reminded us of is that if in theatre and performance studies 'theory' (interdisciplinary or otherwise) and practice connect and complement each other, they nevertheless remain distinct and distinctive fields of knowledge and ways of knowing. Central to this remembering was the instinctive decision we made on the very first day of the very first workshop with Jenny Eclair that rather than simply 'observing' the workshops as we had originally assumed (for reasons we no longer understand ourselves) we would participate in them. This decision was 'instinctive' because in the past both of us have always moved between theory and practice as teachers and sometimes in relation to professional practice and have taken part in similar events. We also have to admit that faced with Jenny Eclair it seemed a lot more *fun* to join in. Subsequently, usually both of us, but occasionally only one of us, always participated fully in the workshops.

The importance of this active participation might seem self-evident, and the influence of PaR was evinced in the fact that other workshop participants often included postgraduate students and younger lecturers. However, we also noted that virtually all the artists seemed extremely surprised that two academics of our generation were keen to understand their work on *their* terms rather than *ours*; through 'hands on' (and other body parts) experience. This might suggest that the 'dialogue' between the academy and professional practice is not yet entirely 'two way', not yet always taking place as an equal exchange.

Towards a notion of 'embodied knowledge'

In the event, our participation in the workshops was crucial in trying to move away from a paradigm of appropriating practice to interdisciplinary theory and towards an idea of what we came to term for ourselves as

'embodied knowledge'.[8] In the context of performance process and practice, the implications of this term may seem blindingly obvious and this,
in a sense, is actually the point, since the implication of the *blindingly*
obvious is often exactly that which is overlooked, especially from a position of the subtle complexities of 'high theory'. Clearly, the notion of
'embodied knowledge' points to modes of exchange and sharing of
knowledge and of understanding orientated towards the experiential,
the physical, and the material and, by extension, to the local and the
specific. For us it related particularly to moments in the workshop when
we literally came to understand something we thought we already knew,
'differently', in ways that involved the body as well as the mind.

However, we want to underline that in pursuing this notion we were
neither simply 'privileging' the physical, nor in any way or rejecting
'theory', interdisciplinary or otherwise. As contemporary feminist academics we would argue very strongly that there is no speaking, writing,
or doing that is not based on some sort 'theory' of the world and of who
'we' are within it. Indeed, for us the notion of 'embodied knowledge'
accepts the impossibility of entirely separating out the 'embodied' from
the abstract, the discursive and the intellectual. Yet this does not mean
that they are reducible to the same or that it is not productive to remark
upon and explore the differences between them.

These differences were apparent from the start of the workshop series
but came into sharp focus most especially in instances where we were
already familiar with a practitioner's work, where the artist had already
been the subject of extensive academic scrutiny. Participating in the
Split Britches workshop, for example, produced a dizzy sense of encountering a familiar object in a totally new light. As we note in Chapter 6, it
was not that our experience of Lois and Peggy's process contradicted the
various feminist and queer theories that have been used to discuss their
work. Rather, what we found was that their process could be said to literally 'embody' these theories, but in a way that was not only distinct
from, but was, in fact, in excess, of them. In short, the creative processes
we encountered in and through these events started to reveal the necessary *limits* of the feminist, queer and postcolonial discourses that we had
used to frame our project *as* theory and in ways that were productive
and conducive to further critical thinking.

These encounters sent us back to the artist's practice with a nagging
sense, not that something may have been entirely overlooked in previous academic discussions (including our own), but rather may not have
been given its proper due. Simultaneously, we re-turned to theory to try
to explore how and why this might be the case. Subsequently, Eve Kosofsky

Sedgwick's *Touching, Feeling*,[9] a book concerned with affect, pedagogy and performativity, became an important influence on our discussions of our experiences in the workshops. Initially, we were struck by the distinction Sedgwick makes between 'knowing' something and *realising* it, especially since she develops this notion as part of a discussion of learning as a 'processural' and repetitive undertaking that occurs in time and space and involves the body as well as the mind.[10] Our encounters with the artists' processes also made us responsive to Sedgwick's critique of what she terms 'theoretical hygiene' within recent queer and feminist – and by extension other post-modern – anti-essentialist theories.[11] While philosophically seeking to 'get beyond dualistic thinking', but inevitably often working in binary opposition to essentialism, too strict an application of this 'hygiene', so Sedgwick suggests, can become 'paranoid' and self-defeating, making it impossible to think beyond the versions of what we already know, or what we have already learned to look for.[12] Nevertheless, she is not suggesting the abandonment of a body of important and influential ideas, which she herself played a major role in formulating. Rather, she performs a 'loosening' and re-opening up of feminist and queer theory, to embrace and revisit other, arguably more expansive, ideas, attitudes and beliefs that have become problematic, even inadmissible, within anti-essentialism. In pursuing this, she offers a non-dualistic paradigm based on the notion of 'beside' – in which 'a number of elements may lie alongside one another though not an infinity of them'.[13] This then is an attempt at a model of thinking that acknowledges differences without either denying the possibility of community and connection or resorting to relativism.

The necessity of 'loosening up' on anti-essentialist 'hygiene' when encountering creative practice and process was evident, for instance, in the radio workshop with Sarah Daniels. As we discuss in Chapter 5, in her writing for this medium, Sarah employs what might be loosely termed 'realism'. Defined as a monolithic category, under the globalising effects of 'theory', both theatrical and interdisciplinary, realism, for some time now, has been characterised as always and inevitably a politically 'conservative' form. In approaching the work of this self-evidently, politically progressive practitioner then, it was crucial to look beyond this thinking, which reduces in advance the (potential) politics of a text entirely to its form. We had to be open to understanding the specific manner in which Sarah expands on aspects of realism to create work that explores issues of serious importance to large audiences and which is profoundly touching and full of hope, mainly because it *does* respect differences, while insisting on the possibility of community.

As this example indicates, the workshops constantly brought home to us the importance of *not* focussing on what we have already learned to look for, with reference to interdisciplinary theories but also to our pre-existing thinking about theatre and performance. For instance, many of the artists not only drew on well-known theatre games and exercises but sometimes on variants of the *same* games and exercises. As such, it rapidly became apparent that we had to resist the temptation to think that we already 'knew' the exercises we were doing and where they could take us, instead of allowing for the possibility of experiencing them anew in terms of the actual process being explored.

A particular revelatory moment occurred early on in the workshop series in 'Performing Words' led by Gilly Adams and Geddy Aniksdal.[14] As a 'training' workshop, this event lies outside the (chapter) scope of this study, but we want to refer to it here because it encapsulated for us the way that *embodying* an idea can carry you to a place of knowing differently. In the abstract, Geddy Aniksdal's insistence that workshop participants keep on (and on, and on) trying to find as many different ways of doing the same movement or speaking the same phrase might appear one of the most basic methods for helping to create what she calls a 'performance score'. Yet, used in conjunction with her emphasis on training and 'technique', designed to explore and to extend the expressive potential of the voice and body, and carried out over hours, rather than minutes, this 'basic' method becomes a rigorous discipline. In this context, it pushes both the mind and the body beyond the comfort zone, beyond ingrained habits of daily life and familiar conventions of performing to pose the question 'What is it possible to do on stage?' Is this blindingly obvious? Perhaps so, since it is (in theory) the 'core' question that drives all aesthetically and politically radical theatre and performance practice. In short, we already 'knew' this, but this question was literally embodied (given voice and body, in time and space) in this exercise in a way that enabled us to *realise* its implications in concrete terms. Above all, these terms include the necessity of working to outwit our own conscious and unconscious assumptions formed in advance, that there are things it is *not* possible (or permissible) to do on stage.

This realisation was one that we were brought to again and again, always anew and always in different ways in all the workshops. While this was not usually directly stated, the overwhelming majority of the tasks and exercises we undertook, or rather the particular *combinations* of tasks and exercises, whether focussed on writing or more physically orientated, aimed to surprise, shock, push, pull, gently persuade or laugh us out of our habitual 'comfort zones', our established and unquestioned ways of thinking and doing. This included ways of thinking and doing established by theatrical conventions and feminist theory, anti-essentialist or otherwise. Like the example Marisa Carnesky gave at the Artists' Forum of not being puritanical and of embracing rather than rejecting contradictions (see earlier), a feature common to all of the workshops was a refusal to self-censor, even when this might 'upset' politically 'correct' ideas of feminism or any other kind of 'ism'. In the enclosed 'laboratory' of the workshop, this eschewal of 'political correctness' was a way of bringing out into the open and being committed to working *through* ideas and issues around which in everyday life there is often silence, because they are so 'challenging'. Overcoming self-censoring, whether political, social, personal, theatrical or academic, is of course, incredibly hard to achieve and rarely sustainable for any significant length of time. To facilitate this, as well as strategies dedicated to moving us beyond our 'comfort zones', workshop exercises, tasks and structures were often designed to prompt ways of thinking and doing that were non-linear, associative, dialectal but without synthesis, or were based on circularity and 'layering' – all very much in accord with Sedgwick's notion of 'beside'. Equally important, and in a sense, reflecting these techniques, was that, as participants, we were constantly working 'beside', *with* and *for* each other, supporting, creatively cross-infecting, disrupting, transforming and re-interpreting each other's work both as co-makers and as 'audience'.

Again we must note that none of this is easy to achieve and sustain, but the moments when, as participants, we were 'open' and fully committed to these processes were intensely exciting, pleasurable and potentially *politically productive*. This was because these moments allowed us to begin to *realise* (physically, emotionally *and* intellectually) the possibilities, not just for coming to know what we know differently, but for *imagining and doing otherwise*. In short, these activities might be said to have embodied or *realised* something like the possibilities of non-dualistic models of thinking and doing, as signalled in the abstract by interdisciplinary, anti-essentialist theories.

Being in the moment

In these terms it is feasible to discuss some of the work undertaken at the workshops through familiar theoretical tropes, such as gender perfomativity, subversive repetition, parody and pastiche, and the crossing and confusing of boundaries between different cultural practices, the personal and the political, and between the fantasy, fictional and the 'real'. However, if as we are arguing here that the workshops 'embodied' and helped us to *realise* some of the implications of the anti-essentialist theories that originally framed our project, this realisation is retrospective. Moreover, it was only achieved because in the course of the workshops themselves we came to a different sort of understanding, frequently achieved via reference to ideas and languages that might, in fact, be deemed 'essentialist'. A prime example of this is the phrase 'being in the moment', which was used by several of the project practitioners and which, as may already be clear above, became key to our thinking around embodied knowledge. This phrase still has currency amongst a large number of theatre and performance practitioners. However, it now tends to be shunned by many academics because it is taken to suggest essentialist notions of 'being' as fixed and singular, and of a 'presence' based on this 'being' which has supposedly been exhaustively deconstructed by a wide range of interdisciplinary theorists. In terms of practice, the meaning of this phrase varies, but most of the time in the workshops we understood it as referring to trying to achieve a state of heightened awareness (of your surroundings, of the people you are working alongside and your audience) by drawing on all of your resources – physical, emotional as well as intellectual – so as to be able to respond to these multiple stimuli as immediately and spontaneously as practicable. In certain circumstances then, 'being in the moment' refers to achieving a state of physical and mental openness which attempts to circumvent any *conscious* distinction or delay between feeling, thinking and doing.

The more theoretically aware may notice that this description of a potentially 'essentialist' phrase, like that of Aniksdal's exercise cited earlier, is beginning to edge towards an idea of the blurring of traditional mind/body dualisms, in ways that once again are very much in accord with the ambitions of interdisciplinary, anti-essentialist theory. Or rather, we could say that it points towards a non-hierarchical understanding of the relationship between mind and body, in which they cannot be wholly 'separated', but are not necessarily reducible to the same thing either. In addition, we would argue that in performance practice, rather than as an abstract concept, it does not necessarily imply 'being' as fixed and 'essential'. Rather, when we came close to *realising* it in the workshops, it was not a moment of consciousness of a 'self' but an embodied sense of intensive *inter*action and *inter*relationship with others and with one's surrounding, in which there is something like a 'pause' in normative consciousness of self.[15]

As this discussion has began to demonstrate, something that *feels* obvious when realised in the context of the workshop can be difficult to analyse retrospectively, without, that is, resorting to the most dense and difficult theory (see note 14). Actually, we would argue that this level of

difficulty confirms process and practice as distinctive fields of knowledge and ways of knowing which may lay closely 'beside' other fields
but cannot 'simply' be appropriated or explained by them. This is, of
course, because if there is such a thing as embodied knowledge it is
transmitted and understood in the localised experience of the specific
moment. In contrast, academic analysis, 'theoretical' or otherwise, not
only tends towards the general and the global but is also, of course,
always either *before* or *after* the moment, or the event, of process and
practice, and never 'in' the moment. Hence our description of the workshops as events that appear to 'embody' certain theories but equally our
insistence that they remain separate and are, in fact, *excess* of these
ideas. In sum, because the workshops were all led by artists who are
ground-breaking, internationally recognised experts in the field of aesthetically and politically radical performance, and because like these
artists' practice, the workshops occurred between actual embodied subjects 'in the moment', they were sometimes more radical than the theories.
That is, they were able to go beyond the theories (including Sedgwick's)
towards *realising* the implications of and possibilities for imagining and
doing otherwise, in ways that theory can only signal in advance through
abstraction or analyse retrospectively.

The irony is that all of this means that the modes of 'embodied knowledge' we realised as participants in the workshops are seldom *directly*
represented in this book. Attempts we made to convey or analyse our
experiences 'in the moment' either ended in description too detailed to
contain in one volume or sent us spinning off further and further from
the actual practice into philosophical speculations that potentially
embrace the fields of phenomenology, psychology, or neuro-science.
Nevertheless, we would argue that these experiences have informed our
considerations of the practice and the process of these [women] practitioners, in important ways – encouraging us to be more 'open' and to
question what we already thought we knew about them. At the very
least, in the chapters that follow, we have tried, as far as possible, to
'embed' the theory which we are inevitably employing, to ensure that it
does not dominate our discussions, and to allow the practice and
processes to be in dialogue with theory but in its own language(s) and
on its own terms.

Thematic concerns

In line with our intention of considering the practice and process on its
own terms, when commissioning each artist for the project we asked

that their workshop should focus on sharing making strategies based on their own work, rather than addressing any particular themes or political issues. However, because all of the artists concerned *are* politically engaged, various 'issues', feminist and otherwise, often emerged and were explored in the course of the work albeit, once again, always in the context and usually within the specific 'languages' of the processes and practice in question.

Individual chapters rehearse and reflect on these points of feminist contact, but we would also like to single out two 'themes' that emerged variously across these events. Overwhelmingly, all the artists introduced making strategies that in some way or another drew on the personal and the autobiographical. Linked in the 1970s and 1980s with 'consciousness raising', this has been a recurring strategy in work concerned with the politics of identity for some considerable time. Focussing too heavily on this point in [women's] theatre and performance, however, risks overlooking the fact that *all* creative production (regardless of gender) is always in some way 'autobiographical' and implicitly confirming the traditional view that [men's] work is by contrast 'more universal', or at very least, has greater scope in its implications. Looking across the chapters in this volume, we would argue that there is much to learn from the variety and complexity of the ways and means by which the autobiographical is 'transformed' by these artists. For instance, it is worth comparing Curious's techniques for connecting local, embodied experiences with global, political questions to create text, with Split Britches' mixing up of the personal with fantasy, and/or using it to 'adapt' another text, and with Vayu's drawing on the personal in finding the 'Rasa' of a 'known story'. In relation to this theme of the autobiographical, it is also notable how many of these artists (Bobby, Curious, Vayu, SuAndi, Jenny) operate through a performance 'persona' that is based on themselves, but then again, how these personas are all 'formalised' in different ways according to the genre of performance and the specific relationship this sets up with the audience.

Second, we note a thematic interest in matters 'domestic', and this despite feminism's repeated challenge over the years to an idea of the 'domesticated feminine'. Bobby, and her 'Daily Life' series of performances, most obviously and centrally articulates a political engagement with the social roles of housewife, mother, and the domestic 'space' of women's lives. Yet the domestic also surfaces in a variety of other practices and thematics: from the 'over-the-garden-fence conversational style' of SuAndi's performance poetry, or the domestic as performance site in Curious's *On the Scent*, to the damaged young girls' lives Rebecca writes about, or the 'female complaints' that source Jenny's stand-up comedy. All of this suggests an urgent need for a more expansive and inclusive view of the 'domestic', one that gets beyond what Sarah's radio director/producer Sally Avens describes as its regrettable '*derogatory*' connotations. Indeed, encountering this as a thematic through process and practice, we would argue for an 'epic' view of the domestic as an important contemporary concern – one which encompasses Vayu's transgessive criss-crossings between the domestic, the feminine and cultures of war, or Jenny's 'monstering' of the commercial cultures' femininity. In short, the domestic (feminine) is no longer a 'home' affair, but in our contemporary moment opens out on to much bigger questions of social and political 'welfare', that most, if not all, of the artists engage with in some form or another.

Website

Over the course of the three-year workshop programme participants generated a great deal of creative material. When we first began to consider the shape and content of this book we tried to include examples of this work as related to particular exercises. However, we came to realise that, given the task of balancing this with our primary attention to the artists' process and practice, we would not be able to give this creativity the space it deserved. Recognising, however, that these responses may clarify and amplify accounts offered in this book, rather than lose these contributions altogether, we decided to post a number of examples of creative work and other project-related documentation on our Women's Writing for Performance (WWP) website: http://www.lancs.ac.uk/depts/theatre/womenwriting/. Within each of the different chapters there are moments when we direct readers to the 'Events Archive' on the website, for additional materials, which variously include samples of creative writing produced in response to set exercises, picture stills, film and audio footage. Our expectation is that this resource will assist with expanding on and illustrating points of discussion or reflection in this book, amplifying exercises through creative application and demonstration.

Voices

Finally, undertaking the 'Women's Writing for Performance' project has been a collaborative process from beginning to end: between artists and participants in the workshops, between participants in the different workshop groups, with the project administrator Susie Wood, and between ourselves in facilitating and researching the programme. In the writing of this volume, marking that collaboration are the ways in which we bring the artists' voices alongside our own, and our endeavours to write jointly about practice and process. In respect of the latter, mirroring the practice of our artists, we have 'processed' chapters between us, working as an outside eye for each other's responses, at the same time as allowing one or other of us to take the lead in realising a final version of a chapter. Ultimately, we have not tried to 'perform' this text as one voice, but have 'created' a textured rather than seamless narrative, marked by sometimes quite different tones and styles.

By the same token, while we had a rough template to follow for each chapter, based on telling an artist's performance biography, and reflecting on her making and performance strategies via the workshops, the differences between the artists means that chapters are by no means uniform, but vary in content to take an optimum account of the specific practice and process in view. In the case of Sarah and Jenny, for instance, both of their chapters required outlining the respective businesses of radio and of stand-up, and the (radically different) gendering of both these contexts, in order to situate the practice (s). For SuAndi, we felt it important to contextualise her work by exploring the problem of 'categorisation' Black British artists can face, both within the arts and within higher education. In contrast, with Split Britches, feminist and queer academic attention to their work meant that Lois and Peggy required relatively little introduction, and we move more quickly on than in some of our other chapters to reflect on their workshop, which was also one of the longer events in the series. Vayu, on the other hand, again required a much more detailed set-up in order to trace the evolution of her performance storytelling practice, especially as this practice may be less familiar (as it was to us) than some of the other theatre and performance arts considered in this volume. Although Bobby's work might be considered very 'familiar', given how much she is taught and studied in the UK academy, we felt that some of the 'ingredients' of her performance had received less attention, and these came to structure the writing of this particular chapter. Similarly, we were on quite familiar territory with Rebecca as a Royal Court writer, and the 'Court scene' required less contextualising than did Rebecca's writing in and for the prison communities in which she works. Finally, the chapter on Curious, Leslie and Helen reflects a difficulty we had throughout: of never being able to cover all of, or say everything about, an artist's work. Orientating their process through site, smell and performance elided attention that might otherwise have been given to other aspects of their work in arts and technology, had this been the focus of their Lancaster workshop.

This brings us to the final point of our introduction. Despite our discussion of 'embodied knowledge' above, we do not intend this study to elide traditional academic accounts of performance practice. Our proposal is that a research through practice culture, as reflected in this book, might enhance our understanding of performance practice, looked at 'beside' other such accounts. Moreover, this study still constitutes *our* interpretation of the artists' practice and of what occurred in the workshops. As such, it is not offered as the 'truth' of these events, or an accurate reflection of the way these artists themselves might perceive their own work. Nor would we like to suggest that having been given the opportunity to be 'inside' the work of these artists makes us in anyway 'experts' in their craft. Instead, it is the element of being taken by surprise, of delight, even at times bewilderment, that has brought us to the point of trying to reflect and think differently: seeing something in the work we had not seen before, 'in the moment', before the necessary and inevitable return to 'theory', after the event. Passionate about the project work we undertook and enthused by the creativity and generosity of all the artists and workshop participants, we present this collection of performance-making stories in order that they might inspire other practitioners, scholars and practitioner-scholars in the way they have inspired us.

Notes and references

1. See for example Judith Butler, *Bodies That Matter: On the Discursive Limits of 'Sex'* (London: Routledge: 1992), pp. 221–2.
2. The other workshops were led by Anna Furse, Jackie Kay, and Gilly Adams with Geddy Aniksdal. Aniksdal and Adams came to us twice with their training workshops 'Performing Words'. In conjunction with an international symposium hosted by the project in April 2006, we also had the opportunity to engage in a one-day workshop with Marisa Carnesky.
3. Lois Weaver quoted in the Split Britches workshop, Lancaster University, 12–15 January 2006.
4. Participants in the workshops came with a variety of interests in and experiences of performance-making. The overwhelming majority of these participants were women, recruited by application, and coming from a wide geographical reach within Britain, and occasionally from overseas. Since the workshops were funded by the AHRC we were able to make them free to participants.
5. Our Artists' Forum took place on 11 November 2006. Artists who formed the panel for this event were Bobby Baker, Leslie Hill, Helen Paris, Marisa

Carnesky and Vayu Naidu. See http://www.lancs.ac.uk/depts/theatre/womenwriting/, Events Archive, Artists' Forum.

6. Ibid.
7. The Research Assessment Exercise (RAE) – originally termed the Research Selectivity Exercise at its inception in 1986, and second exercise in 1989 – is the periodic review used to 'measure' research and allocate government funds accordingly to individual H.E. institutions in the UK. By the time of the third review in 1992, for theatre and performance studies, it had become crucial to find some way of taking practice-based research into account, alongside the more traditional kinds of (published) research output.
8. Originally we 'borrowed' this term from Bill Nichols' writing on the politics of television documentary. We have expanded upon it but an important debt remains; see Bill Nichols, *Blurred Boundaries: Questions of Meaning in Contemporary Culture* (Bloomington: Indiana University Press, 1994), p. 146–7.
9. Eve Kosofsky Sedgwick, *Touching, Feeling: Affect, Pedagogy, Performativity* (Durham & London: Duke University Press, 2003).
10. Sedgwick, *Touching, Feeling*, p. 167; also see pp. 173–5.
11. Ibid., p. 111; also see p. 145.
12. Ibid., p. 166; also see Chapter 4, pp. 123–151.
13. Ibid., p. 8.
14. 'Performing Words' took place from 29 March to 2 April 2004. For details of this event and documentation, including DVD, see WWP project website, http://www.lancs.ac.uk/depts/theatre/womenwriting/, Events Archive, 'Performing Words 1 and 2.
15. In making this point we are (loosely) borrowing an idea from Bryan Reynolds. In February 2006, Reynolds (UC Irvine, US) gave a guest lecture at Lancaster on 'Transversal Performance: Theaterspace, Emulative Authority, and the Force of Subjunctivity'. Reynolds is *both* a theorist and a performance practitioner and we found much of this paper exciting and relevant to our thinking about 'embodied knowledge'. However, in this instance, we decided not to follow up his arguments in detail, since they were rehearsed within a highly complex weave of philosophical fields (including neuro-science) concerned with transversal thinking.

2

A Passionate Desire to Communicate

Bobby Baker

Bobby Baker in *Box Story*. Photograph by Andrew Whittuck

As attested by the success of her work in experimental, community and mainstream contexts, the varied range of publications that (positively) review her shows, and the level of academic interest in her practice, Bobby Baker is one of Britain's best-known and most widely-acclaimed performance practitioners. When we asked her for her 'top tip' for emergent practitioners, she was taking a brief pause between preparations for presenting two performance pieces which, amongst other things, involved cooking several hundred fairy cakes and meringues.[1] Understandably, her response was '*hard work, incredibly hard work, just work, I know it's a cliché but as Einstein said, its about 1 per cent inspiration 99 per cent perspiration, people like me who have been successful in continuing to make work, we work bloody hard, we really do.*' While this is undoubtedly true, it is important to note that, as Bobby always underlines, wherever and whenever she speaks about her own practice, the vital factors *motivating* this hard work are the *ideas* she is '*passionately attempting to communicate*'.[2]

Finding the medium

While, like Split Britches and Curious, Bobby's work is now usually described under the general category of 'performance', in the past it has been defined as performance *art* or 'live art'.[3] It has been analysed by numerous feminist academics, not just those situated within drama, theatre (and now) performance studies, but also by those in a variety of fields, including art history, social geography, and critical studies.[4] The critical attention from art historians is because Bobby originally studied painting at St Martin's School of Art in London between 1968–72 and is part of a 'pioneering' generation of practitioners who were crucial to *producing* the field of 'performance' by crossing genres and mixing media in ways that not only interrogated traditional distinctions between art forms, but also the distinction between 'art' and 'life.' In the 1970s, she notes that her 'colleagues' '*all came from a fine art background* and *described themselves as performance artists*'. However, Bobby might be seen as starting to embrace aspects of a more specifically 'theatrical' tradition when she took a '*fundamental decision in my 30s to move away from being the sole author to deciding to look for people to work with*'. Nevertheless, the fact that she initially entered the field of performance from the direction of fine art is illuminating in exploring what is particular to her practice and to her process, especially as experienced through the workshop she led at Lancaster.[5]

While interested in drama at school, Bobby says that apart from going to see performers such as Joyce Grenfell and Flanders and Swann, a production of Shakespeare for her O-levels and some musicals in her 30s, she never went to the theatre.[6] However, when Bobby says '*I saw none of the famous work*', she is referring specifically to work such as that of Pina Bausch's groundbreaking Tanztheater, which in the 1980s strongly influenced British experimental performance practitioners of both genders. During this decade Bobby had an eight-year break from making work while she had two children, returning to find '*there had been this really exciting development of performance going on*'. With the help and support of Lois Keidan[7] she (re)-joined this development and subsequently '*has been influenced by a lot of the work I've seen*'. Nevertheless, these influences have been '*added in with what was there before*' and Bobby acknowledges that her fine art background not only '*informs my whole structuring of the work, the visual element*' but has also '*given me a slightly different perspective on where I have come to [...] coming to it that way has given me a certain freedom [...] my lack of knowledge about the form within which I eventually arrived has been very enabling.*'

With characteristic self-deprecation, Bobby explains that by the end of her time at St Martin's, '*I now realise that I had become quite accomplished in drawing and painting*'. The techniques she learnt of '*looking and making marks and considering colour*' can still be seen to inform her shows. However, if as a student she undertook '*lots of drawing*' and '*a whole year of colour studies, absolutely repetitive colour studies*', it was actually to '*fill in*' her time, '*because I knew I couldn't do what I wanted to do through painting somehow*'. Elsewhere she has referred to '*an idea I had very early on of wanting to make work that related to moments of time where just for a split second you experience an extra-ordinarily complex set of realities, associations [...] I tried painting that moment but it didn't work.*'[8]

In the months after she left St Martin's she famously had a 'revelation' when she made a baseball boot out of cake and this led to the '*extremely liberating idea that I would use food as a medium, which was very subversive, irreverent but seemed to totally mesh with my own experience.*' Since then, food has featured centrally both as a material and a thematic in her work, in ways that, as has often been noted, may be subversive and irreverent but are often serious and disturbing at the same time. This was already in evidence in her 1976 installation piece *An Edible Family in a Mobile Home* (1976) which, by the final day of exhibition, resembled the aftermath of a massacre.[9] Looking back, Bobby realised that the 'family' she had created had echoes of her own, but the importance of her work '*meshing with her own experience*' really struck her during a series of 'tea parties', where, as she told Marina Warner in 1997, she offered her friends *elaborate confections*. Although in 'staging' these events she made '*fun of herself*', she was '*utterly distraught*' when people '*laughed immoder-ately*', this experience made her realise that *I had been turning myself inside out yearning to be other than myself* and '*I had to go back into myself, use that and work with that and put it into my art – and I could do that any-where*'.[10] This realisation also led to a focus on the 'rituals' of everyday life, and in her 1979 solo performance piece *Packed Lunch* for the Hayward Gallery and in *My Cooking Competes*, shown in 1980 as part of the 'About Time' exhibition at the Institute for Contemporary Arts, the 'rituals' she explored were those of feeding a large crowd of people [the audience] and the baking competition.

Feminist consciousness raising and the autobiographical impulse

This latter exhibition was organised by feminist activists and dedicated to the work of women artists, and if previously, *as* an artist, Bobby had been trying to be 'other' than herself, this might partly be attributed to a context indicated by the *Time Out* review for 'About Time', which opened with the words 'Whether as model, mistress or muse, the woman's role in the arts has largely been a supportive one. Nowadays you will also find her in the service industries as a critic, dealer, historian or exhibition organiser – more active but still, by and large, fostering the male practitioner'.[11] Women's marginal or 'supportive' role in the art world can be explained by the predominance of attitudes whereby, according to a 1980 edition of *Spare Rib*, a member of the all-male Arts Council panel for awarding grants could blithely assert 'women don't have enough depth to be artists'.[12] The autobiographical impulse in Bobby's work, and within that of many of the other women artists who contributed to 'About Time', can therefore be perceived as part of a fem-inist consciousness raising: a foregrounding of the relationship between the personal, the political and the professional. What this exhibition and other similar events also revealed was a massive explosion, or per-haps, a massive *surfacing* of women's art practice across all areas but especially in the 'newer' fields of video and multimedia, installation, and performance (art).

For artists of *both* genders at this time, there was a political dimension to embracing live or performance art, in so far as its 'liveness', its ephemerality, its temporary and transitory nature, meant that it resisted the processes of commodification and commercialisation of the art object within the gallery and auction room. More specifically for women artists, who with rare exceptions had been excluded from these spaces, part of the attraction of performance lay in the direct and immediate relationship it afforded with an audience. Amongst other things, this presented an opportunity to challenge and interrogate the socio-historical discourses which had defined what counted as 'art' and 'who' had the right to the position and title of 'artist'.[13] In short, performance art provided an ideal space to critique the manner in which women had traditionally been objectified within fine art practice and for women artists to claim their right to the position of the speaking subject'.

These sorts of political concerns were already clearly in evidence in Bobby's early work, but materialised even more powerfully after her eight-year absence from performing, during which she had found the experience of motherhood to be *'profoundly isolating'*. During most of this period she worked in the commercial sphere as a stylist alongside her husband Andrew Whittuck, a professional food photographer, who might be said to have been collaborating with Bobby since 1974 when he began documenting her work. However, it was the team work involved in these commercial activities which made Bobby *'realise the power of collaboration and the point of working like that'*. Nevertheless, her acclaimed *Drawing on a Mother's Experience* (1988) was another solo piece and, while conceptually highly complex, had a very simple staging (a sheet, food products, Bobby). Her 1990 piece *Cook Dems*, while still a solo show, was far more ambitious technically and it was this factor that originally led to her collaboration with Polona Baloh-Brown, a long time friend with shared personal and feminist political interests who had a background in performing arts.[14] Brown initially offered to help out when the logistics of touring *Cook Dems* became too much for Bobby to manage alone but her response to the 'creative' aspects of the work also proved invaluable in helping Bobby overcome her *'terror'* over the *'uncertainty over whether what I was doing was effective'* due to *'the lack of feedback'*. This led to an ongoing collaboration which runs through all of Bobby's later, large-scale pieces of work, starting with a series of five shows based on (mostly women's) 'daily life': *Kitchen Show* (1991), *How to Shop* (1993), *Take a Peek!* (1995), *Grown Up School* (1999), and *Box Story* (2001). For this work Bobby also now had crucial administrative support from Artsadmin[15] and these shows have become increasingly elaborate, both technically and aesthetically. They have also involved more collaborations with other performers and artists, ranging from film maker Carole Lamond to composer Jocelyn Pook. In addition, Bobby has continued to make other, smaller-scale, solo pieces such as *Pull Yourself Together* (2000) and her series of *Table Occasions* (1997-), works which in line with her 'realisation' in the 1970s, she can and does indeed *'do anywhere'*. Added to this she indicates,' *I've also become increasingly engaged with website projects and radio, as really effective ways of communicating ideas'*, has done several pieces for Radio 4 and a short film entitled *Spitting Mad* (1997). At the time of writing, her most recent larger-scale show, *How to Live* (2004) in which she co-stars with a frozen pea with a personality disorder, is based on the ideas of founding her own 'Therapy Empire'. Like all of her work this piece arises from her personal experience and is a comic, often surreal, but simultaneously serious critique of the 'rituals' of mental health provision, exploring the ways in which the big, silent P's (Psychiatrists, Psychologists and Psychotherapists) can crush the little p (patient) underfoot. Mental health issues are also the subject of other works currently in development.

Integrity: the essential ingredient

If Bobby's work 'communicates' to a wider public than is usual for 'experimental' performance this is because her focus on the objects and rituals of everyday life, the play of humour, and above all her famously 'endearingly eccentric' stage persona, render her work 'inclusive' and provide numerous points of identification. Yet, Bobby's shows are multi-faceted and densely layered and her relationship with the audience is far more complex than might first appear. Even while she uses self-deprecation and self-parody to encourage laughter at her claims to knowledge and expertise on the basis of her years of experience of being a mother and a housewife (or a patient), she transforms everyday domestic items into highly evocative and aesthetically pleasing 'art objects', through the power of her *extra-ordinary* skill as an artist *and* a mother *and* a housewife (*and* a patient). Her 'endearing' persona then is deployed ironically to persuade the audience to question social and political assumptions about social roles and identity categories but the 'discursive' is explored through the local, the specific and the material. In many shows, she engages in actions which foreground the ways in which discourse acts on the body in a manner which can verge on the violent and masochistic, for instance forcing a tin of anchovies into her mouth in *How to Shop*, or pouring a whole bottle of tomato sauce into her mouth in *Spitting Mad*. At these points, it is not unusual for spectators to gag in sympathy, but such acts can also create a sense of unease or embarrassment at such excessive behaviour. Similarly, her shows frequently touch on serious, even distressing autobiographical material in ways that can give a discomforting sense of complicity in witnessing the public exposure of profoundly personal and painful experiences. In short, as the feminist critical response to her practice suggests, Bobby's work often manages to produce the *affect* she sought as an art student that is the *'experience* [of] *an extra-ordinarily complex set of realities, associations'*,[16] not least in relation to the profoundly ambivalent, intellectual, emotional, and physical experience of being gendered in our culture. The production of this affect, however, is a matter of aesthetics as well as politics, of 'art' as well as 'life'.

'Hard work' comes into this equation and it can take her years to develop a show; for instance, she says, she started to think about the concept of the pea in *How to Live* about 10 to 15 years ago. This may be partly because as she indicated in an interview in the 1990s, Bobby is engaged in '[a] *constant searching for shape and pattern, an almost mathematical concern for form, that you might be able to put ideas together, arrangements which you imagine, in a rather fantastical way might become perfect* [...]'.[17] At the start of the Lancaster workshop she introduced us to her list of 'ingredients' for 'Making the Perfect Performance', which is divided into two parts: 'Essential Concerns' and 'Process'. The first ingredient in the 'Essential Concerns' section is 'Integrity', a term for which she offered a number of definitions from the dictionary including *'no part or element missing'*, *'original perfect condition'*, *'complete'*. In talking us through this list, it became clear that for Bobby the notion of 'integrity' also embraces all the other 'Essential Concerns' and 'Process'. 'Integrity in all its meanings is then a pre-eminent principle within her own process and practice and can be understood to include an understanding that a passionate desire to communicate important ideas involves a commitment to searching for the appropriate (if not perfect) form through which to express them. This sense of integrity and a concern for form counter-balances the deeply-felt autobiographical and sometimes 'taboo breaking' or disturbing nature of work, allowing her to engage with the audience in a way that moves between distance and identification, so as to take them *'on a journey that is somehow safe, based on trust and not abusive'*.[18]

Bobby's stage persona

As has often been noted, Bobby's stage persona is a matter of playing 'herself' but her style of achieving this is noticeably much 'rawer' than that of younger performance practitioners such as Leslie Hill from Curious in *Smoking Gun* and *On the Scent* (see Chapter 3). Leslie's style probably owes much to the influence of artists of Bobby's generation but can be seen as closer to that of Laurie Anderson (an acknowledged influence). It might also be seen in relation to the development of a contemporary 'hyper-naturalism' as evinced by companies such as The Wooster Group in the US and Forced Entertainment in the UK. By contrast with these others, Bobby's style of delivery remains more rooted in her origins in performance art of the 1970s and 1980s, with its emphasis on the position of the artist as 'author' rather than performer, a stance that was often part of an aggressive anti-theatricality; one clearly not shared by Anderson. While certain 'themes' associated with this stance may have always informed Bobby's practice, as already suggested, in recent years, she has been happy to embrace aspects of the theatrical. Indeed, in developing *How to Shop*, which, unlike her previous works, was to be shown in larger venues, Bobby went to well-known theatre voice coach Pasty Rodenburg to improve her vocal technique. She reports that after a couple of sessions Rodenburg dismissed her saying, '*Honestly Bobby I'm just going to do more damage than good. Do it the way you do it. It's working.*' Bobby's apparent lack of technique, reflected in a slight physical and vocal 'awkwardness' as a performer, works because it guarantees the 'ordinariness' of her persona in ways that invite trust and identification and 'authenticates' the show's experiential and political content. Yet, at the same time, as noted above, there is always a degree of self-parody and ironic self-reflexivity in this persona that implies an acknowledgment that she is playing a 'role'. This same contradiction emerges very clearly in one of the 'trademarks' of her stage persona, the white coat or overall, which she has worn throughout all her shows, except for *Box Story* in which it was dyed blue.[19] Discussing the white overall, she has said previously:

> An important part of creating a performance is to decide how best to encompass a complex range of ideas within an appropriate form. I found it irritating to 'clutter' ideas with clothes. That carried too many associations. The white overall offered an inexhaustible range of associations to play with as well as a certain blankness.[20]

As exemplified by her use of a 'pea suit' in *How to Live*, in the course of a show this overall is occasionally cast off in favour of another more 'theatrical' costume but only temporarily. More importantly, the overall is always 'personalised' through hair, makeup, shoes or jewellery, 'details' which she often draws attention to and which, thrown into relief by the blankness of the overall, become, as she indicates in *How to Live*, highly significant. Nevertheless, the formality of the white coat creates an impersonal distance, making space for introjection and projection on the part of the audience that goes *beyond* Bobby's specific identity and experiences due to its associations with social 'roles', as opposed to individuals. In various shows therefore, it can be said to have suggested the cookery demonstrator, the housewife, the (domestic) science lecturer, the patient and the psychotherapist.

The centrality of the 'action'

Bobby's '*almost mathematical concern for form*' is especially evident in a tendency to structure her larger-scale shows around a particular number of 'actions', with for instance *Kitchen Show* being based around 13 actions, *How to Shop*, 7 actions, *Box Story*, 10 actions, and *How to Live*, 11 actions. Sometimes the number of actions is significant. For instance, in *Kitchen Show*, 13 is a 'baker's dozen'. However, in other shows the meaning of the number, if any, is less clear and Bobby has suggested that the rules she imposes on herself may be '*arbitrary – a conceit* [...] *it's the fact that I'm organizing or imposing a form on an event that is important* [...]'.[21]

These actions are sometimes 'attached' to autobiographical stories, which again, tend to provoke a personal identification with Bobby and have often been the focus of critical attention. Yet Bobby points out '*there's not always a story – I'm thinking of* Pull Yourself Together *(2000) which is entirely an action and there's no story. Shows that I really cherish don't necessarily have stories. The next piece I'm doing – a new website – I've got none of my stories in it. The live piece I'm working on is not going to have my story in it. So the story bit comes and goes.*' For her the *actions* are at the core of both her work representing and expressing the overarching ideas or a '*concept around a particular detail or feeling about what it's important to try to open a debate about.*' Using *Kitchen Show* as an example she says:

> I got very angry and frustrated about the way these daily actions, these daily routines and rituals are not observed and cherished in our society. I could see how fundamentally complex they were and how they related to things like the butterfly effect in chaos theory, or the Blake thing 'the world in a grain of sand', the idea that the minutiae contains the enormous.

The concept of the show emerged from '*wandering about*' thinking about this and more specifically during a moment when she had a fantasy about of having '*a world satellite link*' to her washing a carrot, an 'action' that featured in the show.

Usually once the action is completed, it is represented by a 'mark' made on (or through) her own body and Bobby then '*make[s] a pose, just for a moment, for a fraction so that people can observe the mark. It's an essential part of the performance because it gives people that moment to reflect on what's happening.'*[22] While the 'pose' occurs live in *Kitchen Show*, in other of the large-scale shows it is sometimes also shown in the form of slides of still photographs taken by Whittuck. The pose and its doubling in the still photographs, then interrupts the flow of the live performance and is intended to promote reflection on the ideas Bobby is *'passionately attempting to communicate'*. As such, the 'actions', their marking and the posing, can be said to function like the Brechtian notion of *gestus*: a gesture which materialises the social and political 'gist' of the scene or section or of the whole. At the same time, these strategies and devices reflect Bobby's earlier positioning within the 'live art' part of the performance continuum, which (is still) often focused on 'body art', human sculpture and 'actions', rather than narrative, whether 'fragmented' or otherwise. Similarly, the manner in which Whittuck's photographs are *part* of the shows and also available separately as 'documentation', which in turn might be perceived as self-contained 'performances' in another medium, is in accord with performance *art* practice.

As all of this suggests, it is possible to identify certain formal and thematic continuities across the body of Bobby's work but her search for the 'appropriate' form for each piece has led her to employ an enormous variety of media, stagings and performance techniques. As noted, she has worked in film, radio, drawing and websites, and her live shows have incorporated pre-recorded and live feed video, computer animation, still photographs and specially-composed music. Across various shows, she has engaged in lip synching, dancing, theatrical 'flying', slap stick and all sorts of contortions, gymnastics, attaching things to her body, strapping herself to the back of vans, etc. In a fashion similar to but predating Curious' work (see Chapter 3), she has frequently experimented with the use of smell and taste in her work,[23] and although this is seldom discussed, the vast majority of her pieces have actually (in different ways) been 'site specific'. This reflects her early desire to do her shows *'anywhere'* and she has said that by preference she would always perform in public spaces in daily use, such as churches and school halls.[24] This site specficity extends not only to smaller-scale pieces like the *Table Occasions* but to most of her larger-scale shows. So, for example, *Kitchen Show* premiered in her own kitchen, *How to Shop* premiered in a lecture hall and *Box Story* premiered in Bobby's own church, St Luke's in Holloway. Created with these spaces in mind these shows were later adapted for touring.

Transforming the everyday: the workshop

In line with Bobby's interest in 'public spaces' our first task as a group at Lancaster was a shopping trip to the campus supermarket. This was the first step towards fulfilling the main aim of the workshop, which was to encourage us to make something significant and transformative out of the 'everyday'. In framing this trip Bobby introduced herself by telling us the 'box of cornflakes' story from *Box Story* (action No. 1), one of her earliest childhood memories, and by performing action No. 3 (throwing a ripe pear) from *Kitchen Show*, using the wall of the studio as a substitute for her kitchen cupboards. She also presented us with her list of ingredients for making the perfect performance (cited above), which under 'Essential Concerns' lists 'Integrity, Content/issue, Structure/form, Site/audience, Authenticity, Practical viability, and Duration' and under 'Process' lists 'Devising, Writing, Rehearsing, Directing, Editing, Pace/timing and Performance skills'.

Our supermarket visit was intended to provide material for the second 'essential ingredient' – that of content/issue. We were instructed to find three items related to memories and personal stories, but Bobby emphasised that we should not think about this before arriving at the shop but should browse the aisles to see what struck us and what ideas or associations might surface. This exercise was clearly designed to encourage us to be open to being 'inspired' by the everyday, but in relation to autobiographical work it was significant in that the starting point was a response to external stimuli rather than drawing on something from 'within'. We returned to the studio with, amongst other things, flour, curry powder, oranges, After Eight mints, pork pies, vegetable oil, spaghetti, Mars Bars, peas, tinned rice pudding and a coconut, and were each instructed to pick one item and to tell the story associated with it to the rest of the group. A large proportion of these stories were based around childhood memories. Nevertheless, the fundamental role that food plays in all our lives, the evocative nature of its smells, tastes and textures and even its packaging, produced a diverse range of narratives, expressing a wide spectrum of emotions. At this stage, some participants started using the food products to 'illustrate' their story and our next task was to construct an 'action' either using this same item and its related associations or choosing another one.

This exercise started to direct attention to issues of 'structure/form' as well as site/audience from Bobby's list of 'making the perfect performance' ingredients. When showing 'the throwing the ripe pear' action, Bobby had remarked on the 'health and safety' issues that must be taken into account when performing such actions in close proximity to an audience. When showing our actions, our enthusiasm and sheer delight at being 'given permission' to play with food, led some of us to accidentally splash or hit others with liquid or particles. In response, Bobby gently but firmly reminded us of the crucial importance of '*taking care*' of the audience. This was a point she returned to throughout the workshop and it was clear that this 'taking care' is not just a matter of the physical but also of the emotional and intellectual, in line with Bobby's concern '*with taking the audience on a journey that is somehow safe, based on trust and not abusive*'.[25] When making our choices in the supermarket Bobby had stressed that we should give careful consideration as to whether the associations with products were ones which we would feel happy sharing in public. Nevertheless, while no bar was placed on dealing with serious, difficult or painful material and some participants' work did touch on these registers, Bobby indicated that, above all, it was crucial to avoid constructing a relationship with the audience that was aggressive, manipulative or might otherwise represent an abuse of power.

Yet at the same time, Bobby *also* encouraged us to experiment with ways of '*arranging*' the audience and three things began to emerge from these presentations. Most participants incorporated their 'actions' into stories but some were more abstract, focusing on the action rather than attempting to tell the narrative. Interestingly and inevitably, the ones that focussed on either the action (e.g. washing the 'hair' of a coconut) or revolved around a strong image (e.g. a Mars Bars meticulously cut up into thin slices) were the most striking and memorable. Secondly, the smell of food products pervaded the space in a way that was very much part of the fabric of the presentations (some smells lingered throughout the workshop). Thirdly, some of these showings immediately began to involve 'audience participation' and this became a characteristic of the majority of subsequent presentations to a far higher degree than in any other workshop in our project series. Over the course of the event, this spanned from simply 'arranging' us in the space and/or in unusual ways in relation to each other and to the presenter, to directly involving us through interaction with the presenter, each other or with objects. At one point, for instance, we all had our feet washed by the presenter. At another, we were each given a biscuit with the instruction to hold it whole in our mouths without biting or chewing until asked to do so. A large proportion of presentations then, experimented with spatial dynamics and became interactive experiences that worked directly on the body, rather than resembling more traditional 'theatrical' styles of performance. Even the experimental realm of 'performance' still frequently involves end-on staging and/or observes a physical separation between performer and audience. The interactive tendency in this instance was without doubt prompted by Bobby urging us to experiment with the arrangement of 'site/audience', combined with her emphasis on 'taking care of' the audience and with the sensually-evocative nature of food as a material.

Authorship and collaboration

However, ultimately the sheer *variety* of different types of response to this first exercise, touches on one of the most notable aspects of this workshop which can also be seen to reflect something of Bobby's own process. Most of the tasks we undertook were actually fairly 'open' in structure, being designed to prompt 'inspiration' and encourage experimentation, rather than being directed to a very specific outcome. Equally, Bobby's responses to what was produced were largely 'non-directional' and facilitatory as opposed to 'directorial', mostly offering positive reinforcement, rather than evaluating how (and if) the exercise had 'worked' for individuals or suggesting how ideas could be taken further. This contrasts with more 'interventionist' approaches taken by some other workshop leaders. It is not our intention to compare these approaches favourably or unfavourably, since in different contexts *both* are equally useful and productive. Rather we are interested in how the 'openness' of the exercises we undertook reflects Bobby's description of *'wandering about thinking'* about certain ideas at the start of developing *Kitchen Show* and the way her non-directional approach may connect back to her fine and performance 'art' background.

While the collaborative nature of most *theatre* practice has always problematised the ascription of authorship, for several centuries the work of (fine) art has usually been clearly understood as the product of a 'sole artist'. Even though Bobby has increasingly moved towards working with other practitioners, in contrast for example, with the processes employed by Split Britches which are intensively collaborative from the very start, Bobby says *'I work on my own for a certain period of time, come up with the images and the ideas and then involve other people.'* This was something she says she had to come to terms with early on in her working relationship with Polona Baloh-Brown or 'Pol' as Bobby calls her. When Pol suggested an 'alternative' ending to a piece Bobby was still developing, Bobby's immediate response was *'No'*. She says:

> it was very difficult to negotiate that reaction but [Pol] was extremely generous. I said it's only really going to work if it's my images and my vision.

I found it very difficult because it was like I was saying 'I need your help, but don't do the fun bit.' There have been stages where all that has got rather muddy and I have lost the lead in what I was doing – not only in terms of Pol's input, but other people's input and I would say that some of that work is not as clear as the later work.

Giving the example of Pol's role in the work with reference to *How to Live*, Bobby explains how Pol would get *'involved when everything was mapped out, everything was planned and then we had to make it into a kind of performance.'* In programme credits over the years, Baloh-Brown has been described either as director or co-director but, Bobby explains, *'after endless discussion, she is now described as the performance director but I don't know that that entirely covers the fact that she really is involved in the text and structuring.'*

In a later exchange we had with Baloh-Brown herself, she indicated that she is still not entirely comfortable with the term performance director.[26] Reflecting on this in general, she says,

Alongside the development of the genre of performance and of the artist/maker/author/performer, has been the evolution of significantly different types of collaborations required for this kind of work, one of which is the new role of the 'director'. As the term 'actor' became problematic in live art performance, so the term and role of director is inappropriate.

Instead, Baloh-Brown favours what she admits is a more 'cumbersome' designation, that of 'outside eye'. In this role, she says,

I perceive myself as a catalyst through which the work progresses and passes, and this catalyst helps channel it without destroying its original form, without challenging its basic shape, depth or colour [...] An outside eye is also the bridge between the performer/author and the audience.

Baloh-Brown's working relationship with Bobby is obviously a close one, based on trust and developed over a long period of time. As such, it is flexible and can vary according to the needs and demands of the specific show. However, Baloh-Brown says often, at the point she comes in, 'There is always a clear pre-determined structure with 9, 13, 11 sections', but 'the order may still be vague or up for grabs.' She describes their working process as one of '"dialoguing" the performance into existence', initially through discussion and then rehearsals in which Baloh-Brown's focus is on 'what works, the gaps, the links, the pattern'. Her 'creative input' then occurs in helping to connect 'the parts into a whole', while letting 'the performer find the performative space and the persona'.

If this role of 'performance director' or 'outside eye' is distinct from that of the 'traditional' director, equally it differs from that of a 'co-devisor'/ performer who engages in the work from the start but also 'steps outside' to act as 'director/editor'. It is notoriously difficult to negotiate this role, although some, such as Lois Weaver, achieve it very successfully. It is worth noting that some other 'solo' performance practitioners (who also sometimes collaborate with other performers and/or artists) also draw on an 'outside eye'. Japanese performance artist Kazuko Hohki,[27] for example, occasionally works with freelance director Mark Whitelaw in a similar way to Bobby and Pol. This sort of collaboration is therefore, well worth considering, especially by those primarily working as solo artists.

To return to Bobby, the other artists and performers she collaborates with also work from her *'vision and images'*. This is sometimes made available to them in a form developed when Bobby was working on *How to Shop*. During this process she found it very difficult to *'convey my images'* to Carole Lamond who created the filmed extracts and *'to the production manager and lighting designer and so on'*. At Lamond's suggestion, Bobby produced a five page 'storyboard' of the type often used in film and realised that this was a *'useful way of communicating to people what I was working with, what I saw in my head – much more effective than words.'* Looking back recently, she noted that these five pages represented the *'images pretty well as they happened in the show'*. Since then, although she *'didn't formally start drawing regularly […] I would do a series of drawings building up to the shows.'* We have not seen these drawings but some of them are described by Marina Warner in her article on Bobby's work and they appear to be similar to those shown in Bobby's 2006 exhibition of 'Diary Drawings' at Psi#12.[28] She started making these drawing on a daily basis several years ago, whilst attending a mental health day centre and *'the reason for having this exhibition of 30 carefully selected drawings out of 600 drawn so far is because I am so passionately trying to communicate what it's like to be in my position and I suddenly realised that this might help. It might help other people, it might help me just to say what's going on.'* At the same time, she acknowledges that *'I think what's happening is that I'm beginning to realise how effectively they cover some of the thinking that goes behind the performance work. So they've become another kind of bolt-on to the whole movement of making work.'* At first glance, these drawings seem far away from the warmth, humour and inclusivity of the live shows. They sometimes depict Bobby's body literally 'in pieces', or her tearing off her own face, and powerfully convey extreme mental and psychical anguish, anger, violence and profound desperation. Yet, these emotions *are* always detectable in the live shows even though they are never as directly expressed and tend to be offset and 'made safe' by the show's form and by Bobby's appealing 'persona'. Moreover, as Bobby indicates '*a lot of the drawings on show are very funny – they certainly make people laugh out loud*' and even in the most disturbing ones there is an element of contradiction in play between *what* is being expressed and a subtle, even delicate use of colour, a lightness and fineness of line, and above all the angular and witty stylisation of Bobby's self-representation. In terms of *form* and affect then, these drawings can be seen to echo the sorts of expressive strategies evident in the live shows.

We did not discuss or experiment with drawing or storyboards in the workshop, and aside from technical assistance and audience participation, all participants concentrated on developing their own material by themselves. Generally, Bobby's feedback focused on encouraging us to explore these ideas further rather that intervening in them conceptually. Before our 'final' showings, working with us 'one to one' she did offer advice in the structuring of our pieces in performance but in a fashion that was probably close to Pol's role as outside eye.

Authenticity

Issues of 'authorship' were again entailed in two exercises we undertook on the second day of the workshop, in ways that related to 'content/ issue' and to 'authenticity' from Bobby's performance ingredients list. First we were asked to prepare and give a (strictly timed) one minute talk on an issue that we feel passionate about. These talks covered a wide range of topics, including ecological concerns, rape, the Iraq War, homophobia, and the British perception of people from the countries involved in the war in the Balkans in the early 1990s. In an apparent change of tack, we then split up into small groups to tell each other a personal story based on an especially 'dramatic' incident. Choosing one of these stories, each group member attempted to recount this incident to the rest of the participants as if it had happened to them, the point being for the others to guess as to which of the tellers the story 'really' belonged. Interestingly, the 'original' storyteller was only guessed correctly one out of four times. This might have been a simple matter of 'acting ability' but it also raises questions concerning the importance of *actual* 'authenticity' in autobiographical performance. It is unlikely that there would have been the same confusion over the 'original' speaker had the exercise been based around the 'issue speeches' which preceded it, unless, that is, other participants felt as equally (personally *and* politically) passionate about exactly the same topics. In many instances (e.g. British perceptions of people from former Yugoslavia) this was unlikely. Embedded in these two tasks then, was a (for many) familiar lesson about the limitations of the 'dramatic' for its own sake. What was underlined for us was how far the *'passionate desire to communicate certain ideas'* is not only the driving force of Bobby's practice but is that which gives it its 'authenticity', rather than simply the autobiographical nature of her storytelling.

'Making something happen for the audience'

In fact, the point of these two exercises was to start to move us 'beyond' storytelling, beyond the personal, or the autobiographical for their own sake and indeed beyond the notion of the 'action' as 'simply' either expressive or illustrative of these things. Our next task was to use either a favourite kitchen implement we had brought to the workshop, and/or the food items or other objects in the room to 'experiment' in constructing an action which symbolised what the object meant to us, but which crucially was in some way significant and 'transformative' for others. As Bobby put it, this was about *'making something happen for the audience'*. With reference to Bobby's own work this notion of 'transformation' might (once again) be most easily understood through reference to a version of Brechtian 'alienation', or to a Butlerian notion of subversive repetition. In a very general sense this means being prompted to see something familiar or taken for granted afresh, but also in relation to how this might function as part of a larger process of politicisation. This is very much a matter of the 'integrity' of the relationship between form and meaning. When for instance, Bobby undertakes the washing the carrot action in *Kitchen Show*, she provokes us into seeing anew by drawing attention to and encouraging us to appreciate the qualities of colour, texture and the play of light and sound that combine within this 'everyday action'. This is not simply an aesthetic transformation for its own sake, but rather in foregrounding and celebrating the 'art' of usually invisible and undervalued, domestic labour (still predominantly carried out by women), this action points to a wider feminist discourse on the deprecation and marginalisation of all that which is traditionally associated with the feminine.

In contrast to previous presentations, while some of the subsequent showings did involve speech this was used only to make a specific point, rather than to tell a story. The vast majority were abstract, focused on interacting with the objects and on movement and spatial dynamics. In general, however, the group struggled to find an integral relationship between *what* was being expressed and *how* it was being expressed. As a result, rather than '*making something happen for the audience*' many of us found ourselves, once again, either using the object in an 'illustrative' mode, or focusing on aesthetics to the extent that it was extremely difficult for the audience to grasp what might be being communicated. Nevertheless, striking images were produced: a woman standing motionless with a corkscrew in her mouth, or a colander being spun and held up like a chalice.[29] After all, this was an 'experiment' around a highly complex praxis.

Our final instruction for the last day of the workshop was to construct a presentation, considering either the issue we had spoken to, or something else we felt passionately about and to draw on what we might find 'useable' from the other work we had undertaken. Once again Bobby referred us back to the primacy of the principle of integrity as an essential ingredient for making performance. She also strongly advised us that once we had the ideas for our presentations that we should 'write down' the verbal elements, not necessarily as a 'script' but as a means of helping to tighten them up. Speaking personally (as Elaine and Gerry), while like many other participants we had struggled with the previous task, with time to think, the combination of the notion of 'transformative' actions and 'issues', was inspiring and we both experienced moments when the concept for these final pieces came almost fully formed into our heads. Equally, the fifteen minutes Bobby spent with each of us while rehearsing these pieces was extremely useful because she immediately grasped and offered solutions to structural and performance problems.

As in all of the workshops, in these final presentations it was possible to see a number of different sorts of 'journeys' arising out of the way that over the three-day workshop period participants kept returning to particular stories, or (food-) objects, or ways of interacting with the audience. Stylistically, these final presentations were equally diverse. Some veered towards the 'theatrical', involving some sort of 'acting out' of a social role (the housewife who offers instructions for combining the domestic and the exotic by cleaning the kitchen while practicing belly dancing, or the lecturer who drinks milk from a bra and stuffs oranges down her knickers while speaking of phenonmenologist Merleu- Ponty).[30] Others were closer to a live or performance art tradition, being based around actions firmly taking place in the 'here and now' whose meanings were more associative and contiguous (paper arrows made from women's magazines are thrown, which propel the performer forward, walking on a trail of sugar cubes which are crushed, until she reaches the studio sink. From the sink she takes out and pastes on the wall more pictures of models from these magazines).[31] This variety, of course, reflects Bobby's own practice.

Interestingly, in her groundbreaking book on performance art, RoseLee Goldberg sometimes refers to the late 1960s to early 1970s generation of artists who rejected traditional fine arts methods and material to embrace, installation, video and live art or performance, collectively as 'conceptual artists'.[32] In the public realm, this term is now mainly associated with figures like Damien Hirst and Tracy Emin. While it may sometimes (potentially) be aesthetically and politically 'subversive', it lost much of its 'radical' edge when championed by figures like Charles Saatchi in the 1980s and 1990s, and was firmly recuperated to the values of the commercial 'art market'. Nonetheless, certain aspects of Bobby's process and practice can still be allied to the notion and methodologies of 'conceptual art', although this is counter-balanced by her drive towards collaboration with other artists and more 'theatrical' staging in her larger-scale work. Her incursions into film, radio and websites, as well as her decision to exhibit her drawings, might suggest that, 'formally' her work is moving in other directions. However, as a body of work this is nevertheless 'coherent' because what drives her formal experimentation is the search for 'integrity', as part of a passionate desire to communicate ideas in ways that open up a debate about important social and political issues.

Notes and references

1. This was at the Performance Studies International Conference (Psi#12) held at Queen Mary's, London University, 15–18 June 2006. In 2005 Bobby was awarded a three-year Creative Fellowship by the Arts and Humanities Research Council, attached to the Department of English and Drama at Queen Mary's. During the Psi conference she presented a preview of a new piece entitled *Ballistic Buns, Mad Meringues* and exhibited her 'Diary Drawings' referred to later in this chapter. Bobby also created 'Meringue Ladies' for the Women's Writing for Performance project's 'Artists' Forum' held at the Theatre Museum, Covent Garden, London, 11 November 2006.
2. Interview with Bobby Baker, 16 June 2006. All quotations are from this interview unless otherwise stated.
3. The distinction between performance and performance art is a contested one and some of the work of Split Britches and Curious (see Chapter 3) could be

described as 'performance art'. However, we are making the distinction in terms of background and training and how far (some or most) of the practitioners' work embraces aspects of the theatrical.

4. For a list of some of the academic publications concerned with Bobby's work and for more information on her shows, see her website www.bobbybakers dailylife.com/.

5. Bobby's workshop at Lancaster took place between 4 and 9 May 2004.

6. The inclusion of Joyce Grenfell (1910–1979) on this list may be significant. This celebrated singer-songwriter and comic monologist, provided a 'role model' for other female performance practitioners (such as Rose English) who grew up in the 1950s, a period in which successful women solo performers (of any genre) who created their own material were extremely rare. The duo Michael Flanders (1922–1975) and Donald Swann (1929–1994) were also comic singer-songwriters.

7. Since the 1980s and in a variety of roles, including working for the Arts Council, The Institute for Contemporary Art in London and, latterly, as a founder member of the Live Art Development Agency, Lois Keidan has been a key figure in supporting and facilitating the development of Live, Performance Art and interdisciplinary practices in Britain. In the late 1980s, she encouraged Bobby to enter her work for the National Review of Live Art, an annual event established in 1984, under the direction of Nikki Millican to provide a platform for emergent artists. The NRLA is now based in Glasgow, for details see www.newmoves.co.uk. Keidan is also cited by SuAndi as a key figure in encouraging her to develop *The Story of M*, see Chapter 4.

8. Quoted in Lucy Baldwin, 'Blending In: The Immaterial Art of Bobby Baker's Culinary Event', *The Drama Review*, 40: 4, Winter (1996) pp. 37–55, p. 38.

9. As Bobby indicated during the talk she gave to students at the time of the Lancaster workshop (4 May 2004), this took place in a prefabricated house in which the walls were covered in newspaper treated with sugar. The 'family' was made of cake and spectators were invited to eat them. By the end of the week the whole thing began to rot and, in the pictures Bobby showed, what was left of the 'family' resembled violently dismembered corpses.

10. Marina Warner, 'Bobby Baker: The Rebel at the Heart of the Joker' in Nicky Childs and Jeni Walwin (eds.), *A Split Second of Paradise: New Performance and Live Art* (London: Rivers Oram Press, 1998) pp. 68–87, p. 74.

11. Quoted in Rozsika Parker and Griselda Pollock (eds.), *Framing Feminism: Art and The Women's Movement 1970–1985* (London: Pandora Press, 1992) p. 224.

12. Ibid, p. xiv.

13. See RoseLee Goldberg, *Performance Art* (London: Thames and Hudson, 2001), chapters 6 and 7. This book was originally published in 1979. Also see Parker and Pollock (eds.) *Framing Feminism*, originally published in 1987. While holding to the notion that live performance resists commodification, the political efficacy of 'simple' visibility in feminist performance practice was later questioned by the Peggy Phelan in *Unmarked: The Politics of Performance* (London and New York: Routledge, 1993). In the late 1990s, Philip Auslander went on to question if the 'liveness' of performance could still be understood as a guarantee of resistance to commodification. See *Liveness: Performance in a Mediatised Culture* (London and New York: Routledge, 1999). These works have been highly influential in theorising around performance. They have

not, as far as we are aware, had any influence (direct *or* indirect) on Bobby's thinking or creative practice.

14. For a biography of Baloh-Brown see www.bobbybakersdailylife.com/.
15. Artsadmin was founded in 1979 by Judith Knight and Seonaid Stewart to provide much needed administrative support for experimental performance practitioners. They have been important facilitators for many of Britain's most notable companies and practitioners. For more information see www.artsadmin.co.uk/. Videos and DVDs of some of Bobby's shows are available through Artsadmin.
16. Quoted in Baldwin, 'Blending In', p. 38.
17. Bobby Baker in Adrian Heathfield, 'Risk in Intimacy: an Interview with Bobby Baker', *Performance Research: On Cooking*, 4:1, Spring (1999), pp. 97–106, p. 102.
18. Ibid, p. 101.
19. See Elaine Aston, 'Feminist Performance as Archive: Bobby Baker's "Daily Life" and *Box Story*', *Performance Research: On Archives and Archiving*, 7: 4, pp. 78–85.
20. Quoted in Baldwin, 'Blending In', p. 44).
21. Quoted in Heathfield, 'Risk in Intimacy', p. 102. The nature of the imposition of form as a 'conceit' in Bobby's shows is evident in *How to Live*. While we have said that there are 11 actions in this show, Bobby includes two extra 'poses' (see main text below) an introductory one and a summative one, so that in terms of Whittuck's photographs, this produces another 'Baker's dozen'. This has been done so that the first letter of the first word of the written text that accompanies each of these 'poses'/still photographs spells out the words 'Watch Yourself' in the manner of old fashioned poetic 'conceits' and/or riddles.
22. Quoted in Baldwin, 'Blending In', p. 43.
23. From *An Edible Family in a Mobile Home* onwards many of Bobby's performances have involved giving food to the audience, in ways that often foreground smell as well as taste. For instance, in *How to Shop* she fried garlic croutons on stage, filling the auditorium with their smell, before giving them to the audience.
24. Warner, 'Bobby Baker: The Rebel at the Heart of The Joker', p. 82.
25. Quoted in Heathfield, 'Risk in Intimacy', p. 101.
26. All quotes from Baloh-Brown are from email correspondence, 17 November 2006.
27. We became familiar with Hohki's practice as she held a one-year 'Time and Space' Fellowship with our Nuffield Theatre at Lancaster. Hohki also got involved in our project, taking part in Vayu Naidu's workshop and speaking at our project symposium, April 2006.
28. See note 1.
29. For a selection of 'striking images', see WWP website, http://www.lancs.ac.uk/depts/theatre/womenwriting/, Events Archive, Bobby Baker.
30. Both of these examples are available on the WWP website, ibid., as film footage clips.
31. Still images available on WWP website.
32. See Goldberg, *Performance Art*, p. 152.

3
Being Curious

Leslie Hill and Helen Paris

Helen Paris. *On the Scent* © Curious

Leslie Hill. *On the Scent* © Curious

Curious is the performance company of Leslie Hill and Helen Paris. Formed in 1996, the company's ten-year production history reflects a commitment to digital arts and performance; to exploring the possibilities of the web for performance, of creating multi-media performances, or performances that bring together arts and science. *'What's interesting about the work of Curious,'* explains Helen, *'is the way we cover so many different types of media. We do live performance, and at the moment* [2005] *we're doing a lot of live performance, but our work also incorporates internet and film and video and publishing.'*[1] *'I suppose we're called Curious'*, Leslie states, *'because we often start projects with questions, something we're interested in, and I think that's why we work across so many different forms, because we start with a question and then you sort of find the best way to address that question or explore that question for yourselves and to open out that exploration to an audience.'*[2] For the last ten years, Leslie and Helen have been busy 'being curious' about a range of questions and issues that include Leslie's curiosity about facts or science, or Helen's interest in communication – all kinds of communication, the human and the technological, or the interaction of both of these. Whatever the latest subject or object of curiosity, it is likely to connect with contemporary culture in a way that is edgy, interrogative and politicising.

Leslie and Helen both come from academic arts and theatre backgrounds. Leslie grew up in America, completed a degree in English and philosophy at the University of New Mexico, and then moved to England to study for an MA at The Shakespeare Institute, Birmingham University. Whilst completing a doctorate in Film, Theatre and Television, Leslie gained an artist residency at the Centre for Contemporary Arts, Glasgow, and began to build up a performance repertoire.

Helen graduated in English and Theatre Studies from the University of Ulster at Coleraine, and formed her own theatre company, Out and Out Theatre in Belfast (1987–90), before embarking on a solo performance career in London in the early 1990s. Helen and Leslie met at the ICA where they were both showing solo performances as part of the 'Its not Unusual' season in 1994 and the 'Jezebel' season in 1995. They formed Curious in 1996. Helen later did a PhD ('Visceral/Virtual: Performance') at the University of Surrey alongside her work as co-director of Curious in the late 1990s.

While Leslie and Helen are artists first and foremost, they have also benefited from their academic theatre backgrounds which encouraged them to think in terms of theory, criticism, and writing about theatre in general. A transatlantic contemporary avant garde has always been characterised by those who engage performatively with writing and with writing about (their) practice – Tim Etchells, Fiona Templeton, Goat Island, the Wooster Group, to name but a few. Leslie and Helen follow in this tradition and have not only made work but have collaborated on collections about contemporary performance. To date they have published two essay collections: *Guerrilla Performance and Multimedia* and *Performance and Place*. Each of these collections is put together with both scholarly and professional communities in mind.[3] These publications are also representative of two recurring concerns for Curious: the role of multimedia and digital technology and the effect that these have on ideas of place and site specificity in performance.[4] Often the one is interrogated through the other, as in projects which make use of the internet as a performance venue, for example, but linked to real place, real time events: *Lost and Found, Shanghai*,[5] or the *Seaside Towns Project*.[6] An idea of place therefore maps with a sense of what Leslie describes as *'place-lessness'*, which in a more general way she also attributes to the *'gypsy-like'* character of performance and live art practices.[7]

Since the 1970s, there has been a strong and very broad tradition of women working in multi-media performance both in Britain, North America and elsewhere. This was very much in evidence in the ICA 'About Time' exhibition (1980–1) (see Chapter 2, p. 23) and in the work of figures as diverse and diversely geographically located as Simone Benmussa, Catherine Elwes, Carlyle Reedy, Carolee Schneeman, Joan Jonas, Valie Export, and Orlan. All of these women practitioners (amongst others) can be considered as pioneers in this field but their innovations in terms of medium and form are frequently overlooked either because feminist critical focus on this work has often been first and foremost on its gender politics, or because it has more generally suffered from the marginalising effects of being categorised primarily as *women's* work.

On the other hand, up until fairly recently there has been relatively less involvement by women artists in *computer*-based technology in performance, which is of particular interest to Curious. In part this is a reflection on the way in which, as Leslie observes, this means *'choosing to play with some of the boys' toys'*.[8] There are some notable exceptions to this including one much admired by Curious, the internationally-acclaimed super star, Laurie Anderson, whose multi-media performances drew on computer-based technology as early as 1983. More recent examples include the visual arts and object animation company Doo-Cot (Nenagh Watson and Rachel Field) and artists such as Toni Dove, Monika Fleishman and Victoria Vesna, all of whom are experimenting with interactive digital technologies. Many others, like Bobby Baker, have begun to engage in website performance and to exploit the advantages of cyberspace as an accessible, alternative space in which to perform.[9] As a company, it is also the case that Curious play a part in encouraging the use of technology by offering training possibilities to other artists.[10]

Overall, however, although technology plays an important part in their work and for documenting the work – on the web or in film, video or DVD formats – Leslie and Helen are both clear about the importance of the live and of the communication between performer and spectator. Even though technology clearly is impacting on and changing how we communicate, as Helen explored in her early show, *Vena Amoris*,[11] it is still the human element of communication that is important to Curious. Leslie, in the spirit of Laurie Anderson who argues that '*technology is simply the campfire around which we now tell our stories*',[12] writes:

> *In 1994 I found a message in a bottle on the beach on Arran island off the west coast of Scotland, it was scrawled in pencil and decorated with Jelly Babies; in 1995 I scattered tape recorded messages in bottles throughout my performance installation; in 1996 I posted my first hypertext, Deus ex Machina, onto the Internet in much the same spirit as one might cast a bottle upon the waves.*
>
> *One can, of course, classify these different forms of communication as 'real', 'performance' and 'virtual' or as examples of place and placelessness or site specific and cyberspatial experience, but the salient point, as far as I'm concerned, is that the common denominator of both sending and receiving still resides in* living, breathing human bodies [our emphasis].[13]

R&D – arts and technology

'Being Curious' means that some of the questions that Leslie and Helen seek to explore through performance – especially given Leslie's interest in science – take the company into substantial periods of laboratory-based research. A research and development phase for a particular project can mean that instead of an initial stage of working that is just Leslie and Helen together, the artists are working as part of, or drawing on the expertise of, a bigger team of relevant experts. To give a couple of examples: for *On the Scent* Curious joined Dr Upinder Bhalla and other scientists at the National Centre of the Biological Sciences in Bangalore, India. Here they spent time in laboratories observing how scientists work on the sense of smell, trying to see how smells are artificially re-created and whether it is possible to create a particular smell that can be 'performed' and repeated for audiences – though the impossibility of this, because of the ways in which smells contaminate each other so eas-ily, was something that 'defeated' both scientists and artists.[14] In this kind of cross-disciplinary team work it is helpful to Leslie and Helen if those working in science have a creative approach to their discipline which might in turn make them 'curious' about the artists.[15]

Prior to *On the Scent* Curious had been working in another laboratory environment out in Arizona State University in the US – one that was dedicated to the arts and technology. For a three-year period they worked in this laboratory environment which although exciting for them in lots of ways, also created difficulties for them as artists. Leslie explains:

> [A]t the end of three years, we were feeling as though we could hardly do a single line or move without being presented with a 45 page alogorithm by an engineer about how this was going to affect such and such. When you do work with so much technology you're working with a really big team of people and it's hard to be spontaneous or hard to make changes that you think might better serve the piece because you are so involved in the soft-ware writings and the hardware programming and so forth.[16]

Coming out of the large team environment, Leslie and Helen were, therefore, pleased to be getting back into the live performance work for *On the Scent* and their two solos, *Family Hold Back* (Helen) and *Smoking Gun* (Leslie). This was their work that was current at the time they came to workshop with us and both solo shows were performed in our Nuffield Theatre. *On the Scent* (Helen, Leslie and Lois Weaver) took place in a private house in Lancaster.[17]

As we stressed in the introduction, it is important to recognise that we are not aiming to, indeed could not succeed in, documenting all of a company's or practitioner's process and practice, but are rather focusing on certain aspects of the work. While the role of place and technology is something that the company is arguably well known for, in this particu-lar instance, given the company's return to studio-based and site-specific work, the workshop explorations with Curious were more particularly focused on their strategies for processing live work, for 'writing' place or site into practice, and, given their recent experience of making and per-forming *On the Scent*, the possibilities of smell for making, creating and 'placing' work.

'Curious feminists'

'Curiously' for us at this time of encountering Leslie and Helen's practice and process their shows were also explicitly political, indeed feminist political, pieces. Leslie's *Smoking Gun* works a personal family history into a critical take on the Bush/Blair politics of war. Helen's *Family Hold Back* uses the setting of an English dinner party to explore gender and class in the boys-only-club cultures of nepotism and espionage. Helen talked to us about their desire to be political coming from a deep-felt anger: of wanting to protest against the Bush/Blair politics, of '*being on the marches and not being heard*', and equally from the frustration of teaching groups of young women that are '*terrified of feminism*', and wanting to do something about that. What we felt we needed to understand working with Curious was their relation to feminism – particularly an understanding of feminism in relation to the company's longer production history.

Coming from a younger generation, Leslie and Helen have quite different experiences of feminism and feminist theatre to practitioners such as Bobby Baker or Sarah Daniels who 'grew up' with feminism. Starting a performance career in the 1990s coincided with a time when women's companies were 'out of joint', closing down, or occasionally going mainstream in the interests of survival.[18] Feminism was either 'done', 'dusty' or 'dirty'. Whilst identifying as feminists in their own lives, Leslie and Helen did not, therefore, present their company as feminist in way that an earlier 1970s women's company might have done. As the body of work that Curious has produced has tended, Leslie argues, not to offer a '*primary engagement* [...] *with women's issues, then the company doesn't really seem to be "feminist" to me in the sense in which many female companies have been feminist*'.[19] On the other hand, feminist issues have been woven into the fabric of several shows, some more explicitly than others. For example, in one of their early collaborations, *Three Semi-Automatics Just for Fun*, Leslie and Helen juxtaposed a 1950s style of the feminine with violence and guns, sourced by the somewhat astonishing (to us) *Women & Guns* magazine.[20]

One of their most explicit engagements with feminism is the web-based *Guerrilla Performance Locator*.[21] This is a website, commissioned by BBC1 and the Arts Council of England, designed to 'locate' or to map activist activities and performances around the world. Click on the red dots in different countries and you can bring up features of artists and activists who are willing to make public spectacles of themselves in the interest of a political cause. Click on the movie clip and you will see the US Capital building and America's Whitehouse, with Leslie and Helen, wrapped up as a 'human letter', posting/protesting to the American government. This is their homage to the original performance art activists, the suffragettes. It was they, Leslie 'teaches' in another quick-time movie clip on the locator website, who invented performance art and not Jackson Pollock, or the later body art feminists such as Orlan or Annie Sprinkle. In claiming performance art as the invention of the suffragettes, Curious are endorsing a view of this kind of performance as explicitly political and feminist in 'origin'. The activist tactics of the suffragettes, their politicising of the personal, their performative use of the body to 'display' the suffrage cause and their guerrilla-style invasion of public places and spaces, form an important feminist heritage for Curious's contemporary performance-making strategies.

Physical texts/writing texts

As the 'wrapped up' suffragette couple, Leslie and Helen are stuck together, but at the same time appear to be having quite different experiences, or so it would seem, given Leslie's agitated state and Helen's relatively calm, ethereal, looking away from her 'partner-in-suffrage-crime' pose. While the two women contrast with the architectural representations of American, male-dominated politics, they also counterpoint each other. This is an important point in terms of performance composition for Curious as, stylistically, Leslie and Helen bring quite different elements to their shows.

Like the suffragettes, Helen's work has always been firmly rooted in the body and in ideas of performing the body to challenge the feminine:

> *Much of the content of my solo performance work deals with the straitjacketing manipulation of socially constructed ideals of the 'feminine', including concepts of the 'body beautiful'. Through the use of my own body on stage, I strive to subvert stereotypes by appropriating them.*[22]

She also acknowledges the influence on her work of Jo Anna Isaak's case studies that argue subversive comedy as a strategy for female artists.[23] Her *'instinctive reaction to something that terrifies/angers/frightens'* is to *'"extreme it"*: [t]he terms "camp", "drag", "masquerade" themselves posit an element of play'.[24]

When she is making live work, Helen especially likes to do *'a lot with the body'* and also to *'work through movement'*. Although the Lancaster workshop was structured around a series of writing exercises leading up to an exploration of smell, memory and place (see below), Curious also took us on a brief detour so that we might experience the ways in which Helen particularly likes to create text through focusing on body parts. Working through a body part is not uncommon in physical making contexts. Split Britches, for example, used body parts to get into improvisations (and Peggy Shaw especially likes to focus on 'talking' from a body part – see Chapter 6, p. 111). With Helen it was a question of lying on the floor focussing on the body part in a meditative fashion, to explore the memories associated with it and then finding a movement to express them, which we gradually built up and exaggerated. This body memory/ movement was then fed into the writing of a piece of text, which in turn was performed using the movement not as a means of 'illustrating' the words but to provide another 'layer' of expression and meaning.[25] Similarly, another exercise had us finding two or three movements associated with some text already written, which were then stylised and used as a 'performance score' when delivering the text. Instead of relying more on a relish of the word itself, as for instance in some of Rebecca Prichard's writing or Jenny's Eclair's comedy exercises (see these chapters for respective details), in these exercises corporeal expression interacts rhythmically or in counterpoint to the spoken word. Writing out of the body in this way makes a stylistic difference to delivery and as a process allows for another layer of interest and surprise and associative meanings.

Leslie, on the other hand, who does not regard herself as having an equivalent kind of physical skill and presence to Helen, whilst always willing to engage with Helen's physical routes to making, has a preference for approaching performance through writing, and through particular issues or ideas that she wants to write into a performance. She likes to '*stalk different topics*' and to try '*doing lots of little things that kind of circle around a central idea*'. With writing as her preferred way into process, Leslie likes to have a period of setting and sharing-writing exercises. She explained how this works for the new piece Curious were working on (*Lost and Found*)[26] with Lois Weaver:

> *My process is mainly through writing but like with the new piece that we're making with Lois where, what we do when we meet up is we make up exercises for each other, like the* [Lancaster] *workshop exercises. We've got these little notebooks that we all have – (laughs) these matching notebooks! We went on a retreat and the idea was we would do certain things all together and we would each take responsibility for designing a couple of exercises and they're all with the ultimate aim of making this piece of work. So they're all questions and interrogations around 'What is that space like?' 'What do you think that space looks like?' 'What is an action?' 'What is a*

piece of text?' 'What do you think is happening?' So that's quite fun because you're all working towards the same thing but it's nice to give over to somebody else's way of coming at the topic.

Writing for performance

Mirroring Leslie's writing approach, we began the Lancaster workshop with a number of sharing-writing exercises. One particular exercise involved focusing on the task of scripting someone else's story. This was a paired writing activity in which you were given a few minutes to tell your partner a story that was a response to the title 'a difficult journey'. As a creative stimulus, the focus on a journey very much connected to Curious's interest in place, or getting to places. What this involved practically was that each participant had to write her partner's story.[27] To partner somebody that you do not know well, or not at all, allows for more surprise: stops you from thinking you already know what might be coming. To be entrusted with somebody else's story is also insightful in many other ways. For instance, there is a sense of responsibility in being given something personal that belongs to someone else. How far can you go with someone else's story? What dramatic licence do you feel you can take? When you hear your own story retold, what do you hear, or hear differently? What do you want to keep from this re-telling? Or what can you not bear to hear?

The exercise was also instructive for the ways in which it highlighted several writing for performance issues. It particularly encouraged participants to think about what helps to turn a story into a text to be performed. Crucial in our reflections were, for example, ways in which stories for performance can benefit from:

- Using the first person voice/narrative.
- Presence of the teller.
- Attitude of the teller: their relationship to the story, are they positioning themselves 'inside' it, or outside it, living it or reporting it?
- Repetition as a means of assisting with rhythm and helping to image the story being told.

In developing bursts of writing material in this way, participants were, nevertheless, ultimately coming back to, or keeping a hold of, their own stories, but possibly seeing them differently, or sensing possibilities in the material that they would not have otherwise felt, seen or been aware of.

Collaboration and process

This is illustrative of the ways in which Leslie and Helen process work together to assist in each other's creativity. In other contexts we have seen how important it is to have some kind of process collaboration, whether this is Sarah Daniels working with Sally Avens in radio, Bobby Baker with director Polona Baloh-Brown, or Jenny Eclair with her comedy sparring and writing partner Julie Balloo (see respective chapters). Through our experience of running the Women's Writing for Performance Project, and as we explain in Chapter 1, we are all too aware of the number of young, emergent women artists who want to make their own solo shows,[28] but equally of the difficulty of finding others, may be just one other, to work with. This is an important consideration, one especially important we would stress, for those, ironically, going into solo work.[29] For Leslie and Helen how they work together is by trying ideas (more through practice than discussion) out on each other. So practically what this means is that *'I might literally bring Leslie in and say, "What do you think about this? I'm trying this, do you think it works?"'* Each keeps the *'integrity'* of her own work whilst drawing on feedback from the other. *'It's interesting then,'* Helen explains, *'negotiating how you can use the other person and I think we have quite a natural rhythm in doing that, but we don't bring each other in as the director or outside eye even, really.'*

Because Leslie and Helen adopt an approach that means that they facilitate but do not direct each other, each is able to keep a hold of her own 'voice', her own materials, both in their solo shows or for solo moments within a collaborative piece, such as *On the Scent*. In practice this does (as we suggested earlier) make for distinctive performance personae. In the solos and *On the Scent*, for instance, Leslie works in a register that might be described as 'hyper-naturalism', in a stage persona that gives the sense of being closely based on herself as she makes informal, occasionally direct interactions with her audience, while Helen's performance style is far more physically-orientated. As a result her use of language appears more formal, stylised, 'theatrical' even, than Leslie's. At the same time, engaging in a process that allows for this difference in approach, style and persona, political and aesthetic connections are made by looking for the points of *'crossover'*:

Helen: *One of the things about* Smoking Gun *and* Family Holdback *is that we talk about this special relationship, which is to do with the content, to do with the US/UK special relationship in terms of Blair and Bush, but it's also that the pieces can absolutely be seen independently of each other. We could have them programmed separately, though, at the same time, one of the things we were interested in doing and playing with was having a code that you could follow through both. Now we didn't necessarily sit down and say: 'We'll do this together,' we didn't do that. We made our own pieces, and they are very distinctive, our styles and our stories. [...]*

Leslie: *So that was us both making our own scripts and then seeing what we had, and jettisoning some things and playing up other things where there was some crossover.*

In brief, the solos are illustrative of the possibilities that come from having someone to work with or 'off'. As a collaborative making process it is one that enables each artist to 'keep' her own style in practice: to be distinctive from, rather than having to merge with, the other.

From the personal to the global

As much as many of the ideas that Leslie '*stalks*' attend to matters of science, technology or facts, a point of '*crossover*' for Leslie and Helen, but coming from, as we have now established, their quite different performance directions, are their personal stories and histories. In common with all other practitioners in this study, Curious value the personal as an important creative source. Early on in the workshop, Leslie set timed writing tasks that required a response to questions such as 'Where do you come from?' or 'Where are you going?' How we 'place' ourselves past, present and future is open to a vast range of writing responses, from the literal to the figurative.[30] Again, it is the pressure of having to write in a particular moment, to respond immediately and spontaneously without pause for reflection or intellectualisation that enables the surprise, the shock, and the unexpected. It is in this way, as it is in many of these timed writing exercises that personal responses get creative makeovers. Biographical sourcing is not just a personal truth, but, to borrow from Lois and Peggy, a creative truth: one in which the 'real', the fantasy, the fictional get mixed up together (see Chapter 6, pp. 111–113).

More particularly, however, for both Leslie and Helen the impulse is not to make shows that are autobiographical as such, but to source the personal into a bigger, global picture. Helen, for instance, argues that the autobiographical does not '*drive*' FHB, rather the autobiographical is '*the means to an end*', and that end is political. For Curious, personal stories are then a means to connecting us to '*bigger things*'; to make the personal political. Whereas an earlier feminist phase of theatre-making might have explored and extrapolated the personal in the interests of a women's-issue-based piece, Leslie and Helen are drawn to the personal stories for the ways in which they offer *'little jumping off places'* from which it is possible to make *'connections, like how do you as a person in the world feel about things that are going on'*.

In the workshop, therefore, Leslie set writing tasks where she was getting us to 'map' personal responses with 'bigger things'. To give an example: we were set a series of family writing tasks. Each exercise was strictly timed in order for responses to be immediate and not reflective. The idea is that you have so many minutes to write down a story about your father's side of the family. Then you have to respond creatively with a story from the maternal side of your family. Each of these, the paternal and the maternal, has to have a contrasting mood or tone. Perhaps you follow the instruction for the father's story to be a happy one and the mother's conversely to be sad, or vice versa. Thirdly, you have time to make a quick list of family connections to public histories, to the 'bigger picture' of national and international events. Then again, strictly timed, you select bits from all three of these into one piece of writing.[31] What is particularly interesting about this 'mapping' of the personal with the bigger, political picture are the shifts between the familial, the social and the cultural. This gets heightened by the severe mood swings from light to serious and back again. When this gets performed – and everyone got to try out their personal-political writing pieces, performed individually and with a microphone which functioned to amplify or distance the personal into the political – what we observed was that it was the mood swings and content shifts that made for the possibilities of playful delivery.

Smell, memory and emotion

These kinds of writing tasks encouraged us to 'place' personal memories in a way that opened them up and out to the political and in doing so helped us to understand the processes by which the personal maps on to or with the political in the solos, *FHB* and *Smoking Gun*. Leslie's 'kitchen solo' in *On the Scent* similarly reflects a mapping of the personal with the political as the kitchen space is evocative of both a domestic present and past memories of home that mingle with the politics of America's nuclear industry.[32] Yet it also brings us to the other ingredient of the Curious workshop: the stimulus of smell. This was the main driver for the making of *On the Scent* in which Leslie and Helen, joined by Lois, got curious about the relationship between smell, memory and emotion. With Leslie in the kitchen, Lois in the living room and Helen in the bedroom, the decision was that each '*performer would occupy each of the three rooms, creating a smell-scape and a related narrative of personal memories and emotions for their room*'.[33]

Using smell as a stimulus or drive for generating performance material is something that Helen particularly likes to use in the making of work, although Leslie is also happy to follow her example in this. As someone '*sensitive to smell, smell associations*' Helen might, Leslie explains, '*bring a smell into the space where she was working*', just in the way that '*someone will put on a CD and play around to find movement or text*'. In the workshop Leslie and Helen set writing tasks that got us thinking about emotions and memories of smell. They set us some very simple writing tasks such as to think about early smell memories or to think about a smell that you have a strong reaction to or association with. Often it may be hard to describe a smell, but it's easier to feel for the associations, particularly also if you then begin to *place* these: to think about where the smell comes from. 'Placing' the smell begins to unravel memories, emotions and the stories that go with these. As Helen observes, '*[s]mell is placeless, ephemeral, unpindownable and at the same time, smell can transport us back to a moment in our past more vividly than any other of the senses*'.[34] What was especially revealing were the connections between childhood, home and family. This was a connection that Leslie and Helen made in their research process for *On the Scent* and one that helped them to solve *where* their piece should be performed, which was not in a gallery but in a home space:

> There's no way that we could think of to make the sense of smell really interesting as a gallery installation because in a way, without context, it just isn't that emotive and I think a smell that would be pretty emotive for you wouldn't have that effect on me, although there are certain smells that have a nostalgic effect on a lot of people.
>
> We decided to put it in a house and as soon as we decided to site the piece in a house everything fell into place and we made it really, really quickly. We decided to site it in a house because we thought, ok well our first question's 'What's the relationship between the sense of smell and memory and emotions' and the site of so much memory and emotion is your house, your home, and for a lot of people when they talk about the sense of smell they talk about childhood. Childhood homes.[35]

This point is reinforced in the performance when in the closing sequence to *On the Scent* the audience is invited back into Lois's living room space with its smell-scape of lilies, chocolates and 'Evening of Paris' perfume, for her to ask them questions about smell. Just as we had started working with the personal in the workshop, Lois draws the audience into the performance, asks them to give something of themselves by telling her something personal. *'I want you to think of a smell,'* invites Lois, *'It could be the first smell that comes into your mind. It could be a smell that reminds you of something significant in your life. It could be a smell that reminds you of home, or makes you feel homesick. Or it could just be a smell that makes you sick.'*[36] As a sensory experience, a smell is something that can pull us unexpectedly back to a childhood memory or childhood home. All homes have their own particular smells, it is just that it takes a particular level of (smell) awareness to experience what they are.[37] In brief, looking at those audience responses that Curious have already 'bottled' to DVD[38] it is easy to see how important the home is as a milieu for smell, memory and emotion.

On the other hand, what can also be revealing and useful in creative ways are those smells which you cannot place but come back to haunt you. Leslie talked about one such example when they were interviewing people for their 'Essences of London'[39] project in which they set out to capture the 'essences of city life' by asking Londoners from the boroughs of Brent, Hackney, Lambeth, Newham and Tower Hamlets, about their associations of smell with the capital city:

> [W]e spoke to a woman from Uganda who said: 'You know it's so strange because I walk down the street to get to college and it's a really ordinary street, it's really plain. There's really nothing about it that makes me feel anything at all,' she said 'but every time I walked down that street I would become tearful and I didn't know why. So I stopped walking down that street. I'd go out of my way not to go down that street. I wasn't quite sure why.' And then she said once she was late so she had to take the quickest way and she walked down that street and she saw somebody coming out of the house and she realised it was a house of a Ugandan family who were cooking a particular type of millet that really reminded her of home. But it was so subtle that she couldn't quite work out what was affecting her so it was just this displaced thing that was giving her an emotional trigger effect without her even being sure why. I think we're really interested in the stories of transgressing and surprising you and acting as a ghost or sneaking up behind you.[40]

Writing site and smell

Thinking about place and smell featured in our final workshop task. Here we were required to draw on the experience of the writing exercises to make a short piece for showing and sharing in which the piece was stimulated by and orientated through place and smell. Site-specific work by visual and performance artists allows space to be 'written' into performance; to become meaningful or to come to mean differently. Driven by the economics of the theatre industry, and by a politics and aesthetics resistant to theatrical conventions of stage, script, and character, etc., the desire to perform in non-theatre spaces is one that a number of contemporary practitioners share. While not unusual then to move out of conventional theatre space for performance, what made the explorations of place distinctive in the Curious workshop were the ways in which these were combined with the stimulus of smell.

Given that we were working in a campus environment we did not have access to domestic spaces. Rather, choosing a place on campus in which to perform mostly involved participants in ways of re-configuring or intervening in institutional spaces; exploring and exploiting the possibilities of campus architecture – the ways in which the various educational and social 'meanings' of the campus environment can be brought out, commented upon or be fictionalised as something else altogether. Working as part of a group, this also meant that our 'audience' for the moments of showing and sharing were larger than the more intimate configuration of the four person audience experience of *On the Scent*. Despite these differences, in a majority of cases the pieces that were 'made' for showing and sharing used space and smell in personal, evocative ways that took us to the 'place' of a past intimate experience or memory. For example, one participant located a piece of poetic writing in a dustbin enclosure where place and smell were used to perform the detritus of a failed love affair.

On the other hand, there were also participants who more completely combined site and smell with the Curious strategies of writing the personal out to the political.[41] Gerry made the most of this opportunity, for example, to explore the gender politics of her personal passion for cycling, a theme she had begun to explore previously in the final sharing task of Bobby's workshop. For the Curious workshop she staged a monologue about Beryl Burton and the Rossendale Ladies Cycling Club in a men's urinal.[42] Despite some 'natural air freshener' (some freshly picked twigs and leaves, that we were invited to hold under our noses as an antidote to the stench of male 'pee' and that were also meant to signify that we were actually in the public toilets near Epping Forest), the stench of the urine and the toilet location were overwhelmingly repellent and ghosted all kinds of (bad) memories into the space. All of this layered into her story of historical (and not so historical) prejudice against the lady cyclists. Like Leslie and Helen in their suffragettes-coupled-together against American politics, Gerry, dressed in her cycling gear and pointing up the gender politics of cycling, made a 'spectacle of her-self' as a feminist protest against misogyny and sex discrimination. Transgressing the strict gender segregation of a public space (toilet) had its own kind of guilty (we are not supposed to be here) pleasures. But the political impact of Gerry's story really occurred through the smelling rather than the telling. The mal(e)odorous stench lingered long after the moment of showing.

With more time and opportunity this would have been the moment to record our responses to the urinal smells, a moment to interview the group about their personal associations, stories, and reminders, mirroring the way that Lois asks the audience questions about smell at the end of *On the Scent*. Such a moment of asking would argue for an opening up, rather than a closing down – a moment of doing what Curious likes to do best – ask questions.

Notes and references

1. We interviewed Helen Paris and Leslie Hill on 20 March 2005, Lancaster University. Quotations are from this interview unless specified otherwise.
2. Leslie Hill, public talk presented at 'Artists Talking the Domestic', Symposium, Lancaster University, 4 March 2005.
3. Leslie Hill and Helen Paris (eds.), *Guerilla Performance and Multimedia* (London: Continuum, 2001), and Leslie Hill and Helen Paris (eds.), *Performance and Place* (Basingstoke: Palgrave Macmillan, 2006). *Guerilla Performance and Multimedia* aims to offer a range of practical advice to emergent performance artists. *Performance and Place* has contributions from scholars, artists and those who work in the arts on the topic of place in contemporary performance.
4. For more on this topic see, Leslie Hill, 'Push the Boat Out: Site-Specific and Cyberspatial in Live Art', *New Theatre Quarterly*, February (1998) pp. 43–47.
5. For details go to www.placelessness.com/china/, accessed 30 June 2006.
6. For details go to www.placelessness.com/seaside/, accessed 30 June 2006.
7. See *Performance and Place*, p. xiv.
8. Leslie Hill and Helen Paris, 'Being Curious' in Elaine Aston and Geraldine Harris (eds.), *Feminist Futures?: Theatre Performance Theory* (Hampshire: Palgrave Macmillan, 2006), pp. 56–70, p. 69.
9. For examples of women using the web for performance visit the Magdalena Project's 'web queen' Helen Varley Jamieson's site http://www.creative-catalyst.com/did.html, accessed 30 June 2006. Work through the site to find details of the four women cyber-performance company Avatar Body Collision and information on software developments for creating a web-based performance venue.
10. See DV and DVD training information posted on the Curious website, http://www.placelessness.com/, accessed 30 June 2006.

11. For Helen's reflections on this show and on performer-spectator communication and relationship see Helen Paris, 'Crossing Wires, Shifting Boundaries' in *Women and Performance*, Issue 24, 12:2 (2002), pp. 159–174. Available on line at http://www.placelessness.com/works/index.html, accessed 30 June 2006.
12. Leslie Hill, 'Deus ex Machina', *New Theatre Quarterly*, February (1998), pp. 48–52, p. 52.
13. Leslie Hill 'Push the Boat Out', p. 47.
14. For further details see Leslie Hill and Helen Paris, 'On the Scent', *Performance Research*, 8:3, pp. 66–72. Also available on line in a PDF file at http://www.placelessness.co/works/index.html, accessed 30 June 2006.
15. Ibid.
16. Leslie Hill, 'Artists Talking the Domestic'.
17. *Smoking Gun* and *Family Hold Back* were performed at the Nuffield Theatre, Lancaster, on 5–6 March 2005. *On the Scent* was performed in Lancaster 8–9 March 2005.
18. For more on this point see Elaine Aston (ed.), *Feminist Theatre Voices* (Loughborough: Loughborough Theatre Texts, 1997).
19. Leslie Hill and Helen Paris, 'Curious Feminists', p. 56.
20. In 'Curious Feminists' Leslie details *Three Semi-Automatics Just for Fun*, and also discusses *Guerrilla Performance Locator* and *Random Acts of Memory*.
21. Available at http://www.placelessness.com/guerilla/index.htm, accessed 30 June 2006.
22. Helen Paris and Angela Ellsworth, 'Humour in the (Juxta)Posed Body' in *Women's Comedy*. Available on line at http://www.placelessness.com/works/index.html, accessed 30 June 2006.
23. Ibid. For Isaak's case studies see *Feminism and Contemporary Art: The Revolutionary Power of Women's Laughter* (London: Routledge, 1990).
24. 'Humour in the (Juxta)Posed Body', http://www.placelessness.com/works/index.html.
25. See WWP website, http://www.lancs.ac.uk/depts/theatre/womenwriting/, Events Archive, Curious, 'Body Part Performance, My Left Knee'.
26. Ideas of what gets lost and found in life are a recurrent preoccupation of Curious – particularly in relation to other people's lives, not just their own. Curious first considered this topic in relation to Aids, working with Lois Weaver on the development of a website for World AIDS Day in 1996. Their more recent DVD, *Lost and Found* (2005) brings together some of their work on this topic, including, for instance, responses from communities in England's Black country to what has been lost and found in their lives, and documentation of their Shanghai residency which looked at a city going through a period of rapid change.
27. See WWP website, http://www.lancs.ac.uk/depts/theatre/womenwriting/, Events Archive, Curious, 'Exchange Stories About a Difficult Journey'.
28. This is not just a national trend, but the emphasis on young women wanting to make solo work is something that appears to be happening internationally. This observation is based on our experiences and conversations with emergent women practitioners at the international women's theatre festival hosted by Julia Varley: 'Roots in Transit', 15–25 January 2004, Odin Theatret, Hostelbro, Denmark.

29. See also the discussion in Chapter 2 on the working relationship between Bobby Baker and Polona Baloh-Brown, which is also relevant to this point.
30. See WWP website, http://www.lancs.ac.uk/depts/theatre/womenwriting/, Events Archive, Curious, 'Where do you come from?' and 'Where are you going?'.
31. Ibid., 'Something Funny About Your Father's Family', 'Something Sad About Your Mother's Family', 'The List – You and World History' and 'Microphone Piece'.
32. This is on account of the way that Leslie tells stories of her family from New Mexico interwoven with factual information about New Mexico's involvement in the making of the atomic bomb: '[T]hey made the bomb in New Mexico and then, to see if it worked, they dropped it on New Mexico. That's the kind of place I come from. Mal Pais Badlands'. 'On the Scent', *Performance Research*, 8:3, pp. 66–72, p. 71. As she performs this moment, she turns on the popcorn maker in the kitchen to create her own kind of domestic, atomic explosion.
33. Leslie Hill and Helen Paris, 'On the Scent', ibid., p. 69.
34. Helen Paris, 'Too Close for Comfort: One-to-One Performance' in *Performance and Place*, pp. 179–191, p. 187.
35. Leslie Hill, 'Artists Talking the Domestic'.
36. From On *the Scent*, DVD recording *Curious Presents Essences of London* (2004).
37. An example which comes up in the DVD footage, ibid., is when you come back home after having a holiday. Having been away, we then have the home/smell to come back to and have a heightened awareness of this.
38. Ibid. The DVD includes a selection of audience responses to Lois's questions on smell.
39. Ibid.
40. Leslie Hill, 'Artists Talking the Domestic'.
41. See WWP project website, http://www.lancs.ac.uk/depts/theatre/women writing/, Events Archive, Curious, film footage, 'Parachute' and 'Joan of Arc' clips.
42. See WWP project website, ibid., for images.

4
Speaking Out

SuAndi

SuAndi. Photograph by Paul Jones (www.pauljones-photographer.com)

First and foremost SuAndi describes herself as a performance poet and this practice was the focus of her workshop at Lancaster.[1] In this field she is part of a highly influential generation of artists which includes Jean 'Binta' Breeze, Benjamin Zephaniah, John Agard, and Lemn Sissay. In addition to this work, like several other practitioners in this volume, SuAndi has worked within and across a wide range of other creative forms and media, and is particularly known for her activism and artistry in a number of diverse, often socially disadvantaged, communities.

Acts of achievement: Ms Obe?

For the last twenty or so years, SuAndi has toured nationally and internationally as a performance poet and published several volumes of poetry.[2] During this time she has collaborated with small-scale theatre and dance companies such as Lip Service, the Extemporary Dance Company and Themba Theatre. Since 1994 she has received international acclaim touring with her live art piece *The Story of M*.[3] More recently, she has found herself operating in 'high culture', mainstream environments. In 2000, she was commissioned to write the libretto for an opera based on the life of Jamaican Mary Seacole, a Black nurse who was a contemporary of Florence Nightingale.[4] Before touring, in 2005 *Mary Seacole* played to packed houses for six nights at Covent Garden, and was followed by another libretto for a work entitled *The Calling*, composed by Tunde Jegende. This intra-cultural, multimedia piece premiered at the Bridgewater Hall with the BBC Philharmonic Orchestra with SuAndi performing as narrator/orator alongside a Malian singer, an opera singer, and a jazz singer.[5]

Meanwhile, back in 1985 from her base in Manchester in the North of England, she joined and almost immediately was heading up Black Arts Alliance (BAA), dedicated to 'raising the profile of Black work and to networking across different Diasporic communities – from Africa, Asia, the Caribbean and the Americas – at the same time as respecting the diversities, the social and cultural specificities of each community'.[6] Through BAA, SuAndi has co-ordinated and taken part in initiatives such as 'Revelations of Black' at the Royal Exchange Manchester (1987 and 1988), the annual series of 'Acts of Achievement' events which take place as part of Black History Month, and the first Black-led forum on live art, artBlacklive (2001). She is an active member on the boards of several influential artistic and public organisations and, amongst other activities, led the first Arts Council of England initiative for Black people and disability, entitled '*There Are No Limitations*'.

Sometimes as part of, sometimes alongside her work with BAA, SuAndi has also led innumerable community art and education projects with all sorts of age groups in all types of sites, situations and venues. These range from working with Asian women suffering domestic violence, an early pregnancy project, a project working with women with visual impairment, and more recently in Lancaster working with over three hundred local children, leading the 'arts outreach' team for the 2005 Slave Trade Arts Memorial Project (STAMP). An especially high profile example of this type of work arose out of a successful bid she made for a three-year grant from the National Lottery Charities Board in the late 1990s. This money funded a series of creative workshops led by established Black artists, aimed at the young men of Manchester's Black communities and designed to enable participants to work through issues of self-esteem, parenthood, identity, employment, religion and violence. The project culminated in *In My Father's House* (2001) shown at Manchester's Contact Theatre, a performance which involved over one hundred of the workshop participants.

As a creative and public figure SuAndi has attracted several prestigious awards and honours including an OBE in 1999, the Windrush Inspirational Award in 2003 and a NESTA Dreamtime Fellowship in 2006. Yet *as* 'SuAndi, O.B.E.', on at least one occasion when speaking in public she has found herself being introduced as 'Ms Obe'.[7] She tells this anecdote (largely) as a joke and while this mistake might, to an extent, be attributed to the fact that she goes by a single name, it might also indicate that twenty years after its founding there is still a need in Britain for organisations like BAA with the remit 'to remove the marginalisation that Black arts and cultures can experience within the mainstream arts infrastructure'.[8]

If we have felt the need to start this chapter by strongly underlining (some of) SuAndi's achievements and activities, it is partly because this marginalisation is also reflected within the British Higher Education infrastructure. As a result, despite her public profile and awards, like that of so many other Black British artists, SuAndi's creative work has received little academic attention. There are issues of 'genre' and categorisation bound up within the processes of this marginalisation which are 'political' and which have inevitably impacted on SuAndi's creative career.

The limiting nature of categorisation

Considering the breadth of her own activities, it is not surprising that one of SuAndi's 'tips' for emergent practitioners is: '*Say yes to everything,*

*then go home and think hard about it. Turning down any work opportunity –
then you might as well go work in Woolworths. Ask for help, don't be shy, be
courageous.'*[9] Her recognition of the need to 'be courageous' might be
seen to reflect the way that throughout her career SuAndi has had to
contend with the fact that in the world of the arts *'If you're Black, you're
always emerging'.*[10] As she has suggested, this is largely due to the way

> *Black Arts get represented and positioned – especially by funding bodies.
> [...] The ever- changing arena in which the arts infrastructure places our
> work has only served to further frustrate our creative endeavours. In the last
> 20 years we Black artists have been named as 'Multicultural', 'Ethnic
> Minorities', for the briefest period of time 'Black', then elevated (or so they
> claimed) to 'Cultural Diversity', and then hammered down again to the
> anagram of 'BME' (Black Minority Ethnic).*[11]

Behind this process of re-definition is undoubtedly a worthy and liberal
attempt at 'progressiveness', but it can produce a constant shifting of
ground beneath the feet of Black British artists and others from so-called
'Ethnic Minorities'. More importantly, while these changing categories
do not necessarily reflect the way these artists might view their own
practice, they can have a significant impact on the conditions of its production, reception and perception. As SuAndi indicates *'culturally
diverse, means diverse from the "norm", which is white',*[12] so that, *'When we,
Black Arts Alliance wanted to do work with elements of dance, music poetry
etc., we were called Community Arts or General Arts. What we did wasn't
recognised as an art form'.*[13] Similarly, she quotes playwright Sonia
Hughes as having to admit to herself that, 'I do write from a
Caribbean/British perspective, I was just scared to acknowledge it in case
it was thought of as folksy, community-not art. But it is'.[14] In effect then,
these successive shifts of categorisation may be a matter of replacing one
limiting definition for another; of upholding a process of 'minoritisation'
which re-marks in advance the work of Black British artists as 'other' to
the norm, and as 'folksy', as community, not (proper) art.

Born of Nigerian and British heritage, on a personal level SuAndi has
always had to deal with the pernicious effects of labelling: *'I was born
half caste; I grew up coloured; I became Black; I became an artist; I could join
the ethnic minorities; I could be multi-cultural – a whole list. I had to peel off
those labels used to hide and disguise me'.*[15] Clearly, despite her dislike of
labels, SuAndi still refers to herself and others as 'Black' and indeed
'Black British', a category that as the BAA policy statement cited above
indicates includes 'Diasporic' subjects of African, Asian, Caribbean heritage,

or with roots in the Americas. As this heterogeneity and the language of the statement signals, for SuAndi as for many other Black British artists and activists, in line with Stuart Hall's arguments in 'New Ethnicities'[16] and 'Cultural Identity and Diaspora',[17] the term Black is therefore used to signal a *political* identification. It is not intended as a 'homogenising' term that reinforces an essentialist discourse of 'race'. Rather it functions as a signifier of political solidarity and resistance amongst highly diverse cultural groups, whose commonalities arise from the historical legacy of being colonised, exploited and/or enslaved, and from still being the target of the deeply rooted *racism* that persists in 'Western' cultures and societies. Interestingly, SuAndi puts a large measure of her own political radicalisation down to her entry into the arena of the arts in the 1980s, asserting,

> *My first lot of writing was very confident, sexy – I was slim, I was popular, I was a 'frock' (bought a dress every Saturday night). I knew who I was. It wasn't political. [...] I didn't want to deal with race. I think actually if I'd never come into the arts I would never have woken up politically. It was the arts that woke me up. In the arts you get the dirtiest, underhanded, second agenda [...].*

In discussing Vayu Naidu's work in Chapter 8 we stress the political potential of the cultural hybridity of Diaspora subjects in a fairly 'celebratory' fashion, and this reflects the tone of much academic writing on this concept. Yet this issue of shifting categorisation in the arts also serves as a reminder that, as Naz Rassool points out, if 'Black Cultural hybridity can be perceived as a challenge to a society constructed around an ethnically homogenous norm', then equally this can be the result of the way 'that in an ongoing quest for rootedness within a society so fundamentally hostile to their presence, Black people have to learn to adapt, adjust and change their cultures, their customs, behaviours and cultural consciousness, in order to belong socially as well as to identify culturally and politically within the dominant culture'.[18] Further, like all theoretical categories, in practice the concepts of Diaspora subjectivity and cultural hybridity can easily slip into becoming homogenising in themselves, glossing over the very multiplicity of identities, histories, localinalities, and modes of cultural expression to which they supposedly refer.[19] For example, it is easy and tempting to construct a comparison between Vayu and SuAndi, and indeed we have already begun to do so. Both can be defined as culturally hybrid 'Diaspora subjects' and *historically* storytelling and performance poetry are closely related, even at times indistinguishable, forms. Yet, in many ways a comparison between SuAndi and Jenny Eclair or SuAndi and Bobby Baker is just as illuminating[20] and the similarities between Vayu and SuAndi are outweighed by the self-evident ethnic and cultural differences and the disparate and highly particular ways in which each has developed her own *contemporary* creative practice. In fact, as practitioners, at least some of the apparent 'similarities' between SuAndi and Vayu are the effect of the way that the genres within which they work have tended to be categorised and defined within the arts and academic infrastructures as 'folksy and community'.

'Giving voice' to other histories

We are not suggesting that the diversity of SuAndi's artistic and political activities simply reflect ways in which she has been forced as an artist to adapt and adjust within a hostile culture. Or rather we are not suggesting this in a purely re-active, negative or passive sense, since the issues identified above *have* inevitably impacted on her career and her artistic practice. Yet, as an activist and an artist her response to such pressures has been defiantly pro-active and affirmative. As she puts it, '*Racism does not position us in society, we achieve out of rebellion*'.[21] Her advice to emergent practitioners to say '*Yes to everything*' and her working across a wide cultural spectrum can be seen as part of a determined policy of resistance; a refusal to be bound by the limits that social and artistic categorisation can impose and reproduce. This is not only for herself but is also on behalf of many of those who in various contexts are labelled and defined as 'other' from the norm, whether by dint of 'race' gender, class, disability, age or regional location. Artistically, one of SuAndi's key strategies is to literally 'give voice' to the multiplicity of histories and everyday stories that such labels conceal and suppress. In her community and outreach work this is achieved by facilitating people to speak for themselves: to establish their own multifaceted and complicated identities in positive terms, beyond the stereotypes.

The performance piece *In My Father's House* project exemplifies this strategy. It was conceived in response to the way the BBC TV series *Babyfather*, first aired in 2000, was focussed around the (stereotypical) notion of the absentee Black father. As John McGrath, artistic director of Contact Theatre explained, the project's final performance was an opportunity to hear 'the under-represented voice of Black British men speaking positively and with mutual support about the complexities and triumphs of their lives – and particularly about the complexities of fatherhood'.[22] The same refusal of 'types', *'the celebration of humanity in all shapes, colour and laughter'*,[23] an emphasis on the giving voice to marginalised and underrepresented histories, are equally core to all of SuAndi's work. This obtains whether thinking of her libretto for *Mary Seacole*, a figure who was largely 'forgotten' until the latter part of the twentieth century, her performance poetry, or her live art piece *The Story of M*.

Standing for 'M for Margaret,/M for Mother,/and now M for Me'[24] – *The Story of M* details her white, working-class Liverpudlian mother's attempt to bring up her two 'mixed race' children with a sense of pride in *all* aspects of their identities and inheritances. Inevitably, much of the story revolves around the racism and the class and gender prejudice that M faced, but told mostly in M's 'own voice' it is full of warmth and humour, defiant determination, and hope in the face of ignorance and stupidity. At the end of the piece SuAndi switches to her own voice to pay tribute to M, this 'One special woman', whose legacy to her daughter is her pride in 'carrying the spirit of my ancestral people' and the supreme confidence with which she can say,

> So if any of you think that all mixed raced people
> Grew up confused, without identity
> Think again. [...]
> I know exactly who I am –
> I am a Black woman
> A mixed race woman.
> I am proud to be a Nigerian daughter
> whose father loved her.
> He loved me so much,
> And I am equally proud to be the daughter
> Of a Liverpool woman of Irish descent.
> Confused? Get out of here.
> If you're loved, you're loved.[25]

As with the poems SuAndi read to us in the workshop which gave voice to a wide range of 'characters', including a young girl with learning difficulties and 'Darren', a pregnant teenager, a striking characteristic of *The Story of M* is an adamant refusal to accept the position of 'victim', even in the face of the most blatant attempts at victimisation. This same approach is evident in works that touch on some of the more traumatic aspects of the histories connected to her African ancestry, such as the poem *I Feel My Presence*. Written in more 'formal' tones than *The Story of M*, this piece looks back at the horrors of slavery but is ultimately a celebration of strength in survival which ends with the exhortation 'And rejoice that Africa lives on in me'.[26] While SuAndi stresses that *'we cannot afford to leave our histories behind'* her gaze is not purely retrospective; filling the 'voids' of history is important because *'otherwise tomorrow will be tainted and bloodied over and over again'*, but equally *'telling stories of our achievements against the odds weaves stories of the past into the present. The "keeping" of community blends the old and the new. We look backwards to look forwards'*.[27]

Performance poetry: 'getting paid for talking'

Many years before she created the final version of *The Story of M*,[28] it was the death of her mother and a desire to record her own family history that impelled SuAndi to start writing,

> *Because I have no grandparents [...]. When my mother died I thought if I ever manage to have children, I want those children to have a history and my father had left his homeland, gone [...] to the wars, lost all his family. And I really just wanted a family line – and I wrote her life, what I knew about it and everything. And I did it in that way that people do when they're going to be writers – although I wasn't writing for publication.*

Her move into poetry occurred a while later, *'20/21 years ago'* when some friends were doing a poetry performance and book launch with Lemn Sissay:

> *I watched these people read their poetry and thought it was amazing and then I watched them get paid and they got paid, like £1.36. But I thought my god, you can get paid for talking, I'm going to do this. And that's exactly how I came into it.*

However, her own writing *'went on one side for a long while'*, because she got a job with a Manchester-based arts organisation called Cultureword

> *And they were going through a feminist split, [...] of course I went with the women. And we formed our own group which became BlackScribe and I said I'd admin for them for a while – I wanted to write, but I said I'd admin. And then we were doing something one day and I said I'd like to have a go at reading. [...] they were very supportive [but] It probably took me three years before I could say 'I'm a poet'.*

Drawn to the idea of '*getting paid for talking*' it was inevitable that '*[f]rom the out start I knew I wanted to be a Performance poet, my words struggle on a page, without a voice, my voice*'.[29] This is a common perception of performance poetry but this comment also represents a moment of 'shyness' on SuAndi's part. Some of her work *is* produced 'for the page' and is effective in this medium.[30] Nevertheless, having seen her live, the impact of her poems in print is enhanced by being able to imagine her performing them. Similarly, the text for *The Story of M* 'stands alone' in print, but as is the case with most live and/or performance art pieces, especially when they are autobiographical, it is impossible to conceive of anyone else interpreting it.

Nevertheless, at the risk of stating the obvious, SuAndi's remark does underline the distinction between a poetry *reading* and performance poetry, in that the latter is primarily, if not solely, designed to be 'performed' by the poet in public rather than read in private, and in some cases may even be improvised on the spot. Often known either as 'spoken poetry' or 'oral poetry', the spread of the particular term 'performance poetry' can be linked to a variety of movements embracing turn-of-the-twentieth-century, avant-garde experiments with poetry, the American 'beat' poets of the 1950s and the British 'Mersey beat' poets of the 1960s. In Britain from the 1960s onwards, the aim of the vast majority of performance poets has been to rescue poetry from the rules, conventions and typical content of the white, middle-class, literary canon; to allow it to reflect contemporary life and everyday language(s), thereby (re)opening poetry to a broader, even 'popular' audience.

However if, like storytelling, performance poetry has sometimes been perceived as 'folksy' and community it is perhaps because both are rooted in ancient 'oral traditions' with, for instance, SuAndi connecting her craft back to that of the African 'Griot'.[31] As Benjamin Zephaniah indicates, 'People in the west tend to see the oral tradition as something from the past and not relevant in the age of the internet, but elsewhere the tradition thrives, where there are restrictions on people's abilities to speak, or when they have no access to the media'.[32] Like storytelling, performance poetry can happen anywhere, at any time, since all that is required is a poet and an audience. It has a very long and culturally broad history of being used to express and disseminate social and political resistance, both in the West and elsewhere. Zephaniah's own work, like SuAndi's and that of other Diaspora performance poets who emerged in a political climate of 1980s Britain, especially fraught in terms of issues of 'race' and class, is very much within this resistant tradition. These artists were also leading figures in transforming and revitalising

this genre. However, with one or two notable exceptions, as with virtually all other arts, up until very recently this medium has tended to be a
male-dominated one.

   This has gradually changed, not least because of a new burst of energy
at the turn of the century in this field in Britain, facilitated by the spread
of 'open mic' sessions (where aspiring performance poets can turn up
and try out their work in front of an audience), and with the arrival of
'slam' from the US. 'Slam poetry' is sometimes referred to as a sub-genre
of performance poetry, along with categories such as hip hop, jazz po,
punk poetry, dub poetry, pop poetry and stand-up poetry. However, the
term 'slam' arises from live poetry competitions which are judged by the
audience. The structure of these events recalls the rather 'gladiatorial' set
up in stand-up venues such as the Comedy Store in London in the 1980s
and 1990s.[33] Nonetheless, this set-up was effective in engaging younger
audiences and in regenerating stand-up as a form, and the same might
hold for slam. Engaging in slam competitions is potentially a useful way
of getting started as a performance poet. While SuAndi welcomes them
on such grounds, she also sounds a note of caution: '*SLAM poetry is entertaining but it does not allow the depth and breadth of any one writer to be
enjoyed by the audience. SLAM is about the loudest applause (or indeed boos).
A poet-for-life will quickly leave the SLAM stage*'.[34]

   As this indicates, SuAndi has a strong sense of the particular param-
eters of her 'craft' as a performance poet. Nevertheless, there is some
crossover of performers between stand-up and performance poetry and
some general commonalities. In both areas it is common to find oneself
sharing a bill with several other performers and therefore having limited
time in which to make an impact. In both cases this is usually achieved
by means of a distinctive stage persona, quick wit, verbal dexterity, or a
'relish for language', with the use of theatrical devices or any form of
'staging' being consciously rejected.[35] Rather than any specific 'training', like most stand-ups SuAndi's craft has been developed from years of
'hands on' experience, during which she admits that she sometimes
found herself '*running out of the theatre by the fire door*'. However, despite
these similarities between the fields, in her workshop SuAndi told us of
a disastrous experience when she found herself appearing on the same
bill as the comedienne Jo Brand. Humour plays an important role in
SuAndi's work and she is concerned to include and entertain all her different audiences, but she does not shirk from presenting them with 'serious', emotionally demanding, controversial or politically challenging
material that goes beyond the sort of subversion and transgression
enacted by Brand. SuAndi's use of humour ranges from that which

provokes the laughter of recognition and inclusion, to something edgier. For example, one of her poems is about a wealthy white woman who finds herself in prison after an addiction to sun tanning leads to her being mistaken for Black. While this poem is 'comic', the character's shock and outrage at the way she is treated is an implied critique of the ignorance on the part of many white British subjects of the consequences of institutionalised racism, a point that might be a bit too close for comfort for some (white) members of the audience.

SuAndi's performance persona

As a performer, SuAndi can give a vivid sense of character. She acknowledges '*I'm trying to build up that personality, that image. There's a bit of knowing the colour of the hair, the eyes, the weight of the character that I'm writing in. And there are moments in the dark theatre, when [...] I sort of believe that you can make an audience see something. If you believe it strongly enough [...].*' However, she does not consider herself an 'actor' and while she does frequently and intentionally (but only temporarily) create confusion between the characters' voices and her own, ultimately they remain distinct. This is because while these 'voices' appear to be exclusively female and SuAndi's work is unquestionably feminist, this is a feminism that acknowledges and underlines the social and cultural differences that can divide women as a category. If, as we argue above, none of her characters are prepared to take up the position of 'victim', equally, some can reiterate attitudes and behaviour which are not always sympathetic or 'politically correct'. SuAndi's performance persona is then crucial in marking a difference between the characters and herself and also in negotiating between the audience and these figures.

As with Jenny Eclair, Bobby Baker and Leslie Hill (see respective chapters), this persona is *directly* rooted in SuAndi's own personal history and identity, but this is not purely a matter of 'being herself' and is a conscious projection of certain aspects of her identity. In each instance, as well as striking differences in style between these performers, there are (sometimes) slight, yet significant differences of function and meaning which relate to the performance conventions within or against which they are operating. SuAndi's persona is notably without any of the different degrees of formalisation of clothing, make-up, voice, and other staging devices, that we have identified with Eclair, Baker and Hill. With SuAndi, perhaps, formalisation is provided through the structure of the poems and by their characterisation, but this aside, her performance persona makes even Baker's appear relatively 'theatrical' by comparison.

Part of this is that SuAndi is literally, a *sit down* poet. Her preference for performing seated focuses attention on the expressivity of her voice and face. It is also a key element in creating an intimate relationship with the audience in which she addresses them in what she describes as '*an over-the-garden-fence conversational style*'. This draws on gendered, Northern British, working-class, 'domestic', oral traditions, rooted in the family and the community, and produces a persona marked by directness, warmth and self deprecating (but not self *parodying*) humour. This persona provides a fundamentally unthreatening base line from which SuAndi can perform the poems whilst simultaneously marking a distance from the characters they voice. However, SuAndi's consciousness of projecting an aspect of her 'self' in this persona is also a means of maintaining a sense of personal distance from the performance *as a whole*, so that paradoxically, she can respond to the audience 'in the moment'. For SuAndi this is a key characteristic of performance poetry. In the workshop she said '*It's like kids dressing up, it's spontaneous, reacting to the audience, it's* live *poetry and it's important that the set is 'open' and can change according to what's happening in the room.*'

Reacting to the audience is obviously crucial for the performer in any live medium but the more a performance moves towards the theatrical and is 'scripted' or 'scored', if only by the need to identify cues for light, sound, visuals or other performers, the less scope there is for spontaneity in terms of the whole. SuAndi's poems might be understood as 'mini scripts' but in the choice of poems, their delivery and in the scoring of the set overall, there is much potential for improvisation which, once again, strongly aligns performance poetry with both storytelling and stand-up. In SuAndi's case, she takes advantage of this potential, to negotiate a relationship with each particular audience, which is often a finely judged balancing act between inclusivity and political challenge.

The workshop: making an entrance

Negotiating her relationship with the Lancaster workshop group, SuAndi began by chatting casually and then seamlessly slipping into the following:

> *My name is SuAndi and I am a poet. I am. I'm a poet and I am very proud of it, the fact that I do it and I don't mean anything rude by it. I mean that I am a poet. Because I can't spell and I don't speak very well and as for my grammar – well. But despite all of that it is a fact that I am a poet. But I haven't got a garden full of autumn breeze or a stream to wander or a cosy*

eave so I write about the streets and the people I meet because I'm an urban poet. I live in Manchester. And the moon in June doesn't make me swoon or birds singing in tune but a political rap about all governments traps. I like that because I am an anarchist poet. And love has never hit me like a fist full of feathers but I never pull really nice fellas so I write out in verse all the things about men that are worse, Hiyah Men because I am a feminist poet. Now as you can see I haven't got blonde hair or hazy blue stare I am totally black so it's a natural fact that I am a Black poet.[36]

Throughout the workshop SuAndi stressed the importance of 'making an entrance'; taking control of the performance space, introducing yourself and *'getting to the first poem'*, which she emphasised *'should not be too long'*. This 'introductory' piece above fulfils most of these functions in one swoop and we have heard her use it on other occasions – although not always, because as we have indicated, she tailors her performance to the particular audience, venue and context. For aspiring-performance poets then, SuAndi advises that key questions are: *Who is your audience? Where are you performing? Who are you performing with?* If possible, she suggests spending time observing the room to work out the audience dynamic and best way to make an entrance. She later described to us another 'entrance example' from a performance in Amsterdam:

And the third night was four ten minute slots. These ten minute slots are really quite difficult for me because my poems are long and, you know, I don't just want to go on and be the angry black, feminist poet – I want to show different sides. And I was thinking oh my god – and obviously because it's a Dutch audience – will the English survive, will it carry, will the humour work? And the stage was really high and everyone got up on it inelegantly, which meant I was going to do it worse than anybody else. But I'd got a little fan club with me that had been to all of the four gigs and there was an older African guy there, so as I got up, I pushed him out of his seat and indicated that he had to help me to the stage, which he did [...] and I did whatever the intro was that night and then I said to him 'Sidney, what time is It? Sidney I need you to tell me when there are three minutes left because I would hate to finish before you'. ... And I got him to keep time for me and I played that a little bit with him. Sometimes it doesn't work, you have to find different ways – that's why I like to sit at the back of the room and work out what's going on.

Having achieved her entrance, as demonstrated in her start to the workshop, SuAndi will get to the first and all subsequent poems, by 'chatting' in her intimate and 'domestic' style, often around the background to the poem or issues related to it but without explaining the 'meaning' of the poem itself. She then segues into the poem usually without marking the transition and sometimes without an immediately perceptible change of tone. Alternatively, she will either perform this whole preamble in the 'character' from the poem or again, as she speaks, gradually slip into character and from there into beginning the poem. All of these strategies mean that she does not usually give the titles of poems when performing (hence our inability to refer to or cite those of the poems she offered as examples in the workshop).

These strategies date from very early on in SuAndi's career when she noticed that many poets reading or performing their work would say,

> 'Oh I think the poem speaks for itself' and then go on to talk about it for five minutes, explaining it! And I also didn't like the A4 file that was held very regally under their noses, like teachers do, you know. [...] I asked for something to put the file on next to me because I don't like to read, but so that I could put my hand on it as a safety measure. And I didn't introduce the work. And when I came off, they all said, "that's just not the way to do it, you're meant to explain why you've written it." Where I'd just start talking and then halfway through think have I got to the poem yet, I can't remember, I'd better start it. So that just became my technique in performance and [...] when you realise that that's what you're doing, you begin to craft that technique. So that's my whole idea that you lead into it, so that the journey begins from the moment I begin my set.

The journey – surprises, inversions and reversals

The notion of a 'journey' through the set indicates that an important part of SuAndi's 'art' lies in 'shaping' the performance *as a whole*. As she indicated in the workshop, the selection of the mix of poems in the set is obviously part of this shaping, but so too is the way the poems are introduced or linked together. The ease of the slide from 'just talking' to the poems indicates how far, like Bobby Baker, SuAndi takes her material and her language(s) primarily from the ordinary and the everyday. As a result, it is sometimes possible for the listener to miss this transition, only realising that the poem has started after a slight delay. Yet, this delay retrospectively *foregrounds* the fact that a transition has taken place and the sense of surprise this produces can be pleasurable and comic but it can also be unsettling. Talking about the preamble to a poem which starts with SuAndi asking apparently seriously, '*Does any-body want a drink?*' she says '*sometimes, particularly the barmaid, when somebody has absolutely fallen for it and answers back – and it's just the luck of God how that works, some people realise they've fallen for the joke and they don't like it. It's such a fine line.*'

Some of us did fall for it in the workshop – we thought she was offer-ing to make the coffee (!) – and the realisation of the joke did provoke some embarrassment. However, a more striking example of the potential effect of this technique emerged when SuAndi performed at the Symposium that was part of our research project.[37] The audience con-tained invited guests from the US, and some British participants looked on horror-struck as, after having been introduced and having made a few general comments, 'SuAndi' apparently launched into a complaint about the vulgar style and loud behaviour of American tourists. The 'game' only became apparent when gradually, she adopted an American accent and slipped into the poem proper, so that it became clear she was actually speaking in character. One of the *points* of this poem (like virtually all of SuAndi's work) is that it questions assumptions about the ability to 'read' identity, either from appearances or through 'categories', includ-ing that of national identity. As such, SuAndi's preamble 'performed' or 'embodied' this point for this particular audience through a technique that aimed at surprising, or even shocking us into recognising that these issues were not just 'problems' of the fictional characters in the poem, or for other people, but for us in the here and now of the Symposium event.

The poems themselves also often work to create surprise on the level of narrative structure by using reversals and inversions, by withholding information, or 'twists' that are only revealed at the end. This is demon-strated in *The Story of M*, which is constructed with enough ambiguity throughout to allow and even encourage an assumption that M herself is Black, up until the close of the performance when SuAndi comes out of 'character' and shows a photograph of her mother. Equally, it is evident in the poem SuAndi performed at the Symposium (and also at the work-shop) as discussed above. Initially, this appears to be based on a charac-ter who makes prejudicial judgements on the basis of 'race' and class. Gradually, it is revealed that this woman is living in the deep South of the US in 1960s, where she witnesses a violent racist attack in response to one of the famous peaceful 'sit-ins' at Woolworths lunch counters, by young Black students protesting against segregation. This experience causes her to re-evaluate her attitudes, but the twist revealed in the last lines is that this is not the story of a white woman who is appalled into questioning her own prejudices, but of a Black woman who is politicised into resolving never again to play into the structures of racial oppression by opting to 'pass as white'.

SuAndi's introductory and 'linking' strategies can then be described as alienation or foregrounding devices that aim to encourage us to reflect on our own assumptions and 'blind spots' around the issues addressed in the poems. The potential in performance poetry as a 'live' art to respond to different audiences, venues, and contexts is crucial in producing this effect. SuAndi's introduction to the 'passing' poem at the workshop was different to the one delivered at the Symposium, where as noted its impact partly depended on the presence of US citizens in the audience. However, considering the Symposium context in general with its audience of (overwhelmingly white), politically engaged practitioners and academics, she perhaps also judged it necessary to be more provocative than in the workshop in order to work against any potential sense of complacency concerning our own political progressiveness. Similarly, when performing in the South of England, SuAndi says that she smoothes out the broad Northern accent of 'Darren', the pregnant teenage girl, and moves her up a class, to try to avoid the audience reading the poem through received stereotypes of Northern, working-class people and thereby dismissing this piece as not relevant to their own lives.

However, if SuAndi employs alienating devices she is careful to structure a 'journey' through the set, whereby the more challenging material is off set by the *'over-the-garden-fence conversational style'* of her persona, her use of humour and a mix of poems that includes various tones and moods. As she states in her Amsterdam anecdote cited above, *'I don't just want to go on and be the angry black, feminist poet – I want to show different sides.'* This is not least because once identified as *'the angry black feminist poet'*, she has been labelled in a manner which for some might make it easier to dismiss what she is saying.

Finding our own voices

Because many of these techniques are so specific to SuAndi's particular style, for some of the workshop, she focussed on demonstrating them followed by group discussions of the general considerations that they threw up for aspiring performance poets. When it comes to writing the poems, inevitably her process is solitary. As she indicates,

> *If it's going to be a performance piece, it's completely written in my head. If I write it on to paper, it will always be a piece I can only read. I do write*

them down eventually – but only after I've completed them in my head [...]
because even though I'm having to repeat it to keep hold of it, I'm already
hearing the delivery of it. [...] If you write it down you get busy with how it
should look on the page. [...] I might not write for ages and ages and then
in one night I might write eight pieces – by writing I mean both, on paper
and in my head.

The technique of 'writing in the head' is a difficult one to demonstrate
or share with others in the workshop situation. However, SuAndi did
lead us in exercises designed to encourage us to experiment with finding
our own 'voices'. For instance, she presented the group with a blank
piece of white paper and asked each participant to give a very brief verbal response to it, indicating what it made us think of, or feel. Responses
included 'creative anxiety', 'school examinations', 'whiteness', 'bore-
dom', 'new beginnings', and were written down on the paper by SuAndi,
who then read them out as a 'poem'. It has to be said that the surprising
success of this 'poem' depended largely on SuAndi's skill as a performer
and on her ability to 'find' a rhythm in this text. Nevertheless, this task
can be compared to the 'paper' exercise in the Split Britches workshop
(see pp. 114–115). In both instances the aim was to encourage the imagination through 'making something' together and, in this instance, to
demonstrate that poetry does not have to conform to the sorts of rules
and conventions she parodies in the introductory verse with which she
started the workshop. Rather, this exercise shows how, using ordinary
speech, poetry can be created from and about literally 'anything'. This
goes along with her insistence in the workshop that *'It's called perform-*
ance, do what the hell you like so long as it works.'
In relation to writing poems this extended to the use of rhyme. As
recognised in oral traditions, rhyme can be highly effective in retaining
listeners' attention and in facilitating understanding, but in more 'literary' poetic circles it is often negatively associated with the popular and
the populist. During the workshop, one participant with a background
in *written* poetry described it as 'liberating' to be given permission to use
rhyme 'if it worked'. Having noted this, however, we should point out
that like most other contemporary poets, where SuAndi uses rhyme it
tends to be irregular and the majority of her poems actually depend on
rhythm. Yet, rather than drawing on established poetic conventions,
these rhythms draw on those of everyday speech, bringing out the
'poetry' of 'ordinary' voices.
In terms of 'content', SuAndi encouraged us to find material based
on people that we have encountered through our daily lives, indicating,

'*None of my characters are invented, I mean I might not know them in a personal relationship, but it might be I've just watched somebody on a train journey and you fabricate who they are.*' For a further exercise, our brief was then to focus on finding and reproducing the 'voices' of family, friends or acquaintances, thinking about personality, expression, vocabulary and rhythms of speech. This task was later developed, this time asking us to write in someone else's voice, and also in response to a single word given to us on a piece of paper, with SuAndi stressing that, above all, we should try to '*avoid the obvious*'. One participant later commented 'My slip of paper had the word "OLD" written on it. The instruction to write in another's voice was challenging and, because it isn't the mode in which creative thought normally occurs for me, it probably pushed me towards making a less stereotyped persona'.[38] The stimuli SuAndi provided were designed to challenge us to look *genuinely* to the everyday for our inspiration rather than falling back on stereotypes, and while she reminded us to think about the use of pause, silence, and rhythm in creating the 'voice', she also stressed that '*it's a distraction to try and make it "poetic"*'. Interestingly, the participant cited above went on to say, 'However, whilst I could hear the rhythm in my head as I wrote, I found hitting this intonation when speaking the poem very difficult indeed – which is perhaps the flip-side to the compositional strategy, as the persona was almost wholly alien to me'.[39] This might suggest why SuAndi prefers to 'write in her head' in the first instance but it also underlines the *performance* challenges involved in this genre.

Towards the end of the workshop, SuAndi set us the task of writing a poem on an emotional, even 'tragic' theme that was 'close' to us, this time using our own voices. This produced some striking results, but also raw emotion and tears, which again reflects something of SuAndi's own practice. She describes how, whenever she performed *The Story of M*, the section directly touching on M's death always made her cry, except once, and '*that's how I knew that it wasn't a good performance*'. When we saw it some of the audience were crying with her, especially those of us who have lost a loving and much loved parent. If this seems dangerously close to essentialism via the dreaded emotional identification, so be it. This does not detract from the fact that in the context of its narrative of the everyday casual violence that arises from the divisions produced by socially-constructed identity categories, this moment of shared grieving seemed to mark the possibility for community. Moreover, in *The Story of M*, SuAndi very clearly speaks of *her* ancestry and family history, in a way that is specifically located in time and place and not easily open to appropriation by others. Instead, this was a moment that encouraged us to reflect back on our own histories and losses to recognise our differences but also our commonalities.

As importantly, it takes courage to risk 'giving voice' to what touches us most deeply or to approach certain 'fine lines' in public, not least when these are the 'fault lines' that divide our culture. SuAndi's willingness to do these things in her practice and her encouragement of others to do likewise is part of her rejection of rules and conventions, categories and limits. Above all, it is part of her insistent 'speaking out' against the processes of evasion, denial and silence that allow racism, sexism and other forms of prejudice to continue to exist at a deep-rooted, structural level in our society.

Notes and references

1. SuAndi's workshop entitled 'Sussed Words' took place at Lancaster, 2–3 October 2004.
2. *There Will be No More Tears* (Pankhurst Press, 1996); *Nearly Forty* (Spike Books, 1994); *Style* (Purple Heather and Pankhurst Press, 1990). Her fourth collection, *I Love the Blackness of My People*, is unpublished.
3. In Chapter 2 on Bobby Baker we have used 'live art' and performance art interchangeably. SuAndi prefers the term 'live' art. The difference between live art and performance art has been much debated. It is often matter of fine distinctions rather than general rules and, so we would argue, can really only be made on a case by case basis.
4. For information on Mary Seacole see http://www.100greatblackbritons.com/bios/mary_seacole.html.
5. These were Kasse Mady Diabate (Malian singer), Gwen Ann-Jeffers (opera singer) and Cleveland Watkiss (jazz singer).
6. BBA policy statement in *4 for More*, SuAndi, Ronald Fraser-Munroe, Mem Morrison and Michael McMillan (Manchester: artBlacklive, 2002), p. 94.
7. SuAndi recounted this anecdote as part of a paper she gave at the 'Women's Writing for Performance' Symposium, 28–30 April 2006.
8. BBA policy statement, *4 for More*, p. 94.
9. From email correspondence with SuAndi, 7 July 2006.
10. Introduction, *4 for More*, n.p.
11. SuAndi, 'Africa Lives on in We', in Elaine Aston and Geraldine Harris (eds.), *Feminist Futures? Theatre, Performance, Theory* (Hampshire: Palgrave Macmillan, 2006), pp. 118–129, p. 124.
12. Introduction *4 for More*, n.p.
13. Ibid.
14. Sonia Hughes quoted in SuAndi, 'Africa Lives On in We', p. 124.
15. Introduction, *4 for More*, n.p.
16. Stuart Hall, 'New Ethnicities', in Houston A. Baker, Jr., Manthia Diawara and Ruth Lindenborg, (eds.), *Black Cultural Studies: A Reader* (Chicago and London: University of Chicago Press, 1996), pp. 163–72.

17. Stuart Hall, 'Cultural Identity and Diaspora', in Nicholas Mirzoeff (ed.), *Diaspora and Visual Culture: Representing Africans and Jews* (London and New York: Routledge, 2000), pp. 21–33.

18. Naz Rassool, 'Fractured or Flexible Identities? Life histories of "Black" Diasporic Women in Britain', in Heidi Safia Mirza (ed.), *Black British Feminism* (London: Routledge, 1997), pp. 197–204, p. 189.

19. For example see Imruh Bakari 'A Journey in from the Cold: Rethinking Black Film-Making', in Kwesi Owusu (ed.), *Black British Culture and Society* (London and New York: Routledge, 2000), pp. 230–8, p. 231. Bakari points out that in the 1990s discussion of 'Diaspora' film making tended to focus primarily on the work and the aesthetics of African and Caribbean Diaspora practitioners, at the expense of ignoring the specificity of British Asian productions.

20. Aside from the similarities between performance poetry and stand-up (see main text below) both SuAndi and Jenny Eclair were born and raised in the North of England and, as well as other issues, both are concerned with class and regional identity. As such both are very aware of the continuing legacy of the historic 'North-South divide' given an early representation in Mrs Gaskell's 1854 novel *North and South*. The more recent existence and effects of this divide were especially in evidence in Britain of the 1980s, when SuAndi and Jenny started out on their careers. Northern cities like Manchester and Liverpool were far harder hit by the economic recession and rising unemployment produced by fundamental shifts within the countries economic and industrial base under the influence of Margaret Thatcher's government, than the vast majority of the Southern region. With *The Story of M*, like Bobby Baker, SuAndi was working in the field of multimedia, 'live' or performance art (see note 3 above), both also share a strong focus on 'transforming the everyday'.

21. SuAndi, 'Africa Lives On in We', p. 122.

22. John McGrath, http://www.nesta.org.uk/ourawardees/profiles/3334/02_profile.html, accessed 6 April 2006.

23. SuAndi, http://www.artscape.orrg.uk/detail.php?id=3045, accessed 4 July 2006.

24. SuAndi, *The Story of M*, in *4 For More*, p. 18.

25. Ibid.

26. SuAndi, 'Africa Lives On in We', p. 128.

27. Ibid, pp. 125–6.

28. As with Bobby Baker, SuAndi cites Lois Keidan as an importance source of support; Keidan was instrumental in prompting SuAndi to write the final version of *The Story of M*.

29. SuAndi, National Disability Arts Forum website: http://www.ndaf.org., accessed 4 July 2006.

30. For example see the poem 'Parents', http://www.artscape.orrg.uk/detail.php?id=3045, accessed 4 July 2006.

31. The Groit (and Griotte) is a poet, storyteller, praise singer and most importantly a genealogist or 'keeper of history' for the community. For further information, see http://www.rps.edu/0205/keepers.html, accessed 4 July 2006.

32. Benjamin Zephaniah, http://www.benjaminzephaniah.com/truth.html, accessed 7 July 2006.

33. For more on stand-up venues, see Chapter 9, pp. 161–163.
34. Email correspondence with SuAndi, July 2006.
35. In fact, props, music, and theatrical devices are banned in some Slam competitions. See Poetry Slam Inc. FAQ, http://www.poetryslam.com/modules.php?name=FAQ&myfaq=yes&id_cat=1&categ, accessed 7 July 2006.
36. Text courtesy of and copyright SuAndi, email correspondence, July 2006. Clearly this piece could be written out as 'verse' but when SuAndi sent it to us by email she did not do so.
37. See note 7 for details, and WWP project website, http://www.lancs.ac.uk/depts/theatre/womenwriting/, Events Archive, International Symposium 2006, for SuAndi performing at the event.
38. See website for full text and for this poem and other examples from the workshop http://www.lancs.ac.uk/depts/theatre/womenwriting/, Events Archive, Sussed Words, SuAndi.
39. Ibid.

5
Women Writing for Radio

Sarah Daniels with Sally Avens

Emma Trevette and Amy Golden in the Chicken Shed Theatre Company production of *Who's Afraid of Virginia's Sister* by Sarah Daniels. Photograph by John Pridmore

While there are any number of practitioners who serve some kind of formal 'apprenticeship' for their writing careers, often a theatre- or arts-related programme at a higher educational level, there are also those who come to their 'craft' more by 'accident' than design. Playwright Sarah Daniels is one of the latter.

Educated at a secondary modern in Greater London on the outskirts of Essex, Sarah was someone who hated school; was likely to be the one at the back of the class not following lessons. Her only source of contact with drama was through English lessons: *'the school thing was terribly boring, dull and a bit intimidating because you'd have to read a scene and you'd be allotted parts so you'd be forever looking to see if you could pronounce the words properly and not make a fool of yourself in front of the class.'*[1] In her fifth form year, however, she got offered tickets to her local repertory theatre. Reluctant at first (this was hardly the 'done' or 'cool thing' for teenagers) a friend eventually talked her into going. However, once she discovered that the theatre bar was less than vigilant when it came to underage drinking and that it was possible to get served a *'vodka and lime'* without the hassle and humiliation of being refused, theatre became a *'habit'* for Sarah – as did the drinking, she joked with us, in her self-deprecating, comic style. While Sarah explains how she can *'remember quite clearly going to see Shakespeare and saying "Oh I'm not coming here again"'*, the repertory system meant that the programme changed every month, so *something* more accessible or entertaining was always likely to turn up. Gradually, *'sort of by osmosis'*, it was the repertory theatre that got her hooked on drama.

Leaving home at eighteen, Sarah moved further into London. This was the 1970s, the decade when there was an explosion of women's theatre and socialist theatre, *'and the great thing about that was that some of it was absolutely dreadful so I would sit there thinking "I could do better than this, even I could do better than this."'* After a time, she began to write her first play, but in secret, *'I didn't do it under my embroidery or whatever Jane Austen was supposed to have done, but I did do it completely in secret.'* Spotting an article in *Time Out* that explained that the Royal Court read all unsolicited scripts, she sent it in. The script was rejected, but the critical feedback she received was just what she needed to carry on with another play: *'the reader's report was, I thought, very complimentary and it absolutely gave me the confidence to think ok, it wasn't good enough, but that one has been taken seriously, I'm going to write another one.'* That next script became her London debut play, *Ripen Our Darkness* (1981), and Sarah's career at the Court was launched.

Sarah 'joined' the Court at a time in the 1980s when, under Max Stafford Clarke's direction, there was notable encouragement and support for women playwrights. It was here, at London's premiere new writing venue, that she began to hone her writing skills, and, alongside Caryl Churchill, came to figure as the most prominent and influential of British-based writers in the emergent field of feminist theatre and theatre scholarship. *Ripen Our Darkness* earned her another Court production (a first Court commission automatically gave you the right to another): *The Devil's Gateway* (1983). She returned to the Court in 1984 with the most controversial of her plays, *Masterpieces* (first opened in Manchester at the Royal Exchange, 1983) and in 1986 with *Byrthrite*. Her Court appearances continued into the 1990s with *Beside Herself* (1990) and *The Madness of Esme and Shaz* (1994).

Also in 1986, as a marker of Sarah's 1980s success, *Neaptide* was performed at the Cottesloe, Royal National Theatre. The director of that production was John Burgess, the anonymous reader and reporter of that very first unsolicited Court script. Burgess recently directed the revival of *Masterpieces* for the Court's fiftieth anniversary celebrations (February 2006), evidencing the way in which Sarah forges lasting and significant relations with her directors. Jules Wright, for example, the original director of *Masterpieces*, later directed *Beside Herself* (1990), while Lawrence Till (director of *Morning Glory*, 2001) is both friend and ardent fan, someone who confesses to having seen *Neaptide* seven times.[2]

We signalled above that *Masterpieces* was, and still is, the most controversial of Sarah's plays. At the time of its original performance the play attracted hostility on account of its radical feminist treatment of pornography. Rather than engage with the politics or aesthetics of the drama in any serious way, the (mostly) male critics objected violently and wildly to the way in which they considered themselves, as 'members' of the male sex, to be under attack.[3] In consequence, they conspired to a view of Sarah as a man-hating lesbian: making it an attack on her person, her views, rather than being willing to consider the argument she makes in *Masterpieces* that there is a need to attack those social structures that aid and abet violence against women in society.

This early, feminist period of her writing was driven by the urgency Sarah felt to say something about the oppressiveness of women's lives; a political and feminist awareness of violence against women '*went hand in hand with* [her] *starting to write*', and '*Masterpieces was written very much from a "right I'm going to write these arguments in a play" and it came out of a real feminist movement and I felt part of something.*' There were particular moments of social violence that especially fuelled her anger.

While she was still at school, for example, a boy from the fifth grade raped a girl at knife point. After admitting to the rape he was sent away to borstal. However, Sarah explains that what happened next was that '*the headmaster stood up in front of the whole school in assembly and said this had happened and it was going to be in the local paper, but what we all had to remember was that it was always a case of half a dozen of one, six of another. And the thing is that in the '70s that was a "completely acceptable" thing to say.*' Later, in the 1980s, Sarah felt angered by the Yorkshire Ripper case and the ineffectiveness of police action as the Ripper continued to murder women. She was later to dramatise the case in her adaptation of the Pat Barker novel, *Blow Your House Down* (1995). These were feminist issues that Sarah felt needed to be talked about and theatre was the forum in which she entered into public debate.

A criterion for political theatre is that it should open up debate beyond the confines of the theatre and *Masterpieces* is one play that can make a serious claim to having achieved this goal. Teaching the play for a number of years, we can vouch for the hot debates it sparks in the seminar room. '*I often meet people who are not the generation of students now, older than that,* Sarah says, '*Who say to me "Oh, that play, I split up with my boyfriend over that." Or blokes come up to me and say "my girlfriend never spoke to me again after that play."*' While the play is less likely to inspire break-ups in audiences today, judging by the post-show discussion after the fiftieth anniversary revival of *Masterpieces*, the pornography debate and violence against women, are issues that young women still find highly relevant to their lives now.[4]

Defining Sarah's early work as political, however, is not just about subject matter but is also a question of form. Following a strong (although by no means the only) Court tradition in Brechtian-feminist dramaturgy, also important at that time to plays by Caryl Churchill, means that as regards their formal composition Sarah's plays work to alienate those social structures and systems that are oppressive and violent to women. This she combines with a style of 'broken realism'. She has been particularly fond, for example, of using monologues in a way that interrupts and disrupts other dialogue-based scenes, creating a pause in the dramatic action. Her monologues are often funny and give voice to characters otherwise silenced by class, gender, sexuality, or any combination of these.

In the rush to condemn rather than to consider the argument of her work and its aesthetics, a crucial point was overlooked: as much as Sarah's theatre was concerned with exposing the wrongs against women, it was also concerned with the possibilities of change and more hopeful futures. Borrowing from Eve Sedgwick (see Chapter 1, p. 10), we can summarise this as Sarah's recourse not only to a 'faith in exposure' tactics, but also to her invocation of the 'reparative': she writes both of the (expected) damage done to lives as well as the (unexpected) futures that her characters achieve by repairing, (re)-making, or putting their lives back together differently for and by themselves.[5] In brief, while Sarah wrote anger and despair at violence against women into her plays, what she also brought to her drama was a note of optimism that came from the '*sea change of women consciously changing their thoughts and having solidarity with other women*'. Women '*consciously changing*' their lives through finding each other arguably themes and structures her play-writing, characterised as it is by women who, isolated by the differences and prejudices of class and sexuality, try to see each other differently in the interests of less oppressive relationships and communities. The reparative possibilities may be less in evidence than the angry protests (the all-women's picnic towards the close of *Masterpieces* or the aunt and her niece escaping to a Mediterranean island at the end of *The Madness of Esme and Shaz*) but they are present and important to her sense of agency and change, a point which we shall return to shortly in the context of Sarah's radio work.

In addition to her Court writing, Sarah has formed other strong theatre associations – with the Watford Palace Theatre (*Morning Glory*, 2001; *Flying Under Bridges*, 2005), or with Clean Break Theatre Company (*Head-Rot Holiday*, 1992), dedicated to improving the lives of women affected by the criminal justice system, and for whom Sarah serves on the board of company directors. Most recently she was commissioned by the community venue Chicken Shed (Southgate, North London), for whom she wrote *Who's Afraid of Virgina's Sister* (2006), a play in which she looks at the inequalities of opportunity for people with 'disabilities' in a relationship between two sisters. Since *Neaptide* she has been back to the National Theatre to take part in the National's Connections seasons which offer new plays for young people by established writers. For these seasons, Sarah wrote *Taking Breath* (1999) on environmental protest and *Dust* (2003) on bullying. Getting young people interested in theatre goes back in part to her own dire experiences of drama in the classroom and the desire for young people to discover theatre in more lively and stimulating ways.

Enter radio

In what has become an increasingly diverse portfolio of work, Sarah also came to write for radio. As someone, as we have described, who began writing stage plays in the late 1970s in the ferment of feminism and fringe theatre, radio seems an unlikely later career choice. Sarah confesses that as a younger writer she would never have thought of writing for radio, even though other women dramatists around her, like Gilly Fraser, encouraged her to think about it. Indeed, she admits that in those earlier years she thought radio dull, unexciting, something only her parents would listen to: '*I remember thinking I'm never writing for Radio 4, only sad bastards listen to that. And now, well this must prove I'm a sad bastard, because I listen to Radio 4 all the time.*'

Partly what changed her view was her growing disenchantment with the writer's position in the theatre. While the 1970s was an exciting time to get involved in theatre (and feminism), Sarah argues that the playwright's role began to suffer thereafter as a consequence of Thatcherite policy-making: '*Thatcher killed off theatres in this country in that everything had to make money, everything had to be a money-making product.*' Playwriting was damaged by what she describes as the '*lottery mentality*': '*you are writing this play which you really hope hits the jackpot*', because the economics of theatre writing mean that unless you have a major (commercial) hit, it is virtually impossible to live by writing alone.[6] Of Sarah's stage plays, *The Gut Girls*, which she wrote for the Albany Empire about the girls who worked in gutting sheds of Deptford at the turn of the twentieth century, has earned her the most income (on account of the amateur rights, which are not at all huge, but at least have been regular). To support herself as a writer she takes on television script writing – episodes for the BBC soap *Eastenders* or the children's programme *Grange Hill* which she has contributed to for over twenty years now.

Moreover, if in theatre she came under attack from the critics on account of her radical feminist politics, these have helped her career in other more positive ways and in particular with beginning a writing career in radio. Specifically, it was the National's production of *Neaptide*, a play which deals with lesbian custody issues, which prompted radio producer Anne Edyvean to commission Sarah to adapt the American novel *The Friends* for radio. The novel focuses on the friendship between two sixteen-year-old school girls who start a relationship. The girls are befriended by a teacher who is then sacked for being a lesbian. The commission came through around 1990–1, and Radio 5, which at that time catered for young people and children's drama, made the broadcast. What is interesting about Sarah's first radio commission is the way that it 'speaks' to a young audience which, as we note above, has been important to Sarah's career, but about issues of sexuality for which her main stage theatre work has been so controversial: '*I don't think they'd do that now. I can't think of anywhere where somebody would say oh yes that's great, do a story for young people about two girls falling in love.'*

After *The Friends* adaptation Sarah started doing more drama for radio and worked with about six other writers on a project called *Stars*, adapting a series of books by Hunter Davies. In the mid-1990s she was commissioned by Caroline Raphael[7] to write an original radio play on post-natal depression, *Purple Side Coasters* (broadcast in 1995). For several years she had a hugely enjoyable time working as part of a team of writers for the world service radio soap opera *Westway*:[8] *'We had such a laugh doing this, I've never enjoyed anything so much. The producers nearly pulled their hair out, because if you get six writers in the room and you give them control – one of us had a magic marker and a board – and we just behaved like very, very naughty kids at a party.'*

Working on *Westway* was also how Sarah came to meet the producer/director Sally Avens. With Sally, Sarah found in radio the kind of successful writer-director relationship that had been so important to her in theatre, with Burgess and Till especially: '[...] *if you work with someone you trust, like Sally produces and directs it all – I still think that's the same in theatre that the most important relationship is between the writer and the director – and if that works and if the other person understands what you want to say and where you're coming from, then it can work really well.'* As someone sharing Sarah's interests in women's writing, Sally had an idea for a series of four plays based on love poems by women writers. Though aching to develop an idea of her own, which was a play about breast cancer (which was refused on the grounds that Radio 4's soap *The Archers* was running a breast cancer storyline)[9] Sarah was persuaded to contribute to the 'Women on Love' series and wrote *Warming Her Pearls*, based on a Carol Ann Duffy love poem.[10] Sarah and Sally have since continued to collaborate: in 2002 Sarah finally got to write her breast cancer play, *Cross My Heart and Hope to Fly* which Sally produced and directed. She worked again with Sally on *The Partial Eclipse of the Heart* (2004) and *The Sound Barrier* (2005).

While Sarah and Sally have both had careers in different media (theatre, television and radio for Sarah; television and radio for Sally) both now feel happiest when working in radio because of the opportunities that it provides the writer (Sarah), or working with writers (Sally). In their jointly led workshop with us,[11] Sarah and Sally introduced us to techniques of writing for radio and outlined the possibilities radio offers emergent writers, reflecting in particular on Sarah's script writing for radio, and more generally on women writing for and in this medium. To have writer and director present meant that we had insights into Sarah's writing processes connected to the business of radio production that Sally oversees.

Women writing for radio

Of all the media we encountered on our project, radio is the most accessible to emergent writers, and radio 'converts' Sarah and Sally advocate it as a medium in which it is a good place for writers to start. This is not least because as Sally argues *'BBC Radio Drama is the biggest commissioner of new writing in Britain. We have the opportunity to produce more new writing than most theatres, primarily because we have so many outlets for it on radio.'*[12] Although, given our interest in encouraging women to write for performance, we must responsibly point out that radio does not provide the writer with an income that it is possible to live off,[13] on the other hand, it is writer-centred; views the writer as core to its business. From Sarah's personal point of view, as someone who had a tough time with the misogyny of the press in the wake of *Masterpieces*, it is also a medium where there is less critical exposure: *'writing for theatre you have to be quite robust to take the flack from the reviews. It's very, very hard sometimes to pick yourself up from that. Radio's more comfortable.'*

One of the things that we learnt from hosting the project workshops was that while many of us may have ideas for plays or performances, very rarely do we get these beyond the ideas stage. What can make the difference is (as we also reflect in both the Bobby Baker and Curious chapters) the possibility of having an outside eye – one that is both critical and encouraging as a means of building up confidence and developing skills. This was crucial in terms of transforming Sarah from an 'I can do better than that' idea of being a writer, into actually being one. Unlike the Royal Court Theatre, not all theatres will offer feedback on unsolicited scripts. However, radio is one medium where solicited and unsolicited scripts will get a response. A writer needs to know that she can put ideas forward for a play – to a BBC department, to individual producers or to the Writersroom (which is the forum for new writing at the BBC), and that she will get a response that will more than likely be critical, but will, nevertheless, show that *'one is being taken seriously'*; encouraging, and enabling the would-be-writer to carry on with her work. The feeling that 'one' is 'taken seriously' is important to promoting the confidence in a writer, while critical feedback is essential to helping her to see what further work needs to be done.

Moreover, the commissioning process for radio is far less fraught for the writer than it is in the theatre. Whereas in the theatre there is a full production team to persuade and to convince of your ideas, in radio there is one key person to deal with: the producer/director. Ultimately it is the producer who takes the work to a commissioning editor. Twice a year there are commissioning rounds at which producers present their ideas for different drama slots,[14] taking forward work by both new and experienced writers. The commissioning editors are like *'the buyers'*, Sally explains, while the producers are *'the suppliers'* who have to *'sell'* their ideas to the network in order to get the budget to make the plays. While an experienced writer like Sarah will be able to get a radio commission on the basis of a proposal, a newcomer can expect to have to keep drafting until there is a full script ready to commission. Experienced, or inexperienced, the producer/director is the person the writer works most closely with: the writer's guiding outside eye from beginning idea through to production, where they (rather than the writers) will oversee the business with the actors and the recording process.

What makes all of these general points resonate on a gender basis, for women writers, is the way in which radio has both a predominance of women working in radio and listening to radio drama. *'There are some really strong women in radio,'* says Sarah, giving Caroline Raphael, Anne Edyvean and Clare Grove as examples. These women tend to work at the practice-end of radio writing, however, rather than in the higher, more powerful roles of radio production, that remain largely male-dominated. According to Sally and Sarah it is the wish for some kind of work-life balance and the desire to stay at the more creative end of the business and in contact with the writers (the higher up you go, the less the contact and creativity) that 'keeps' women at the creative rather than the executive levels of radio work. While this means that in one way there are fewer women rising to the 'top' of the radio profession, on the other hand this increases the likelihood of a strong creative women's team, as reflected in the working relations between Sarah and Sally. In terms of listeners, a broadcast like the Afternoon Play reaches an average audience of 900,000 (although BBC research manager Mike Smith states that '2.4 million people listen to at least one play a week').[15] In the make-up of that listenership, 56 per cent are women who listen to the afternoon plays. Smith explains '[women] tend to listen more often than men, who are less likely to be at home to listen, and most listening is still carried out in the home'.[16]

As a radio producer, therefore, Sally argues the importance of the *'domestic'* to radio drama. *'People often use that word* [domestic] *in a derogatory way,'* she says, *'which I don't think they should.'* *'It's often a realm in which women writers write because they are interested in emotions'*, she explains, '*they are interested in family and relationships and that world and I think it's* [radio's] *a perfect medium for that because you're speaking very directly to a lot of people who are living that kind of life and to whom those things are hugely important and are life changing.*' This is an interesting observation given the way in which women's theatre and performance writing has tried over the years to loosen the ties of identification between the domestic and women's writing. However, it does suggest radio as a place for woman-centred themes or topics; a medium in which breast cancer or post-natal depression, to pick on two of Sarah's 'female' topics, are subjects important to the high numbers of at-home women listening to the drama broadcasts. In the initial notes to Sally for her 'Women in Love' series, for example, Sarah says that she wrote, '*why, with all my experience, can't I just be allowed to write a play which I'm really burning to write about a woman who has breast cancer? It only affects 40 000 women every year and, guess what, they probably all listen to Radio 4!*'

Characters and radio realism

Drawing attention to the domestic is also a way of signalling a dominant perception of radio drama as a more conservative medium than many of the other types of performance practice explored in this volume, although in saying this we would want to stress Sally's comment about not turning this into a negative or '*derogatory*' observation. It does, however, bring us to a point of understanding how Sarah's writing has changed from her early political stage work (as described earlier) as she adapts to a different medium.

Fundamental to this change is that where earlier work opted for a highly politicised style of 'broken realism', Sarah's writing for radio invests more heavily in psychological realism that remains dominant in mainstream media such as television, film, theatre and radio. As we rehearse in Chapter 1, since Brecht, the use of any type of 'realism' has been perceived as antithetical to politically progressive theatre and performance (and indeed our own feminist theatre and performance scholarship has often played a part in contributing to this argument). While we would in no way dispute the limitations of certain types of traditional or mainstream realism, we would, however, acknowledge the possibilities of historically contingent and shifting *realisms*. The psychological realism of Sarah's radio writing is one which is open (rather than closed) to a process of realignment: of 'moving' characters (and listeners) to a place that through experience in the course of the drama, however grim or desperate, is more hopeful than that from which they started. Arguably, the narrative that Sarah makes out of the lives of her radio characters is now less concerned with a feminist 'faith in exposure' than in the reparative possibilities that obtain for both sexes, even while her women characters remain the most central to the writing. Asked recently in the post-show discussion to the revival of *Masterpieces* how she would respond to the view that her attitude to the writing of male characters back then was hostile, laughing, she said she would have to agree with that observation. Today she argues that she is much more '*mellow*' about *all* of her characters, male and female. Also, she admits in a moment of '*being very, very honest*', that the hostility of the criticism back then means she does aim to be far less '*negative*' about her male characters now, adding, '*I always think I get more positive response if I've written a man in a play, than if it's just "all women".*'

In the radio workshop, we learnt that the writing of characters begins as a part of the commissioning process (see earlier). A writer has to make her pitch for a play; briefly present her idea for a drama in order to get the work commissioned. In making her proposal the writer is less likely to secure a commission if she proposes a play about 'x and y' issues. Script editors and producers want to know about characters and storylines.[17] As an example, Sarah presented us with her original idea for *The Sound Barrier*, pitched for a sixty-minute radio drama slot, and initially titled *The Long Silence*. This was a play that we listened to in advance of the workshop, along with recordings of *The Long Wait* and *Cross My Heart and Hope to Fly*, and was a key point of reference in the workshop for understanding Sarah's writing process. Recommended by the *Guardian* reviewer as 'required listening for aspiring radio dramatists', on account of the way that the play 'clearly showed how to build a story and weave different voices together' without 'one note, one moment' being out of place, it is also one of a handful of scripts that the BBC 'Writersroom' has posted on its website as examples to instruct and to inspire other writers.[18]

Her proposal for *The Sound Barrier* has a set of notes on all of her characters as she first conceived them: Audrey, the lonely seventy-year-old widow; Becky the professional single mum with a drink problem, and Colin, profoundly deaf and missing the support of his parents (especially his mother) who have both died. She gives an indication of the 'story so far' (before the play begins) and some idea (for the benefit of the 'suppliers' and 'buyers') of what will happen in the end. While the notes indicate that a range of issues are covered in the drama – child welfare, alcoholism, living with deafness, and so on – her emphasis is on character: who these people are, what their lives are like, what their views on the world are like – all the kinds of small details that put together will make them effective in the drama.

In brief, for this style of production a writer has to know her characters, needs to know their back stories in order for them to come across as credible and personal: characters that are believable; characters that feel as though they are in the room with us. To be effective these types of characters need to embody an emotional truth; to be authentic and moving in a way that persuades the listener to 'believe' in them and to invest in their world. Sarah explained to us that this is more easily achieved in her writing when she works with characters that she feels closer too (though for a contrasting view on this, see Rebecca Prichard, Chapter 7, p. 121). Experimenting with character writing in the radio workshop showed us that those characters that in some way evolve more directly out of the writer's experience can be easier to get inside of, although you do have to take care that they do not just end up sounding like yourself. On the other hand, you may have to work harder at those characters that are less familiar – perhaps in terms of class, gender or race. When she wrote *Partial Eclipse of the Heart*, which has a middle-aged, Black, female character, Sarah was '*proud*' of the character writing, '*especially as the woman who played it was very complimentary.*' Yet she '*still felt that thing of not being Black myself – of looking at it more closely in a way because I'd hate to be racist or anything* [...] *It is difficult – that's a line you have to walk.*' Equally, Sarah would identify writing her male characters as more difficult than creating the women characters in her plays.

The challenge of constructing characters that are further away from a writer's experience may involve some research. This might include checking out various facts – finding out precise details of someone's job, for example. Also, in the interests of making a character believable rather than one-dimensional or clichéd, it means getting to grips with how they speak: what a character would or would not say, depending on their class, gender, age, and so forth. A character that goes outside of her or himself will not be convincing. For example, when Colin, the deaf character in *The Sound Barrier*, suddenly starting talking about his deceased mother as a feminist, Sarah, advised by Sally, came to realise she had made a mistake and cut this kind of detail out. In the workshop we developed an awareness of all of this by trying an exercise that was about how to avoid clichés in radio writing: we were each given a cliché to start with and then had to re-write it in a way that avoided the cliché, but left the group to guess what the original cliché was (e.g. Too many cooks spoil the broth./I don't need any of you men to help me change a light bulb. I'm better off on my own.).

We were also given a character task in which we were instructed to think about someone that we know well and to write down three things that we could hear them saying. Those three things were then passed to someone else to source a character. To help with this we had a twenty questions character checklist (see appendix), and then we were given a few minutes to start a short piece of writing that, in the voice of the character, begins 'Last night I'. This, and other related character exercises, helped us to think critically about knowing a character's back story: not telling the story of a character, but working in the kind of detail that helps to communicate who this person is in a believable fashion.

Monologues

In positioning us in the first person, this latter exercise 'Last night *I*' also encouraged an exploration of the monologue form. The monologue has a particular strength in radio drama. It can be an excellent means, for instance, of creating the voice of self-delusion: a character that is blind to her (mis)readings of other characters and situations. Monologues can also operate not just as a conduit for inner thoughts, but for a character to tell us what has been happening to them and to others in a way that advances the storyline. It is also possible for monologues to include detail about characters that do not have an actual voice in the drama. In *The Sound Barrier*, for instance, Sarah changed her original triangle of speaking characters, Colin, Audrey and Becky, to Colin, Audrey and Jenny, a social worker on Becky's case. The single mother Becky is 'written' into the monologues of the other three as a character we never hear from directly, but is, nevertheless, someone we hear a lot about and form a picture of from the other three characters.

While the monologue, as we noted earlier, has been important to Sarah's theatre writing, and used as a point of disruption in her political theatre, in radio writing she excels in the use of interior monologue, taking this as a means of giving voice to characters in isolation, who 'reach' each other during the course of the drama across their particular points of separation. Written entirely in interior monologue form *Cross My Heart and Hope to Fly* and *The Sound Barrie*r, for example, demonstrate a dramaturgical use of the monologue that encourages an idea of 'gaps' and connections: characters in isolation, by themselves, who also tell us of the contact they make with others that brings about change in their lives and the lives of others.

Sally argues radio as an '*intimate medium*', an art form that despite its millions of listeners speaks to the *individual*. Sarah's fondness for monologues is her particular way (and it does make for a distinctive radio voice) of making this very *direct* connection. Unlike other kinds of realism (see earlier), the listener is not positioned as someone who knows more than the characters. Rather, the business of her writing is to take the listener and character together on an emotional journey. This avoids what is arguably the most problematic form of realism and naturalism: the illusion of being in a position of 'superiority', from which we are able to 'know' others more fully than they know themselves.

Whether working in monologue or dialogue form it is crucial that characters sustain a listener's interest in them: we have to be interested in what happens to them. So it is important not only that they feel 'real' to us, but that they are not predictable, that they can surprise us. Arguably in Sarah's plays characters surprise listeners by surprising themselves. For example, although determined to stay out of Becky's problems in *The Sound Barrier* both Audrey and Colin each experience a change of heart that takes them and the 'action' of the drama in a different direction. So thinking about how characters come to behave differently, can 'change' character, is an important consideration.

Playing status games[19] can be instructive for thinking about how characters change when they are forced to play a status that is at odds with other kinds of status based on class, gender, economics, etc. We discovered that paired status improvisations can be a helpful way of seeing what happens if, for example, a headmaster faced with an unruly pupil has to play a lower status than the pupil he is trying to discipline, or an apologetic single mum being issued with a parking ticket by a traffic warden is suddenly given a higher status than the warden? What is insightful about this is both the playfulness that occurs when status conventions are broken, when tone, mood, character and action are not quite as they should be, but also what can happen to a character in a given situation when a writer 'forces' them to behave in an uncharacteristic way.

Producing the script

While character is an important consideration for radio writing, and was our main route through the radio workshop and Sarah's processes of writing for radio, clearly there are other matters that require attention. Relevant to scene writing generally is the rule that also applies in television and film writing: get into a scene late and come out early. In radio the opening scene is one that requires particular attention. Unlike the theatre where it requires some effort on the part of the spectator to get up and leave before the end of a play, with radio drama it is all too easy for a listener to 'switch off'. An opening scene that grabs a listener's attention is vital. It needs to be both intriguing and clear. As Sarah's idea for *The Sound Barrier* illustrates, when you begin a play you join a story that has already come so far. As a writer you have to decide where to 'start' the story for an audience.

While something needs to grab a listener's attention it is important not to give everything away at once: put the major crisis at the beginning and the story has no further to go. Sally set a (homework) challenge of writing the first minute of a radio drama in which the task is to get your audience 'hooked': *'by the end of 1' we need to have a hook – something that will make the listener keep listening'*.[20] This actually proved a lot harder than it sounds. Common mistakes were either giving too much away (being too descriptive), or not putting in quite enough detail (and therefore being unclear). Nearly all of us forgot about the importance of keeping precisely to one minute and ran way over time.

Ideas about opening and setting a story in a way that grabs and grips an audience does not necessarily mean opening up on to a world of epic events and action-packed drama (it may do, but it does not have to). Rather, to move the action on, which a scene must do to earn its place in the drama, you need to think as much about a changing emotional pattern or state as anything else. This kind of emotional patterning is much more important to Sarah's radio writing than an action-based drama. Even when writing on a more epic canvas, such as *The Long Wait*[21] set in France on the eve of the invasion of Normandy, which has opportunities for fighting, shooting, intrigue and spying, Sarah's approach still tends towards the emotional lives of the characters. Indeed, at the risk of appearing essentialist, Sarah dared to suggest to us that she feels *'men often write more action-based things and women can write emotion a lot better'*.

We got to explore emotional patterning in the workshop through the practice of scene writing and one particular exercise that encouraged us to focus on emotional change. The task was to write a scene for two characters in which the scene has to start with a way of saying 'I love you' and end with 'I hate you'.[22] Noting the golden rule of avoiding clichés, love and hate were not allowed to be stated literally, but needed to be expressed in other ways. What this helped us to see was that importance of an emotional 'journey' as the means for creating dramatic change.

With practice at scene writing comes an understanding of how easy it is to 'overtalk' or to 'overwrite'. Learning to see how much information listeners need and at what point they need it in the drama is essential to good scripting. Drama games that demonstrate how little needs to be said to get a point across can be instructive for heightening an awareness of an economy words. Sarah demonstrated this through an exercise originally suggested to her by playwright Bryony Lavery. This was a paired exercise in which we took a very simple scenario (a cat-sitting friend has to tell her cat-owning friend returning from holiday that her cat has died) and played this out in several different ways, starting with a pair that has lots of dialogue, sparse dialogue, one line, one word, no words, in order to see how much or how little is needed for an audience to get the point of the story.

A similar kind of point applies to the use of sound effects. Used judiciously these offer a way of avoiding lengthy descriptions about settings, or can help to move between settings (as well as be used to create a mood, an atmosphere, etc.) in ways that are particularly economical. However, Sally also warned us about the dangers of abusing sound effects so that they over-clutter and kill a scene off. We were given a very clear example of this as Sally got us to listen to extracts from the radio drama, *This Gun That I have in My Right Hand is Loaded* – a spoof of radio conventions by actor Timothy West, designed to illustrate many of the pitfalls of radio writing. Understanding effects also requires being able to handle these on the page in script writing; getting used to writing in 'FX' (sound effects) as and when you want them to come into play. In trying to think about how, when and where to use 'FX', we felt this was a question of having to hear the effects and to see them on the page. Getting the 'FX' points right on the page links to a more general, but important point: the 'writing up' of a radio script requires careful layout and presentation of the material a writer is sending in (this does actually matter). All of these points are ultimately important in working towards a final broadcasting length which has to be exactly and precisely timed to fill its performance slot. A producer/director can always help with cutting words, pauses, introducing sound effects for effective scene changes, or whatever, but a writer's ability to self-edit (as we discovered in the one-minute opening exercise) is an important skill to acquire in the writing process.

One final production point to mention is that for radio drama a writer can look forward to the possibility of star casting in her plays. High-profile media performers who would not, for example, be in a position (in terms of time or money) to accept roles in the theatre can be tempted into radio parts which require far less of their time (roughly one day's recording for every thirty minutes of script). Pauline Collins, Patricia

Routledge, Caroline Quentin, Harriet Walter, Penelope Wilton, figure among those performers who have taken part in Sarah's radio plays, for example, bringing accomplished female performers to her woman-centred drama. Equally, the difficulty that a theatre writer has dealing with a whole cast and crew of people when a play goes into production is much less of a worry in radio drama. *'It doesn't matter, particularly in radio, if you don't get on with the actors. They're only there two days,'* says Sarah, *'Just as long as they get on with your script.'* On the other hand, this comes back to the role of the director and the absolute necessity of good director-writer relations and a director who really understands a writer's script and can communicate it effectively to the performers.

In our interview with Sarah and Sally we put Sally on the spot, asking her as a radio director of Sarah's work what makes for a good Sarah Daniels' script. Sally's view returned us to the point about the way in which Sarah works on characters to bring them out of their isolated lives; to learn something more of themselves: *'You don't leave a Sarah script going "God I might as well go home and slit my wrists," you go "no, the world is alright" and that is quite a skill I think to pull off and for it not to be sentimental, not to draw characters that we don't believe in.'* This is no longer a question of writing feminism *'with a capital F'* as she did with *Masterpieces*, but it is, Sally concludes, very much about her characters negotiating and coming to terms with *'areas of life that maybe they haven't come across before.'* In brief, it is, we would argue, a reparative realism that dominates the Sarah Daniels' radio script.

The writer within

Sarah's conviction that she could be a writer was in part fuelled from going to see plenty of bad theatre and coming to believe that she wanted to and could do better. When Sarah and Sally began the practical work in the radio-writing workshop, they started with an exercise in 'bad writing': *'Take five minutes to write about a personal object, write anything even if it's rubbish, but write.'* The point of the exercise was to prove that the writing actually was not all 'bad': to convince every participant that she has something to write and can write (though it was also illuminating for the ways in which writing about personal objects made for interesting revelations about ourselves). All of the workshops in our project share a similar kind of commitment to generating creativity: a belief that, irrespective of skills or confidence levels, there is writing in everyone and it is a question of bringing it out. In terms of writing for radio specifically, however, the set-up of the business, the sources of advice, support, critical feedback and the possibility of a mutually rewarding director-writer relationship, such as that between Sarah and Sally, means that an emergent writer has some very real, realistic, professional writing opportunities ahead of her. Top writing tips from Sarah and Sally are to get your '*voices*' out there; to '*by pass your own internal censor*'. Like the characters in Sarah's plays, a writer needs the conviction that she has '*something within* [her] *that is worth bringing out*', and to get it out there. The relatively supportive environment of radio means that she has a realistic chance of finally being 'heard'.

Appendix: character check list[23]

1. Name. (Male or female)?
2. How old are they?
3. Where are they born?
4. Details about their mother and father.
5. Do they have any brothers and sisters and if so how old are they?
6. What do they do? (School? Work?)
7. Are they married or in a relationship if so with who?
8. What is their earliest childhood memory?
9. What makes them angry?
10. What frightens them?
11. What thrills them?
12. What is the most important life event to date?
13. What do they want more than anything in the world and is this a secret or a public desire?
14. Who do they love?
15. Who do they hate?
16. What is their most irritating habit?
17. What do they find irritating in others?
18. What's the most likely thing they'd say?
19. What's the least likely thing they'd say?
20. If they could change one thing about their life so far what would it be?

Notes and references

1. We interviewed Sarah Daniels and Sally Avens on 26 November 2005, Lancaster University. Quotations are from this interview unless otherwise stated.
2. In 'Cake with Sarah Daniels' (programme notes, *Flying Under Bridges* 2005), Till writes: 'I saw the production of her play *Neaptide* at the National Theatre seven times, including three times in one week. She was my Take That'.

3. For an overview and discussion of male criticism of her work see Mary Remanant, introduction to *Plays By Women: Volume Six* (London: Methuen, 1987), pp. 7–12.

4. The post-show discussion was held immediately after the performance on 28 February 2006. The majority of the audience were women, and from a mix of age ranges – mostly either student age or Sarah's (and our) feminist generation. Among the students, many of them were theatre students studying and working on *Masterpieces* for a performance. What was interesting about the debate was that the younger women did not see the issues in the play as dated, but as relevant to their lives. As much as this provoked some lively discussion, it was rather depressing to think that this contemporary relevance points to a failure to have finally addressed and dealt with the pornography industry and general issues of violence against women.

5. Here we are glossing what is a much more complex argument that Sedgwick makes in respect of the paranoid and the reparative positions in *Touching Feeling: Affect, Pedagogy, Performativity* (Duke University Press: Durham and London, 2003), chapter 4, pp. 123–151. Briefly, Sedgwick unpicks the 'faith in exposure' (à la Butler's gender performativity model) which she identifies as a paranoid view, with a strong theory of negative affects, resistant to surprise and reliant on exposure, through a consideration of reparative possibilities, argued via the work of Melanie Klein on the paranoid and the reparative. Although not wishing to extend this point into a lengthy, heavily theorised analysis of Sarah's theatre, we *do* want to draw attention to the reparative quality of Sarah's writing, here and later in the radio drama, as something which we came to through the workshop experience, and subsequently reflected on, via the borrowing from Sedgwick. See also our discussion of this point in Chapter 1, p. 10.

6. It is hard to earn a living from writing for theatre alone, unless you have one huge box-office success as Catherine Johnson did, writing the book for the smash hit musical *Mamma Mia!*, or possibly Charlotte Keatley with *My Mother Said I Never Should*, which got adopted onto the A Level syllabus, or achieve the stature and status of a writer such as Caryl Churchill. Sarah notes for example that when she had her first Court commission for *Ripen Our Darkness* she had a fee of about £2,500, whereas today a comparable commission would still only be around £5,000.

7. Caroline Raphael was Head of Radio 5 until it switched to news, when she joined Radio 4 and was head of commissioning until November 2005.

8. Other writers in the *Westway* team were Mike Walker, Annie Caulfield, Tanika Gupta, Pat Kampo, and Rukshana Ahmed.

9. This actually touches on an important broadcasting point: producers and commissioning editors have to pay attention to storylines and issues in adjacent broadcasting slots. As the Afternoon Play is broadcast immediately after *The Archers* you cannot risk having similar storylines. Hence the Commissioning Editor at the time, Caroline Raphael, turned down Sarah's idea for a play about breast cancer.

10. This was the first in the 'Women On Love' series broadcast in 1999. The other plays in the series were Tanika Gupta's *Coat*, based on a poem by Vicky Feaver; *Lonely Hearts* By Helen Kluger, based on a poem by Wendy Cope, and

The Love a Life Can Show Below by Hattie Naylor, based on a poem by Emily Dickinson.

11. The workshop was held on the 26 and 27 November 2005.

12. Those 'many outlets' include, for example, the Afternoon Play (broadcast five days a week, Monday to Friday, BBC4); the Friday play (evening slot, BBC 4); the Saturday play (afternoon broadcast, BBC4), and Sunday dramas (classical plays and new theatre writing, transmitted on BBC 3). Getting to know these slots and their listeners is important for writers new to radio. Full and updated guidelines about the slots and writing for them can be found on the web at the BBC's 'Writersroom', http://www.bbc.co.uk/writersroom/.

13. A first-time writer can expect to be paid approximately £45 a minute, although more experienced writers will command higher fees than this.

14. See note 12 for examples.

15. Statistics and explanation provided in E-mail correspondence, January 2006.

16. Ibid.

17. There are possible exceptions to this – for example if a writer is making a pitch for a documentary drama where it would be important to signal the particular issues involved.

18. Elisabeth Mahoney, review of *The Sound Barrier, Guardian*, 31 October 2005. *The Sound Barrier* script is available at http://www.bbc.co.uk/writersroom/ insight/script_archive.shtml, accessed 25 July 2006.

19. Sourced by Keith Johnstone's *Impro: Improvisation and the Theatre* (London: Methuen, 1989). See also Chapter 6, note 14.

20. From Sally's workshop instruction sheets. See WWP project website, http://www. lancs.ac.uk/depts/theatre/womenwriting/, Events Archive, 'Writing for Radio', with Sarah Daniels and Sally Avens, audio clips, 'Shopping Trip'.

21. *The Long Wait*, based on a story by Mike Walker, was broadcast in 2004.

22. See http://www.lancs.ac.uk/depts/theatre/womenwriting/, Events Archive, 'Writing for Radio', audio clips, 'George and the Teacher'.

23. The 'Character Check List' is an invention of Sarah Daniels', originally inspired by a 'Pass Notes' column in the *Guardian*, No 2,642 Past Notes, Friday 9 September 2005.

6
Imagining, Making, Changing
Split Britches

Peggy Shaw and Lois Weaver in *Dress Suits To Hire*. Photograph by Eva Weiss

With the possible exception of Bobby Baker, Split Britches has received more academic attention than any of the other practitioners in this volume, so the company's history is well documented.[1] Lois Weaver studied 'traditional' theatre in college but abandoned this in favour of political activism in New York. During this time she also gained experience with members of Joseph Chaikin's Open Theatre,[2] before joining Spiderwoman,[3] a feminist performance company. Having worked as a visual artist and as a social worker, Peggy Shaw's introduction to performance was through a chance encounter with a piece of street theatre by the gay drag company Hot Peaches. As she puts it, this show inspired her to '*run away with the circus*',[4] eventually joining Hot Peaches on a two-year long European tour.

Peggy and Lois's first meeting in 1977 occurred when both companies were in Europe and led to Peggy joining Spiderwoman. In 1980, under the aegis of this company and in conjunction with Deborah Margolin, they developed a piece entitled *Split Britches*, based around some of Lois's more eccentric female relatives. Lois still counts the performance of this show in a Baptist Church in the Blue Ridge Mountains to celebrate her parents' fiftieth wedding anniversary as one of the highlights of her career, because '*It brought together kinds of communities that I never thought would be together in the same place, the closeted lesbians from all over the Blue Ridge Mountains [...] my family, people interested in folk theatre and people who actually knew these women.*' For Lois this was an example of the integrative potential of 'community theatre', and both Peggy and Lois still refer back to this piece when discussing the principles that have informed their process and practice over the intervening years.

In 1981, Peggy and Lois left Spiderwoman to form the company Split Britches with Margolin, and these three created a total of five shows together, the last being *Lesbians Who Kill* (1992). During this period the company were also founder members of the WOW café in New York.[5] This celebrated queer and feminist performance space, which operates as an open, non-hierarchical collective, moved buildings in 1985 and remains an important venue for emergent practitioners to develop their skills and show their work.

Since 1992, the 'core' of Split Britches has been Lois and Peggy but the company has produced shows in collaboration with other artists and companies, including James Neale-Kennerley, Bloolips, the Clod Ensemble and Stacy Makishi. In the 1990s, Lois was also artistic director of the British company Gay Sweatshop and toured a solo autobiographical performance *Faith and Dancing* (1997). She makes regular appearances as Tammy Whynot, a country and western singer turned lesbian performance artist. In 2005, she collaborated with Curious for *On the Scent* (see Chapter 3). Peggy has toured three autobiographical solo pieces: *You're Just Like My Father* (1994), *Menopausal Gentleman* (1999) and *To My Chagrin* (2003–6). In the last few years, a collaboration with Paul Heritage and the People's Palace Project has seen them taking the same techniques and exercises they shared with us at Lancaster into women's prisons in Brazil and in Britain. For Lois this work is a natural extension of their long-term commitment to queer and feminist politics, broadened and re-articulated in terms of 'human rights'. In 2005–6 they revisited one of their best-known shows, *Dress Suits for Hire* devised around text by Holly Hughes and originally produced in 1987.

While over the years, Peggy and Lois have won several prestigious awards,[6] as with the majority of practitioners discussed in this book their financial rewards have been limited. With Split Britches this is exacerbated by the fact that for much of the time they have been based in the US where funding for theatre and performance, especially for experimental or political work, is even scarcer than in the UK. This underlines the importance of spaces like WOW and accounts for one of Peggy's 'tips' for emergent practitioners which is to '*rob a bank*'. However, there is absolutely no sense that either of them regrets the choices they have made. This is evident in Peggy's other tips for emergent practitioners '*Go to where you want to work, find the people you respect, go and find them and offer to do the photocopying – anything, don't be put off by people telling you it's too expensive to live in certain places, follow your desire, don't do what others tell you to do, do your own work.*' Similarly, Lois echoes sentiments often expressed by other practitioners in the workshop series: '*Don't wait for the funding, don't wait for permission, don't wait to be asked, make work in your bedroom, in your living room, don't wait for it to be finished, show people five minutes, ten minutes, let your audience help you shape it.*' Implicit in these remarks is that, as Peggy says, they do their work for '*love*', and their lack of financial security is partly a consequence of a passionate refusal to compromise on their political or artistic principles. It is not surprising then, that the word 'inspiring' occurred in most participants' responses to the Lancaster workshop.

Out of the void

As noted above, over the years their practice has also inspired numerous articles interviews and books, in part because of the socio-political and theatrical context in which they first appeared. This is best evinced by one of the first reviews they ever received for *Split Britches*, which as paraphrased by Lois went something like, '*I would not expect that even Shakespeare would dare to put three women on stage on their own for an hour and expect to hold the audience's attention.*' In short, at the time, both as 'makers' and on stage, women tended to appear only as adjuncts to male characters or practitioners. On the exceptionally rare occasions lesbians were visible in the theatre at all they were objects of aggressive homophobia. As Peggy puts it in describing her work with Hot Peaches, '*We had to start to make our own work from scratch, there were no role models, we didn't have anything from the past to draw on, there was this huge empty gap, this huge chasm where all the women writers and queer writers were down a deep hole. So we were creating material in a void.*' Peggy also acknowledges that the performance style she had developed with Hot Peaches was that of 'in your face' political cabaret, directly expressing the anger and pain provoked by her own experience of marginalisation and social abjection.

With Split Britches, as Lois indicates, they wanted the work to be '*about valuing women, valuing women's stories, valuing the lesbian experience because these things were not valued on stage or elsewhere.*' However, she adds that, if their work was feminist and lesbian, '*it was because we were feminists and lesbians. But we didn't set out to make theatre that was feminist or lesbian, we were trying to make work where these things were a given.*' The terrain of Spilt Britches was to be '*forgotten stories, the marginalized, the eccentric and the invisible*', but, as Peggy notes, Lois proposed a style that was '*subtle and integrated, non-confrontational, based in humour*'. Lois adds: '*We wanted the audience to like the people they saw on stage and then to realise that they liked a lesbian or a butch woman.*' Crucial to this was the necessity that as performers they should 'love' the characters they played even, Peggy insists, those who might be considered the '*enemy*' because, '*We were not interested in setting people up, or being cruel and aggressive* [doing that is] *harsh and empty – but we were not "goody goody" either.*'

Out of the 'void' in which Spilt Britches were operating then, a highly distinctive and innovative aesthetic began to emerge, described by Lois as '*focusing on the details of women's lives and their relationships with other women and some of these details included their relationship with their teacups and their environment.*' The emphasis was '*on these things rather than narrative, detail instead of action and on putting different "moments" together instead of being concerned with* [character or plot] *progression.*' Into this they mixed techniques and influences from the Open Theatre, drew on both Spiderwoman's and Hot Peaches' concern for reclaiming and subverting popular culture, and on the former's interest in fantasy and the latter's interest in queer 'camp' and dressing up.

Interestingly, Split Britches' shows have sometimes been read as if the majority of them were directly autobiographical, even though, unlike Bobby Baker for instance, much of the time Peggy and Lois perform named 'characters'.[7] This confusion may arise in part, because, as evident in the workshop, their process involves a notion of 'creative truth' which draws on the autobiographical but transforms it through layers of fantasy. Indeed, in the workshop Lois explained that they use fantasy as a *'structuring device'*. As this suggests, while Lois's comment on their focus on detail and the environment recalls some 'original' principles of nineteenth-century naturalism and realism as evinced in the work of Emile Zola in literature and Anton Chekov in the theatre, Split Britches' 'characters' are clearly not 'psychologically motivated'. Rather they are profoundly contradictory figures whose 'back stories' and motivations remain illusive, largely because *as* characters they themselves show absolutely no regard for the distinction between 'truth' and their own creative fantasies. Further, while Lois and Peggy have always been charismatic and compelling performers, their mode of embodying 'character' rejects mid-twentieth-century, mainstream theatrical values and conventions (and training) for 'proper' acting.[8] However, while in the shows as a whole there is never any attempt at persuading the audience to suspend their disbelief, some of the 'moments' Lois describes above can carry an emotional weight that does seem to draw on the experiential, or on 'embodied' knowledge, in ways that can provoke identification, not so much with the characters but with their *situation*. This aside, as we note in our introductory Chapter 1, their work may be read as *always* 'autobiographical' in the sense that *all* creative production, *whoever* authors it, *whatever* their gender, sexuality, etc., inevitably draws on the personal. This is relevant to Split Britches' work in so far as one of the things that originally made their shows 'innovative' and which contributes to preventing it from being 'goody goody', was that the theme of female/lesbian sexual desire has always been a central and powerful dynamic. It is also one that has been explored in ways that, especially in the early years, often transgressed or subverted orthodoxies, including those produced and maintained by some feminisms, lesbian and otherwise.

Another element in the mix of the Split Britches aesthetic is that they 'didn't wait for the funding', so that as Sue Ellen Case points out, theirs has often been a 'poor' theatre (in the economic sense) but one in which the power of the imagination transformed necessity into a virtue.[9] Indeed, the power of the imagination could be said to be another key thematic running through their shows, reflecting the political belief that, in Lois's words, *'If you can imagine it, you can make it, if you can make it then you can change it.'*

During the workshop, like most (honest) practitioners, Lois also stated that many of their methods have been *'begged, borrowed or stolen'* from the various people they have worked with over the years and from other practitioners including, most recently, Goat Island.[10] Lois also remarked that there are certain exercises which they have used for some time which remain core to Peggy's technique for creating characters, but which she personally has *'tired of'* (even while she acknowledges that they do have their creative uses). As all of this suggests, while it is possible to discern certain continuities throughout their body of work, Split Britches continue to develop and to respond to the altering socio-political and theatrical environment. This is evident in the re-definition of their political concerns in terms of 'human rights', their work in prisons and in the 2006 version of *Dress Suits For Hire* when compared to the1987 version. The very fact that as performers Lois and Peggy are older, foregrounds themes in this piece which were always present but not originally so dominant.[11] Some of the deliberate 'rough edges' in the staging have been smoothed. For instance, the transitions between the various 'moments' in the show which in 1987 could be abrupt, casual or deliberately messy in a manner that might be described as anti-illusionist and which rendered the piece as a whole 'episodic' or fragmentary, are now more carefully staged, more theatrical. This is very much a *self-reflexive* or meta-theatricality, involving for instance, Lois, apparently 'out of character', speaking stage directions which prompt props for the next 'moment' to drop from above. Yet, while these transitions may still operate as interruptions in the action which work against 'suspension of disbelief' in the characters and their world, these changes do give more of a sense of flow or continuity in terms of the *rhythm* of the piece as a whole. These alterations may reflect a recognition that some aspects of the 'original' aesthetic were of their time, and since then their potential effect has been diluted by the way the same or similar techniques have become widespread. However, the 'void' or 'black hole' Peggy spoke of above has now been somewhat, but not entirely, excavated. As a result, what these changes now seem to reveal is how far this highly distinctive 'postmodern' work, can be related back to a 'modernist' queer theatre tradition, embracing practitioners such as Frederico Garcia Lorca, Jean Genet and Tennessee Williams.[12]

Back in the 'void' of the 1980s and 1990s, the political and community dimension of Split Britches' work combined with their innovative aesthetic, meant that their practice featured importantly in the development of feminist and queer theory within theatre and performance studies. As such, their shows have been drawn upon in thinking through concepts ranging from polymorphous perversity, the butch-femme aesthetic, queer, gender performativity, postmodern feminism and feminist utopianism. This has been to an extent that in her introduction to a collection of Split Britches' performance texts in 1996, Sue Ellen Case acknowledged that these academic debates might seem to 'have moved quite a distance from the actual performances of Split Britches'.[13]

In the light of this comment, Lois's and Peggy's differing attitudes to this academic writing are interesting. Lois describes herself as having a '*love/hate*' relationship towards it. On the 'love' side it is '*exciting*', '*validating*' and has ensured that their work '*wasn't just going to disappear as so much other work has done*'. On the 'hate' side is that as someone '*who in another life might have wanted to be a scholar*', Lois feels she is too '*susceptible to this writing*' and that for instance with *The Salad of the Bad Café* (2003), which they created with Stacy Makishi, '*the theory had started to infiltrate the process*', to the detriment of the show. Peggy simply never reads this work at all, '*I try not to use any intellectual concepts. I try not to get caught up in anyone else's ideas of who and what I am.*' Both then perceive dangers in paying attention to certain types of 'theory' especially theorisations around their own practice, when making work.

The workshop: between chaos and order (effortless creativity)

For some of us who have studied their practice through the frame of these theoretical discourses, the Split Britches workshop was like seeing a familiar object in a totally new light. It is not that the methods they employ in making work contradict the theoretical readings, indeed they can be said very much to *confirm* them while remaining distinct from and 'other' to them. As indicated in the introduction, this holds for most of the practitioners discussed in this volume. If for us it was especially striking in this instance, it may be because of the 'exemplary' position given to this company's work in so much writing. Yet, it also reflects something specific about Spilt Britches' process which focuses strongly on 'embodied knowledge'. While this process might actually aid in *realising* the implications of the theory, equally it is not wholly explicable or containable in the terms of such thinking.

Reflecting something of their differing attitudes towards 'theory', within their practice Lois, who usually functions as director as well as performing, describes herself as '*obsessed with sequence*', while Peggy admits that this is something that *she* constantly disrupts because *she* is *'chaotic'*, has no *'logic or order'*. This accords with our experience in the workshop which suggests an intensive collaboration that does indeed operate through a productive tension between 'chaos and order'. This is also a process that facilitates individual creativity but is always focused around modes of dynamic inter-relation through which *all* ideas are constantly being filtered. At the start of the workshop, Lois indicated that they intended to explore their process under three headings 'Questions and Obsessions', 'Surprise' and 'Creative Truth'. Considering the tension between 'order and chaos' indicated above, it is not surprising that she immediately admitted that these categories 'overlap', nor that other possible headings such as 'impulse', 'fantasy' and 'layering', rapidly started to emerge.

In the early stages of the workshop there was an overwhelming emphasis on 'surprise(ing yourself)', on spontaneity, on impulse and on the privileging of the physical and embodied over the abstract and the intellectual. These methods work towards unsettling habitual modes of thinking and acting, and freeing the imagination. They also produced large amounts of material, in a manner that, as Peggy put it, felt *'effortlessly creative'*. Throughout we were given plenty of space as individuals both literally and metaphorically. We were encouraged to articulate and explore our own particular questions and obsessions and to establish our own 'studio' in the room: a personal space to write, reflect and to collect and eventually present the bits and pieces we accumulated. Nevertheless, the sense of *'effortless creativity'* arose from a constant emphasis on 'responding' to, and thereby gently 'disrupting' and transforming each other's ideas.

Due to this effect and to the amount of material produced, this process did, at times, *feel* rather 'chaotic'. However, if the spontaneous, the physical and the embodied were privileged, this did not constitute a complete *rejection* of the 'cognitive' and the 'intellectual', but instead an embracing of ways of 'thinking' that are associative rather than linear. Throughout the process there was a concern with experimenting with different ways of assembling, layering, juxtaposing and editing material together, and this became more of a focus as time progressed. Even though the workshop could only introduce (rather than develop) this latter stage, for most of us something did begin to emerge in the form of a 'rough sketch' for a performance (solo and otherwise) that made perfect sense, albeit very much *on its own terms*. This reflects the effect of associative thinking, where surprising and unusual, yet nonetheless meaningful connections between apparently disparate ideas, objects or themes can be produced, which might not surface through a more linear approach.

The problem this creates for us (Elaine and Gerry), which is also always one for the 'theory' touched on above, is that in the limited space available, this associative approach is almost impossible to sum up in writing, without imposing some sort of linear structure upon it, and without focusing on some aspects of the work more than others in ways that are artificial and possibly misleading. We shall, therefore, very tentatively, try to identify some 'core' techniques from this workshop on the understanding that, as a whole, the process we experienced was rooted in the *inter*-relationship of these techniques, in the *inter*action between exercises, ideas and participants, and on the various elements of a performance being created simultaneously alongside each other. To reflect this, we shall also offer some examples of the way exercises worked together.

Scribing and writing

On the first day, Lois stressed that keeping a journal or as they call it 'scribing', recording everything said or done by yourself and others, is absolutely central to Split Britches' process. In terms of creative writing, however, like many other practitioners, a core technique is 'automatic' or 'impulse' writing, that is timed writing exercises, ranging from one to ten minutes, in which the pen must not leave the page. As with all their methods, Lois and Peggy underlined the importance of there being no self-censoring, or worry over 'political correctness'; no attempt to avoid repetition or diversion, no concern for making 'sense' or for producing 'good' writing. The idea is to simply keep going and hopefully *surprise* yourself. This writing was produced to a variety of stimuli, including first lines supplied by Lois or Peggy, such as 'If you really knew me, you'd know that', or 'It's too late because', or from physical, visual or verbal images and ideas thrown up by other tasks. When the time elapsed, we were encouraged to outline any parts that struck us for some reason, even if this was only a single word, and were sometimes asked to either share this fragment or the whole piece with the group. When these, or pieces of writing undertaken as 'homework', were read out, the rest of the group were asked to write spontaneous, 'creative responses' of between one and five words. The notion of the 'creative response' is one that has been borrowed specifically from Goat Island but has subsequently been adapted in various ways. In this instance, Lois adds other specific instructions, such as the responses should be adjectives, or 'colours', or 'textures', or 'feelings'. Responses were then given back to the reader and were used to provide further stimuli for later work.

The creative response

This notion of a 'creative response' to each other's work represented another core technique, and one which all participants indicated they found especially useful and productive. These included 'performed' as well as written responses and also (as will become clear) creative responses to these responses. On the last day of the workshop each of us also performed an overall response to another participant's (four days of) work. This technique might be seen as a 'formalisation' of a general aspect of the collaborative devising process. However, in our experience, in some types of group devising, 'responding' to each other's contributions, whether these are represented through improvisation or 'writing', when undertaken through *discussion*, can lead to abstraction and the closing down of imaginative possibilities. By contrast, these more creative ways of responding to each other's work were non-judgmental and focussed concretely on what was actually being produced, rather than referring to a pre-determined conceptual superstructure or pre-conceived direction for the work as a whole. Similarly, as individuals, these techniques encouraged us to be 'open' to what others found interesting, striking or moving in what we produced. This was often surprising, causing us to re-visit ideas, images or 'moments' that we might otherwise have abandoned, and/or to build upon them in ways we had not previously envisaged.

Impulsive bodies

In a less formalised fashion, this notion of responding to each other was intrinsic to the more body-centred activity in the workshop. In these terms, another 'core' technique was based on what Lois described as the 'group body Hoo Hah'. In its basic format this is a well-known exercise. It starts simply by going round a circle with one participant at a time presenting an 'impulse' in the form of a gesture or movement accompanied by a sound, which the rest of the group collectively repeats back to them. This then gets expanded through various stages with impulses being passed around or across the circle; with individuals and/or the group sometimes echoing responses, extending, building on or transforming them. Sometimes the impulses broke out of the circle altogether. At one point, for instance, the group was divided up into four units, with each being placed in a different corner of the room. The aim was for each unit to travel across the room to an opposite corner, echoing the impulses of a chosen 'leader' who could choose to respond to impulses produced by other units and who also had a text to play with in the form of a line from a song. This evolved into a piece of playful, interactive, improvised choreography, reminiscent at times of the famous Sharks and Jets sequence from *West Side Story*. The numbers in each unit were then gradually reduced to the point where we were *all* 'leaders' with our own song lines, travelling in any direction around the room, either moving on our own impulse, or echoing and/or responding to those of others.

In all the variants of this exercise, as with writing, the emphasis was on acting 'in the moment', without hesitation or self-conscious reflection. We were encouraged to take pleasure in moments of collective energy and exchange but also in being the leader; taking centre stage. While the focus was on *physical* impulse – gesture and movement, Lois insisted that these must always be accompanied by sound, to '*keep the mouth open*'. This was because once the group became familiar and comfortable with it, this exercise was developed in various ways to create character and/or to structure scenes or 'moments'. As Lois and Peggy pointed out, having found a physical score for a scene you did not want to have to go back and find a voice as something separate. The use of song was, therefore, partly a preparation for speaking lines while vocally 'riding on' and maintaining the integrity of sound produced by impulse.

Although based on spontaneity, within these exercises distinct and identifiable 'dramatic moments', in the shape of 'exchanges', 'riffs', sequences or 'moods', constantly emerged between individuals or/and the group, before being transformed into something else. This very much reflects the formal structures found in Split Britches' work and the fact that their characters are defined more by their inter-relationship with each other than by their singularity. When lines of text were incorporated into this exercise, or when impulses created within this exercise were applied to text, this was not then a matter of finding 'different' ways of speaking them in relation to predetermined notions of character or meaning. Rather this was a way of finding themes, characters and dramatic structure, associatively and simultaneously.

Part of the point of these 'Hoo Hah' exercises and at the root of their efficacy in liberating the imagination, was that we often found ourselves committed to exploring something produced on impulse, that if working in a more 'logical' and linear manner, we might have rejected outright as too bizarre and overstated, silly, embarrassing, or simply meaningless.

This was also the case with a technique for creation of character from impulse and through the body, as demonstrated in an exercise led by Peggy, which is similar but not exactly the same as the one used by Curious (see p. 48). This started with walking around the space in different ways, gradually identifying a part of our bodies that we were in some way 'aware' of through pain, pleasure or particular associations, and then starting to move in a way that privileged this part of the body and to vocalise a sound that expressed the feeling/sensation/association. This was then personified through a process in which, one at a time, we all asked each other (helpful) questions about 'ourselves' as 'characters', which we answered spontaneously 'from' and 'through' the body part using the movement and sound. Some of the characters who emerged in this exercise became important figures in participants' ideas for shows. Nevertheless, for the less physically-orientated and the more self-conscious amongst us, this task, like some of the group 'Hoo Hah' exercises, was more challenging than it might appear in this account. In fact, while always intensely and pleasurably 'playful', this workshop required a high level of openness to leaving our own habitual comfort zones and of flexibility and of commitment in trusting ourselves, each other, and the process.

Fantasy, immediacy and the creative truth

As with the group 'Hoo Hah', many exercises started off very simply as games or warm-up devices and were then expanded and/or used in conjunction with other tasks as a means to create material. The 'personal inventory', for instance, was introduced as a means of encouraging a focus on the immediacy of 'being in the moment' as a performer, without self-consciousness. A participant stands in the centre of the circle and makes a 'personal inventory', focussing on what they are feeling, seeing, smelling or thinking about at that moment, starting each sentence with I see, or I feel, or I smell, or I think etc., and keeping going without pause until they are stopped. This was later developed into individual work in which we moved around the room, making an inventory, eventually focussing on something in the space that 'reminded us of something else' (a specific memory, sensation or another object) which we then took as an image for a writing exercise. The 'personal inventory' also influenced another game in which each of us picked another participant at random and made 'observations' about them. This started out with 'I see', focusing only on immediate and surface things (e.g. I see Emily is wearing brown shoes) and then moved onto 'I notice' which could bring in past observations and become more personal (e.g. I notice that Maya likes purple). Finally, this became 'I imagine' and we invented fantasies about each other in which we were encouraged to be as extreme as possible (I imagine Jo likes to torture small furry animals, just a little bit). After several turns, we were asked to pick one of these 'imaginings' about ourselves to become the first line of an impulse writing exercise in which we were also to use some words given to us in response to impulse writing from the day before.

The last stage of the 'observation' game points to what is perhaps the most 'key' technique in the workshop. Throughout, we were encouraged to articulate, work with and trust to our 'obsessions', fantasies and desires, however eccentric, extravagant, or politically questionable. Similarly, we sometimes invented equally extravagant or dubious obsessions and desires for each other, which were incorporated into the work. As with the impulse exercises, the simple commitment to continuing to work with, rather than immediately rejecting these notions as ludicrous or unworkable, meant that we did, in fact, start to find 'performance solutions' for ideas that we might otherwise have dismissed as beyond our own skills and abilities, or as unstageable and wildly over-ambitious. These techniques are designed then to encourage the performer/devisor not to stunt the power of their imaginations by confining themselves to what they already think they know is possible, probable or practical, but rather to have faith in Lois's principle, that '*if we can imagine it, we can make it*'.

Fantasy and freeing up the imagination also informed the Butch/Fem games we undertook in this workshop, so that they were not necessarily, or rather *simply* 'about' sexual politics. This work began as a circle game based on contradicting each other as to what might be defined as butch or fem. One participant states that something (anything – ponytails, toenails, singing, cows, depression, scratching, etc.) is 'butch', to which their neighbour replies, 'no pony tails are *fem*,' before turning to the next person to assert that something else (pigtails, biting, dancing, etc.) is butch, and so on around the group. A variant of this exercise played in pairs was then introduced based on a Keith Johnstone's theatre game 'It's Tuesday',[14] mixed with the 'personal inventory'. The wording was switched to 'It's butch' (or fem) – to which the reply is 'It can't be because … ', acting as a starting point for producing a long list of reasons that gradually become more desperate and absurd. This work again became part of the stimuli for impulse writing. In both instances, these games were designed to encourage spontaneity and to undermine tendencies to self-censor in the interests of political correctness. While they do focus attention on the categories of butch and fem they also have the effect of rendering them meaningless, except purely as a starting point for playful and creative interaction. By the same token, in other tasks and exercises, what might be defined as traditionally 'feminine' desires, interests, and concerns, especially those relating to costume and appearance, were taken seriously, or rather as seriously *and* simultaneously as playfully as any other type of 'fantasy' in the workshop.

Yet within the concept of the personal inventory and the later 'observation' game is a sense of anchoring fantasy in the actual, the immediate and the directly to hand. So for instance, for the third day of the workshop we were asked to bring in objects we felt like 'playing with', which were dumped in a pile in the centre of the room. These objects, which included wigs, hats, gloves, masks, playing cards, a rifle and artificial flowers, were used in a number of different exercises around character and structure. For instance, at one point we chose three of them to be combined with any three lines from some impulse writing from earlier in the day, to construct three images for performance. Again in such instances, ideas for 'design', costumes, props and set began to be developed alongside text, character and structure, inspired by what was literally in front of us.

Similarly, the notion of 'creative truth' is not purely the transformation of the autobiographical by fantasy, but also roots fantasy in the embodied and experiential. In one exercise we were asked to think of a 'personal' story that had some connection to a pre-existing text (novel, poem, play, etc.) that we had also brought in. This was used to stimulate impulse writing in which we created a scenario/staging for a scene based on this personal connection starting with the words 'I (or s/he) comes on stage and'. This was not a matter of Stanislavskian 'emotional memory' using the personal to perform pre-existing text, nor was it the direct representation of autobiographical material. Rather it was a method of responding to or 'adapting' another text by passing it *through* the autobiographical and the embodied. In fact, the example given was from *Belle Reprieve*, a text based on Tennessee Williams' *Street Car Named Desire* which Split Britches created with Bloolips in 1991. This first scene of *Belle Reprieve* is based on scene two of *Street Car*, specifically where Stanley rifles through Blanche's trunk, and was created by drawing on Peggy's experience with US Immigration and Customs while working with Hot Peaches. The company were seeking to re-enter the US with a British drag artist (without a visa) who swapped suitcases with Peggy, so that she had the frocks and love letters to men and he had the suits and the love letters to women, allowing each of them to 'pass' as heterosexual.

Sequence and layering

As already indicated and as our examples have began to demonstrate, what was most distinctive about this workshop were not individual exercises or 'core' techniques but the various ways they were combined and spliced together. While from within, some of this initially appeared chaotic, actually it can be seen to reflect Lois's obsession as a director with 'sequence', which was also evident in the way we were often asked to select and work with three images, words, lines of text, or impulse movements. It is also evident in her fondness for 'game structures' as the basis for creating work, something that is reflected in many Split Britches' shows.[15] However, Lois's notion of sequence, once again, tends to be associative rather than linear, so that while tasks were introduced, built on and expanded, feeding and bleeding into each other, work was produced, left and then returned to, only to be disrupted and transformed through combination, contrast and juxtaposition. This produces a gradual build-up of ideas, images and actions in which the influence of earlier work is always visible but through the 'layers' that have accrued on top. This process gives enormous scope for individual expression and creative choices, but it is also clearly guided by a directorial strategy in which, in the early stages, Lois appears to operate as facilitator and/or co-devisor, later taking on the role as 'editor' and shaper of the material that has been collaboratively produced.

For example, on the first day of the workshop we started by imagining a question, an obsession and a delight for someone else in the group, most of whom we had only just met. This was therefore really an exercise in *projection*, reflecting more about 'ourselves' than the other person. We then introduced this person as our 'best friend' (e.g. this is my best friend Kirsten, her question is 'Where should I be?', her obsession is great smells, her delight is a pint of beer). The next stage was to think of three 'truths' about ourselves and then to introduce ourselves to the rest of the group using a combination of these truths and the information invented for us by another participant.

This work was followed first by impulse writing concerned with obsessions, the 'personal inventory' game and the creation of a list of likes and dislikes, out of which we chose one to formulate a question. With all of this work 'in the air' and available to draw on if we wished, we were asked to take a blank sheet of paper and to write down two truths about ourselves: a lie and a fantasy of something we would like to do or be. The next stage was to make an object from this piece of paper (e.g. a snowball, a plane, a guitar, a map) inspired by one or more items on this list. This was presented to the group, firstly as a description ('This is a plane.'), then in three sentences to tell the 'story' ('This is a plane. It has all the evil people in the world on it. And they are all going to die.'). Moving on, in pairs, we drew on these sentences to tell each other a timed one-minute story, with each partner subsequently 'performing' a one-minute response to the *other's* story, using any means they desired. In turn, we each wrote a three-word response to our partner's performed response to our story. These words became the stimuli for writing from which we chose three lines, which were then integrated into our partner's performed response to our story, under our direction.

Lois's headings 'Questions and Obsessions', 'Surprise' and 'Creative Truth', clearly informed this series of tasks. However, while exercises did not all obviously lead on from one another logically, there was an *associative* sense of sequence with ideas being developed and transformed by moving between the personal and fantasy, the concrete and the immediate, our own 'truths' and inventions, and those of others in the group.

Assembling and editing

On the third day of the workshop, Lois started to demonstrate to us techniques for assembling and layering material in a more formal manner. The night before this, we had been asked to gather together everything we had produced so far and to add a piece of music and a pre-existing text (play, novel, poem, etc.) and any objects that we wished. We were also asked to imagine a 'container' (suitcase, box, guitar case, etc.) in which to place this material. The day started with the 'observation' game described above, followed by each of us articulating our fantasies for making a performance, regardless of practicality, feasibility, cost or the limitations of our own skills and experience. This operated as a frame for studio visits, in which each of us presented our individual ideas for shows and engaged in discussion with the group as to possible directions we might take, with reference to these fantasies. For some of us these presentations provided several 'surprises' in relation to our own work as well as that of others. This was surprise at the 'performance solutions' to seemingly unstageable ideas that were beginning to emerge and at the way connections between what might appear as very disparate material became evident. All of this occurred 'effortlessly', without us having to consciously work things through in a linear fashion.

The studio visits were followed by another long and varied sequence of exercises. These included Hoo Hah work as a group and in pairs and a variant on the 'butch-femme' exercise using objects from the group pile.

Most of these tasks incorporated lines of texts from our 'containers' and were aimed at exploring our 'performance fantasies'. This set of tasks culminated in a series of short presentations. In a complete change of tack, we then returned to our performed responses to the one-minute stories from the very first day of the workshop, as described above. The instruction was to incorporate a song within these pieces that disrupted or ran counter to the 'mood' of the piece as we had previously established. Finally, telling us to hang on to *everything* from this session, Lois asked us to create a 'snapshot', an image moving or otherwise, with or without text, which represented something we now wished to develop further.

Again not all of these tasks followed on from each other in a 'logical' fashion but no one in the group showed any hesitation or difficulty in rapidly creating their snapshot. These were means of editing down or condensing material which had already been filtered through various stages, to pinpoint what was central without consciously 'throwing out' anything else on the way. From within the group it was easy to see traces of a journey in these brief snapshots, not just through this last sequence of exercises but through the workshop as a whole. It was also notable, in both the earlier presentations and in the snapshots, that while there was clearly a wide variety of shows with very different themes and styles of performance being created, there was also a high level of cross fertilisation of ideas, images and concerns within the group. These could easily have been brought out and built on should the aim have been the creation of an ensemble piece. As such, this process offers both an excellent model for group devising and for facilitating the development of solo work, although most of the exercises do require the collaboration of at least one other person.

This, like much else in the workshop, in its own terms, recalls some of the academic 'theory', which Split Britches' work has been used to 'exemplify'. This is theory that, for instance, deconstructs notions of essential stable and singular subjectivity and proposes instead models based on *inter*-subjectivity, *inter*-sociality, and the positive and productive *inter*play of relations of similarity and difference. These are models in which identity is always being constructed and reconstructed in a contradictory fashion through encounters with others and with 'fantasy' in the form of representation. Ideas explored through such modelling argue for the potential of butch/fem play to foreground gender categories as performative social constructs that do not necessarily have any grounds in any identifiable 'reality'. The tactic is to reveal that the attributes traditionally associated with gender categories are no more 'natural' or meaningful, than claiming *anything* (pony tails, toenails, singing, cows, depression, scratching etc.) 'for' one category or another. Such theory tries to imagine beyond what is currently thought to be possible, probable or practical, to find more just and democratic social and political structures.

Peggy and Lois's process as well as their practice quite literally seems to 'embody' all of these ideas. Yet, in this workshop, subjectivity and identity were never discussed in any such terms. Indeed, in setting tasks or in discussion Lois and Peggy sometimes made statements or worked on assumptions about the self and the relationship between self and body that could be interpreted as 'essentialist' and therefore at odds with this theory. This apparent 'paradox' arises because Lois and Peggy do indeed ascribe to a radical politics, which in *practice* as well as in 'theory' is concerned with trying to imagine beyond what is currently thought to be possible, probable, or practical. As such, they work on the implicit understanding that in order to pursue this aim it is necessary to continually question and disrupt *all and any* assumptions and orthodoxies, including those established by current thinking within feminism, queer theory, or anywhere else.

Notes and references

1. For more detailed history, performance scripts and a bibliography for Split Britches (up until 1995), see Sue-Ellen Case (ed.), *Split Britches: Lesbian practice/ feminist performance* (London and New York: Routledge, 1996).
2. Joseph Chaikin founded his extremely influential experimental theatre company the Open Theater, in New York in 1963. For information on his approach as a director, see for instance, Alison Hodge, *Twentieth Century Actor Training* (New York and London: Routledge, 1999).
3. Spiderwoman was founded in 1975 by three sisters Muriel Miguel, Gloria Miguel and Lisa Mayo. For further information see 'The Spiderwoman Theater, Archive Materials: On line Exhibit', at http://staff.lib.muohio.edu/ nawpa/spdrwmnarchv.html, accessed June 2006.
4. Unless otherwise specified all quotes from Peggy Shaw and Lois Weaver are either from discussions in the workshop or interviews conducted with them during this event, which took place between 12 and 15 January 2006. Still images form this workshop can be seen at http://www.lancs.ac.uk/depts/theatre/ womenwriting/, Events Archive, Split Britches. This website also gives details of the availability of (edited) video documentation of the workshop.
5. For information about WOW see http://wwww.wowcafe.org/, accessed June 2006.
6. Split Britches have won four 'Obies', prestigious awards for off (and off-off) Broadway shows made by the New York journal, *Village Voice*.
7. For further discussion on this and other topics see Geraldine Harris, 'Double Acts, Theatrical Couples in Split Britches *Double Agency*', *New Theatre Quarterly*,

18: 3, August (2002) pp. 211–222. Also available on line via, http://journals.cambridge.org/.

8. For instance, they both often sing and dance in shows in a manner that is always entertaining, moving or 'dramatic' in its own terms, but which would not be acceptable to the values of the traditional drama school, conservatoire, or popular television competitions.

9. See Sue-Ellen Case, *Split Britches*, p. 5.

10. The US-based company Goat Island have influenced a number of other practitioners through their 'summer schools' and publications. For further information see http://www.goatisalandperfrmance.org/, accessed June 2006.

11. There were always threatening undertones in Hughes' text and in the characters' 'situation'. However, in the late 1980s these tended to be outweighed by the novelty, the vitality and the exuberance of Split Britches' interpretation. In 2006, this piece seems to touch directly not only on the anxieties that come with ageing, especially for women, but also on some of the more 'global' anxieties of our age. This is not to say that it now appears as a 'negative' or defeatist piece. *Dress Suits* was performed at the Nuffield Theatre, Lancaster as part of the Symposium for the Women's Writing for Performance project, 29 April 2006. In a session 'responding' to this performance the following day, a younger scholar/practitioner described her pleasure at seeing mature women on stage, in roles that allowed them to be powerful, sexual and playful. She said this gave her hope for her own future both as a woman and an artist.

12. Amongst other things, such as the use of language, structure, the play on sexuality etc., that inform these comparisons, the 'situation' in *Dress Suits* (two sisters somewhat 'trapped' in a situation, who spend their time dressing up and enacting out fantasies) can be compared to that of Genet's play *The Maids*.

13. Sue-Ellen Case, *Split Britches*, p. 15.

14. See Keith Johnstone, *Impro: Improvisation and the Theatre* (London: Methuen, 1989). This book, which details a wide range of inventive and, at the time, highly original exercises was extremely influential in the 1980s and 1990s. The 'status game' used by Sarah Daniels in her workshop (see p. 93), also comes from this source.

15. See for instance *Lesbians Who Kill*, in Sue-Ellen Case (ed.), *Split Britches*, pp. 185–224.

7
Giving Voice(s) to Others

Rebecca Prichard

Rebecca Prichard © Andreas Bleckmann

Invited to work with us at Lancaster, playwright Rebecca Prichard scheduled a weekend workshop visit that began with her giving a public talk
to theatre students.[1] Their excitement at having a playwright that featured on their contemporary theatre syllabus was palpable. Just as Caryl
Churchill and Pam Gems were seminal to changing the all-male bias of
the academic theatre syllabus back in the 1980s, so Rebecca Prichard is
one of a handful of women writers from the 1990s to challenge the dom-
inance of in-yer-face boys' writing and to continue a counter-cultural tradition of women's dramatic writing. Not that Rebecca, like most other
women dramatists wishes to be confined by the gender label in her writing: '*I feel as objectified about being called a young writer as I do about being
called a woman writer, simply because when you decide to write and if you are
seriously writing then that's what you're doing*'. On the other hand, women
are important to her writing and she takes '*strength from working with
other women and seeing what issues are particular to women*'.[2] Balancing her
optimism about more women writers coming forward in the twenty-first
century, is what she identifies as the need for London theatres to achieve
more equal number of women in management positions. Although she
would not endorse the view that women write only for women, nevertheless there are points of gender identification in theatre writing that
argue in favour of having women in theatre roles that enable them to be
supportive of staging women's writing and women's writing careers.[3]

Like several other women dramatists writing for the British theatre in
the 1990s, Rebecca would argue that this was not an easy decade for
women playwrights to get started in their careers or to get noticed,[4]
given the way in which critical attentions tended to focus on 'masculin-
ity and its discontents', and on an explosion of theatre writing by a new
generation of angry young men.[5] This in part accounts for one of her
'top tips' for emergent writers: not to focus on how hard it might be to
get into the business but to '*make the assumption that it's easier than you
think and just keep going at your own writing and realise that theatres want
your work [...] they want new people to come in.*' Sometimes Rebecca found
herself 'in' the angry young boys' club (along with Sarah Kane and Judy
Upton); brought into the fold of in-yer-face writing.[6] Although an
admirer of so-called 'in-yer-face' writers such as Sarah Kane and Mark
Ravenhill, these are writers that Rebecca knew she had a '*feeling of aims
in common*' with, but at the same time explains that '*we didn't see ourselves as part of a movement*'.

On the one hand it is easy to see why, given her 1990s attention to
teenage disillusionment (*Essex Girls*, 1994) and gang culture (*Fair Game*,
1997 and *Yard Gal*, 1998), that she was identified as one of the 'young

angries' writing about urban violence and disenchantment. On the other hand, what this overlooks is the specificity of her writing characterised as it is by an attention to disadvantaged communities of young women. Caryl Churchill, one of Rebecca's *'heroes'* (along with Edward Bond and Harold Pinter) has repeatedly dramatised the risks to future generations of women, given the relentless march of global capital and society's widespread failure to democratise. Rebecca's theatre has affinities with this, at the same time as being distinctive for the way in which she seeks to write *in* the young voices of female discontent. To stress this point, we would cite, for example, the contrast between Rebecca's approach to character writing and that of Sarah Daniels. Sarah will often feel wary when she involves characters that are further away from her own experiences, gender or ethnicity (see p. 91). Rebecca, on the other hand, aims to get inside 'other' voices in her writing; those outside of her own experiences whom she feels deserve to be given a public voice in the theatre. It was this creation of 'other' voices that was the motivating force behind her workshop and in this chapter is our route through to understanding the process and practice of Rebecca's writing for theatre.

Theatre in the community

This need to bring other voices and other cultures to the stage can be traced back to the inspiration which Rebecca found in the community theatre courses she took with Fiona Macbeth during her time as an undergraduate student at Exeter University:

> When I was at university, the course that I did was very practical and we did a theatre in the community element, which I loved. We went into prisons and places that I'd never been – I'd never been into a prison before to visit anyone or anything and I just found it very engaging the work that we were doing. It was trying to use drama to create change in people's lives, or as a kind of relief or a form of self-expression in difficult circumstances. It was all that sort of training, and I wanted to use it when I left university.

That community theatre training was immediately put to use after university by developing her debut play *Essex Girls* for the Royal Court's Young Writers' Festival (1994). A two-act drama that deals with teenage girls and single motherhood, *Essex Girls* draws on Rebecca's experience of working in various youth clubs in Essex, and in a young single mother's hostel for teenage mums turned out of their homes for getting pregnant. Not conscious at first of how this experience was in a sense 'research' for her play, it nevertheless became a way of 'working' that *'fell into* [her] *writing'*. The connection between community and theatre became more obvious when Rebecca found herself working with the young mums and running drama workshops in the hostel's front room. From a writer's point of view, this makes her feel a mutual *'ownership'* of the work: *'I do definitely feel fed by the environments where I've researched plays and I feel a sense of shared ownership in that way.'*

The *'community element'* endures in Rebecca's writing for theatre, both as a matter of artistic process and output: helping to shape her writing as well as providing her with dramatic 'subjects'. *Fair Game*, an adaptation of Israeli writer Edna Mazya's *Games in the Backyard*, staged at the Court in 1997, for instance, dealt (controversially) with teenage gang rape. It was also a project that took Rebecca into schools, and engaged her in discussion with and feedback from teenagers that fed into drafts of the play. *Yard Gal* (1998) also explored gang culture, but from the perspective of a girl gang. Clean Break, an all-female company committed to women whose lives have been affected by the criminal justice system, commissioned *Yard Gal* and the play went on in prisons and at the Royal Court. As a commission, *Yard Gal* involved Rebecca going into prisons as part of the creative writing process. She has since remained involved in theatre and prison projects, continuing, until recently, to work with Clean Break as a dramaturge and script reader.

Her commitment to theatre as socially and politically interventionist is further evidenced in her activism for 'Artists Against the War'.[7] Her short play *Delir' ium* was performed at The Tricycle (in association with Artists Against The War) and at the Royal Court, both times as part of a series of afternoon readings of short pieces in response to the invasion of Iraq in 2003. Subsequently, the play was also performed in a reading by Alan Williams at the Chichester Festival Theatre (2005). Another recent short piece was her response to the Harold Shipman case (the British GP notorious for murdering his patients), *A Good Doctor*, which she wrote for radio (Woman's Hour, 2003).

Writing feminism in the 1990s

Looking back briefly to second-wave feminist performance and the importance of issue-based theatre at this time, we note that in that moment it was often the case that feminist writers and practitioners with a social conscience would prioritise the political over the creative: think about what they wanted to say, rather than how they wanted to say it. We can recall ways in which at times this lead to some rather odd, non-dramatic moments in which, to give an example, a character in a scene might suddenly break off from what they were saying to deliver a long speech about women's rights, or might engineer a dialogue as a way of giving full postal or telephone details of a feminist organisation. We would have to admit that these kinds of moments, worthy though they were in their political intention, were not terribly convincing as theatre.

By contrast, bringing social and feminist criticism to theatre in the 1990s, Rebecca's writing pays keen attention to the language and voices of her characters that she seeks to put on stage, rather than trying to use them as mouthpieces for her own political agenda. Reviewing *Yard Gal*, for instance, Benedict Nightingale observed:

> If *Yard Gal* had been written 20, 15, even 10 years ago, it would surely have been a different and, almost certainly, inferior play. Few drama-tists of that era would have been able to resist making it abundantly evident that its two teenage characters were victims of society and society itself was in urgent need of institutional reform.[8]

Importantly, therefore, for us to develop an understanding of what informs her theatre writing, Rebecca wanted to direct our attention both generally to a love of language fundamental to the writer's, arguably all writers' craft, and more particularly to techniques that encourage an awareness of how 'others' speak – this with a view to successfully inhab-iting those other 'voices' creatively, rather than merely using them to rehearse social or feminist issues.

Pleasure and power of words

Firstly and fundamentally then, Rebecca encouraged us to think about the sheer pleasure that people get from words. If Jenny Eclair got us to focus on words that sound funny (see Chapter 9), Rebecca offered a more general invitation in the workshop to simply vocalise words that people enjoy, no matter what the reason:

> 'snuggle' (because it sounds like what it is)
> 'gurggle' (because it's fun)
> luscious' (because it's evocative)
> tu'penny/ha'penny (because of the sing-song sounds)

In an exercise early on in the workshop, she organised us into a circle and got us to pass around our words – uni-directional, at first, with each person passing their own particular word around the circle. Thereafter, we got more adventurous and creative by picking any of the group's words, adding to these by word association, and passing them randomly around and across the circle. We also played with breaking the words up, passing on a part of, rather than a whole, word. As an exercise this served to energise words; to encourage us simply to delight in language and, crucially, to stop us thinking about *what words mean*. Any kind of vocal rhythm game is helpful in this respect: any game that encourages pleasure in and playing with sounds, rhythms, syllables, rather than being drawn to words for meaning and content. As with the impulse work that we did with Split Britches (see Chapter 6), it meant that the word-play was not censored and could be as 'silly' and absurd as we wanted to make it.

Secondly, as a development of this point about the pleasure of language, Rebecca argued that a writer needs to be aware of what language 'does' to spectators. She recalls Pinter once stating that a sentence has the power to deliver a punch in the stomach: language has the capacity to make a physical impact on its spectators. A way to encourage an awareness of language as the dramatist's 'tool', or primary medium through which she works, is to try out brief extracts from plays. Rebecca shared examples from a range of dramatic material from Greek drama to modern British playwriting to illustrate language at work in different registers and genres. De-contextualised, not necessarily knowing where a piece comes from, who the writer is, or what the dramatic genre is, encourages us to listen to the words themselves, rather than their meaning. *Hearing* rather than *understanding* the dramatic language invites an awareness of the rhythms that carry language, or the effects that can be created by breaking those rhythms. It further illustrates how, without knowing the background to a particular text, language has the power to evoke feelings in the listener: emotions surface from 'underneath' a text even without knowledge of meaning or context, or creates images through the power and impact of words. In brief, reading extracts aloud in a group offered us a way of being aware of the sensual power of words; the ways in which language has the power to engage us and to affect us emotionally.

Understanding the power of words to affect an audience is something Rebecca learnt when writing her debut play, *Essex Girls*. Although proud of *Essex Girls*, she is also self-critical of the way that as a first play she '*allowed the audience to feel very comfortable in their seats. They could watch the play and see the girls in their own world as quite isolated and apart, and either feel liberal enough to empathize with them or not – it was the audience's choice.'* This realization made Rebecca much more aware of her *'relationship with an audience'.*[9] Similarly, from the workshop exercises on the pleasure and power of language we noted the importance of this for the writer; the need to think not just about the creation of a dramatic world, the characters, the action – but to consider the affect that this will have on an audience as part of the writing process.

Listening to others

In the criticism of her own work, Rebecca identifies that in writing other worlds – in *Essex Girls* a teen culture of desire and disenchantment, for example – a writer needs fully to reflect, or 'live' in, that fictional world in order to carry the audience with it, rather than leave them at a (critical) distance. *'You see clichés about young women in trouble, or you see them as victims in a larger story,'* she argues, *'but not in a way that shows the world from their perspective, that gives voice to their stories.'* A firm believer in people having far more compassion than they are given credit for, she views theatre as a vehicle for putting us in touch with other cultures and experiences, rather than being alienated or cut off from them.

Having learnt from the *Essex Girls* experience, and charged with the task of adapting *Fair Game*, Rebecca was at pains to dramatise the teenage gang rape not as something audiences could walk away from, but as something they were compelled to make a connection to:

> [I] *carved out bits of the play and just set it in a park in the East End, so that if an audience came to see it, they couldn't just take it as something that happened over there* [in Israel], *but they would have to face it as something that was happening in our culture.*

As with *Essex Girls* she engaged in people research, this time going into schools with her director, Roxana Silbert, to gauge teenage reactions to the piece during the writing process: *'Taking the first draft into schools was frightening: teachers stopped them using certain girls to play the central character because it was felt that the part was too close to their experience'.*[10] While the play caused controversy even before it was staged on account of casting teenage (rather than older) performers in the roles,[11] the social realities of the gang rape are what make the piece hard-hitting; the 'real' voices of the teenage gang members are what pack the Pinter punch.

To write 'real voices', Rebecca uses the contact that she has with the disadvantaged communities that she writes about to listen carefully to how members of that community speak:

> *I try to make my work current with slang and language and that sort of thing, so that it feels relevant to young people so that they can identify with it. When I work in youth clubs or work in schools, I keep an ear out for phrases and stuff like that and ... not only that, I just want it to relate to them and for it to bring about discussions that can help young people deal with what's going on in their world.*

Similarly, when, after *Fair Game*, Rebecca came to work on *Yard Gal*, she tuned in to Jamaican slang – listened to the young women she met in prison, so that she could get a feel for and get into their language:

> *There were women from all over, but I think what I picked up on was that, particularly among the young women, there were both Black and white women who had adopted – not really yardie culture, because that was a bit of another league – but Jamaican slang, patois. And it just interested me as well to see white women talking, using Jamaican slang. They really tested my ear out – some of the stuff that they were saying I just couldn't understand. I thought that I'd got into it and could do it, but I couldn't when they really tested me out.*
>
> *But I love that language: it's so rich and I think it's really quite theatrical: it's dark and it uses imagery as well. I really loved it as a language to work with. After I picked the patois up, I consciously researched it and started listening more to radio stations and trying to get into it myself.*

So successful was Rebecca in writing the Jamaican slang that when the time came for the play to go on in Holloway prison, many of the women there were expecting to see a Black writer and were shocked to discover that she was white.

In the workshop Rebecca encouraged us to think about 'tuning into' how others speak as a way of skilling-up for dialogue writing. She recommended noting down verbatim snatches of conversation to develop an awareness of how people converse. While listening to conversational snatches on buses, in supermarkets, or wherever, was something Rebecca advised that we could try for ourselves outside of the workshop; in the workshop itself she set us exercises to heighten our awareness of how people speak with a view to working on character. This has a certain affinity with Sarah Daniels' approach (though Sarah combines thinking about speech with developing a character's back story see pp. 91–92) and SuAndi's 'giving voice' to characters. At the same time it is different and distinctive from the latter: finding voices to inhabit a dramatic world means that those voices exist independently of the writer, unlike live art or performance poetry where a performer's persona comes into play, even when they are speaking in other voices (see discussion of SuAndi's performance persona, pp. 69–70).

In practice, what this required of us was to think of someone that we know, someone familiar to us, but to re-create them through a particular 'quirk' of speaking. For example, someone might have a tendency to insert 'do you know what I mean' into their sentences, or address everyone by a particular term of endearment (at the point of writing, for example, 'babe' appears to be much very much in vogue in teen culture). When you listen to examples of these language 'tics' then you can begin to analyse what they 'say' about the person who speaks: the 'tic' might say something about a person's attitude to others, or about their levels of confidence or lack of confidence, about whether they are really saying what they mean or are masking a truth, and so on. A character begins to emerge just through a few lines working off the 'tic'. Working in a group, we paired up to see what our 'characters' had to say to each other. Listening carefully to each character's lines can also help to place them into a particular place or situation from which to 'act out'. Also we found that pairing people up as opposites was a quick route to creating situations of (potentially dramatic) conflict.

As Rebecca suggested, a way of developing this kind of work is to take the paired opposites in their particular situation and to give them a secret that at first is withheld and then gradually comes out in the scene. What this helps to illustrate is, for example, the value of holding back: of not saying everything at once and of having the audience 'work' in the gaps. Keeping and breaking a secret also offers a way of taking an action in a different direction: of allowing a scene to move in a different (unforeseen) direction. The motif of secrets also makes us aware of the ways in which language is an imperfect tool: the decision to have characters say certain things is in effect a way of making a choice about other things that do not get said. Language, therefore, masks that which is 'unsaid'. When characters speak, we could ask to what extent they are 'lying' through the choices they make about what to say and what not to say. Writing for theatre could, in this sense, therefore, be argued as gradations of lies rather than truths.[12]

The bigger picture

If you work on developing a scene then inevitably you start to question how that scene relates to the bigger dramatic picture. Two comments are relevant here to Rebecca's process: the role of the director in working towards the bigger dramatic picture and thinking about what kind of realism is most appropriate for creating the 'real voices' in a compositional structure that overall aims at social criticism.

Like all of the practitioners in this study, Rebecca values having a sounding-board to bounce ideas off and like Sarah Daniels, in particular, views the director as having a crucial, supportive role in this respect. The director is the *'medium which your work goes through, so it's very difficult if they don't understand your work'*. *'I like directors who [...] are [...] motivated by what motivates me. So it's been good to work with Roxanna* [Silbert] *and also with Gemma Bodinetz.'* She also welcomes the distance that having a director affords the writer. If the director is charged with the task of taking the work forward, then the writer is in a position, she argues, to think critically about her work and possible changes to it. Rebecca has no issues about men directing her plays (*Delir' ium* was directed by a man), and though she might be tempted to direct her own work in the future, is at the same time not sure she *'would ever be brave enough'*.

When Rebecca first submitted *Essex Girls* to the Royal Court's Young Writers' Festival it was only the first act of the play that she had written and she needed to find a second act.[13] It was Silbert, her director's tutor, who helped her to sort out what the second act should do with the 'girls':[14]

> We talked about taking the girls (who were sort of 14) and looking at them when they're older and perhaps setting [act two] in a supermarket or wherever they've ended up. But I just felt that was too concrete and made it seem like their lives were doomed, whereas I wanted the first act to be quite hopeful – as if they could go either way – and then the second act to show different, older girls, and to put the two side by side, so that the audience still remains with some kind of hope.

Rebecca's rationale behind this dramaturgical choice is significant in terms of understanding how she structures her authentic voices into realistic worlds and cultures that invite the possibility of change. Thinking for a moment of Lois Weaver's belief in the idea that 'if you can imagine it, you can make it, if you can make it then you can change it' (see Chapter 6, p. 105), then for Rebecca imagining and making the worlds of 'others' in her theatre is also expressing a desire for those worlds to change. In the interests of change, she argues '*I think sometimes if you write really realistic stuff, that's purely realistic and you stick to traditional structures, you give an expectation or pattern that fulfils itself, as if you are saying everything is doomed.*' So in Essex Girls this meant that she went for a 'different structure' to work against the obvious and the expected, and to hang on to the possibility of hope.

For this reason she is also not in favour of writing social realism in a way that 'cements *reality*': '*If you do pure social realism, it feels to me as if you are kind of saying this is the way it is and all we can do is despair. I'm not satisfied with that as an artist. I don't feel happy with that.*' If Sarah Daniels' radio realism figures the social and the political through its emotional affects and looks to the reparative (see Chapter 5, pp. 89–90), then arguably Rebecca's realism is one that pulls spectators emotionally into the exposure of social wrongs, but through an empathetic engagement with the characters who have been wronged.

Women, writing and prisons

While Rebecca expresses a commitment to social change through her theatre writing, she also gets involved in women's prison projects. Taking theatre into prisons is something that a number of our project artists have experience of: SuAndi undertakes prison projects within a range of community-based work in the North West of England; Lois Weaver and Peggy Shaw have worked in women's prisons in the UK and Brazil, and Sarah Daniels, like Rebecca, has had a Clean Break commission, and also currently serves on their board of company directors.

Two key questions generally arise around theatre and prison projects: how it feels to work with a community that is there to stay when you are free to leave and, generally, how to cope with working creatively when faced with the harsh realities of incarceration. Rebecca feels '*ambivalent*' about the former: '*on the one hand, I'm glad to have worked with some really great women; on the other hand, it always feels bad to leave them.*'[15] In terms of the latter, reactions from practitioners vary from wanting to highlight the possible injustices of the penal system, to wanting, as Lois and Peggy do, to look for the joy in the moment of prison creativity.[16] For Rebecca, a particular joy of working on her Clean Break project for *Yard Gal* was being able to nurture women's creativity and writing. Initially, Rebecca was assigned to HMP Bullwood Hall for a three-month period as a creative writing tutor (from January 1997). That three months turned into the best part of year spent working either as a creative writing tutor for

Clean Break or at Bullwood prison.[17] Published alongside the script of *Yard Gal* are extracts of creative writing – fiction, poetry and drama – from some of the women prisoners Rebecca worked with. In the notes by Rebecca that accompany the writing she again points to the mutuality of this process, the shared ownership of her writing, though noting wistfully, that she wished she '*could have done more*' for the women.[18]

What the women gave *her* was the inspiration to write about the damage done to *young* women's lives: '*A lot of the women in Bullwood Hall were very young and I was quite moved by that really: how they'd ended up in prison so young. I wanted to write about young women.*' She was touched by the way in which when she heard the women talking about their own lives, it made it seem '*as if prison was a moment of stillness out of complete chaos. I mean, I don't know how people survive that sort of life, just constant change and the difficulties of living hand to mouth, knowing that without crime they would not survive, and the fact that they're going to be chucked back out into that again with very little support.*' In sum, '*It feels quite a devastating environment to see young people in. I think that's really why I wanted to write about it.*'

While the workshops that she ran in Bullwood were for the women's creativity, towards the end of her time there and for the writing of *Yard Gal* she held a series of interviews: '*that's a change of gear really. You have to be really open about the fact that you are writing a play and this is about research.*' Inevitably, in this part of Rebecca's writing process some women did not want to get involved – and they had the choice about this. No one was made to participate, it was entirely voluntary. What Rebecca found most interesting were the women who decided to take part in the interviews and then when it came to the crunch '*were really sullen and very unresponsive*'. This actually gave her a creative way into her play:

> ... I found that really interesting as well, like what if a character was like that with the audience and it made me think a lot about the relationship with the audience and people who withhold information. Usually when you come to tell a story or as a moment of theatre, then the audience have an assumption that you want to be a storyteller, but what if these characters are reluctant storytellers and they don't want to tell their story at all and they want to go away as soon as possible? So that gave me an in and I was playing with that.

When *Yard Gal* opens the two young friends, Boo and Marie, are very much the reluctant storytellers. Despite encouragement from Marie,

Boo repeatedly states that she 'ain't telling them [the audience] shit'.[19] Narrating their damaged street lives, and eventually in Boo's case, prison life, *Yard Gal* synthesises all the elements Rebecca regards as important to her writing: an ear for language, for 'real' voices; a social critique of the waste of young lives, and a relationship with the audience that is direct and raw in its engagement. There was no escape; no sitting back from the characters and their world, as Rebecca felt that there was in *Essex Girls*: the play packed a street-gang punch that took the audience prisoner whether they liked it or not.

In the theatre the critics were enthusiastic about *Yard Gal*. More Black women came to the show at the Court than is usual for Court productions, suggesting that perhaps, as in the prison experience, Rebecca's writing 'passed' as Black. It was a production where as much as the girls Boo and Marie talked energetically, albeit at times reluctantly, to the audience about their lives, the audience unusually talked back – shouted out advice to the characters. The response to the play in prisons, however, was more mixed. Rebecca had hoped that it would be the younger women who would respond to her piece *'but it turned out that often the older women in prisons were more engaged.'* She feels that the younger women were often more affected by, and sometimes needed to get away from, the harsh second half of *Yard Gal*, as violent crime leads to sadder, more damaged lives for the girls.

Theatre games and power games

Having described and contextualised the processes of writing *Yard Gal* as a Clean Break commission and all that this entails, back in the workshop, what we explored on the final day of working with Rebecca were the kinds of workshopping techniques that she uses in prisons.[20]

Firstly, she simply wanted us to be aware in a very general way of how basic theatre exercises that are used in any number of writing and workshop activities take on a whole new meaning and produce some very different results when used in prison situations. Briefly, what mostly happens is that theatre games very quickly produce a heightened sense of power relations that are an important feature of prison life. Mirroring a partner, for instance, is a very common drama technique, used in different kinds of workshopping situations. In Rebecca's workshop it was introduced as a way of thinking about power relations. In paired mirroring the aim is to share the mirroring so that no one person leads the exercise, but rather each partner has to *feel* for the movement of the other in a way that encourages a sharing of movements. Such a simple exercise produces complex responses. It is actually hard, for example, not to find yourself leading or following, or trying to initiate a move-ment, because may be you feel not enough is happening, and so on. To be mutually in balance is, therefore, much harder to achieve than you might think.

Like children's playground games, drama games often involve two groups in competition with each other. There are a good number of team games, for example, that are premised on the idea of those who catch and those who get caught; those who try to reach the other side of the playground, and those who try to stop them. One particular game that Rebecca invited us to play required forming two circles – one inner and one outer. The inner circle sits on chairs; the outer circle stands, with one person behind each chair, an arm's length away from the seated inner circle. One chair, however, is left vacant. Those in the outer circle are the jailors; those seated are the prisoners. The prisoners have to try and break out of jail by moving to the empty chair. They can only 'escape' if winked at by the jailor who is 'it' (the jailor behind the empty chair, trying to capture their own prisoner), and if they manage to move before they are 'slapped' on the back by their jailor whose aim is to make sure they stay put.

As a drama exercise this explores dynamics of power and responsibil-ity and creates some very strong reactions at having to be responsible. In our workshop group of writers and performers, for example, everyone preferred being in prison rather than a jailor: nobody felt comfortable with having the power and the responsibility over the prisoner. Played in a prison setting, Rebecca explains, this produces very intense feelings and discussions about power relations: between warden and prisoner, and also the power dynamics between prisoners.[21]

Body as a writing tool

'To bring women to writing' was an attractive, if flawed manifesto adopted by French feminist Hélène Cixous in an earlier phase of second-wave fem-inist thinking and activity,[22] and the idea that women should 'write' and 'write' themselves into 'texts' proved highly influential in the 1980s (espe-cially in cultural-feminist forms of theatre making and performance). However, while the idea that women should 'write' themselves into social, sexual, cultural and artistic 'scripts' was incontestable as a feminist pro-posal, the implied assumption that *all* women would be able to do this, was problematic.[23] The communities of young disadvantaged women that

Rebecca portrays in her drama and that she has worked with in prisons, for example, would be highly unlikely to see themselves as 'writing women', or as having the opportunities to write. Working in a prison context means working with women who are not writers; who have little if any experience of theatre, or any kind of creativity for that matter, who do not even consider themselves as women with stories to tell.

Strategies for encouraging women to come to writing as a form of agency and self-expression need, therefore, to be given very careful consideration. When working in prisons there is every need, Rebecca argues, for techniques that encourage women into creating and making stories which appear to have nothing to do with ideas about drama or playwriting. In this 'writing' situation, rather than starting with language as the writer's tool, she starts with the body as the primary tool for expression. Here too, a number of familiar theatre techniques come into play, but to different effect given the context of working with women whose stories, feelings, experiences have often been silenced, repressed, written off, or out. Body sculpting, for example, is frequently used in theatre work as a means of visualising emotional states, along with freeze frame tableaux that can image a moment of dramatic action, thought, or feeling. Shaping and re-shaping bodies and freeze-frame images produces altered states of feeling or alternative moments of dramatic action. Physicalising a mood, feeling or action, is a means of 'writing' that we are then able to 'read'. 'Reading' the images confirms for us that we are, in fact, 'writing', communicating and making stories.

'Desperately seeking Suzanne'

To bring women to 'writing' also requires finding ways of working that are not too self-revealing: ways of 'writing' that deflect from the personal. One such strategy is to have people create a fictional character as a conduit for stories. Our group created Suzanne: a woman who was meant to be at our workshop but could not make it. With Rebecca keeping notes, the group built up a very basic picture of Suzanne (starting with what she looked like, how old she is, what her job is, whether she is married, or not, whether she has children or not) that gradually got increasingly layered and complicated. The character emerged as a frustrated actress, and the group invented lots of (often quite wild) stories about Suzanne's thwarted dreams; her anger at being a middle child who failed to get parental attention, her feelings of betrayal, and so forth. If at times it felt excessive and verging on the 'unrealistic' (if not fantastic) such story-telling responses were insightful for the ways in which they created a way of discharging emotions, that were familiar to many women in the group, but 'buffered' by the fictional character strategy, and for the ways in which building a character affords a complex linking-up of many interconnecting stories that gradually 'leak' their way into the fictional frame. For a group of women who at the outset believe they do not have stories to tell, this exercise may help to convince them otherwise.

Fast forward, rewind

After 'researching' a character in this way you can begin to dramatise episodes from her life. Avoiding (alienating) instructions about 'writing scenes', a way into this is to build on sculpting and freeze frame exercises to *do* this again in the form of *physical writing*. For example, 'fast forward, rewind' is a very simple, three scene exercise in which you take a moment from the character's life and sculpt this into a still tableau. You then create two further scenes: one from before this moment, showing what lead up to it, and one that comes afterwards, showing what happens next. To begin with, these can all be sculpted, tableaux images, which can then be transformed into moving silent scenes, and then scenes with lines of dialogue inspired by the physical picture-making. In terms of selecting a 'still life' episode it can be productive to locate a moment when the character is experiencing change. A life-changing moment which can come from a character's own shift in outlook, or a change brought about by events outside of her control (accidents, health, bereavement, losing a job, etc.), or a combination of these is helpful to raising an awareness of change. As Rebecca explains, for those young women in prison whose lives have been damaged and laid waste, it is hard, may be even impossible, to see how their lives are to change course in the future. Yet it is through discussion, she argues, '*through talking about it that we can actually bring about change and help people to look at those issues.*'

Moreover, if small groups work on the same trio of fast forward, rewind scenes, then looking at variations between them can be insightful for sensing the different possibilities of dynamics and relations between characters in the story. As a drama technique, again this refuses an idea of theatre writing based on concept, but rather takes character as means by which to generate narrative and stories. Playing with variations further encourages ways of seeing how a character can change depending on who is in the scene with them and what their relationship is to them. This gets us to think about how a character also role plays in relation to other characters.[24]

Finally, one of the most surprising insights from working in this way is how much more sympathetic you feel towards a 'bad' character in a story when you *embody* them. When obliged to play a particular role, however 'bad' that character, you tend to be more sympathetic to their point of view – all of which can generate energetic and interesting debate around different characters in the stories, their motivations and their actions.

Stories and perspectives

Reading images inevitably stirs up a lot of discussion, because not everybody sees and interprets a physical snapshot in exactly the same way. In *Yard Gal* Rebecca had her two characters, Boo and Marie, play with the 'gaps' in memory and their different interpretation of events: '*They would argue about what the story was at various points. There was something about two people telling the story on stage where, with their different versions – they're talking about the past – they could actually achieve something in the present through the telling of the stories which helped their own relationship and helped them come together again as friends.*'

As a final exercise on Suzanne in the workshop, Rebecca got our group to present her 'life' by casting everyone into a role in her story, and then interviewing everybody about her.[25] Working on multi-perspectives in this way brought the character to life in her absence and brought out different versions of life events: different perspectives on Suzanne, her motivations, character, and relationships. As an exercise it felt like some kind of detective-murder game, in which Suzanne, the 'murder victim' is brought back to life: 'clues' about her past life make her present. This is a different, playful way of finding a character's 'back story', and one that moreover brought us back to secrets, lies and truths, and the pleasure and power that the writer has in imagining the unimaginable, and persuading an audience to imagine along with them.

Post script

For Rebecca theatrical imagination must, however, always connect to '*social motivation*'. After the success of *Yard Gal* she had lots of offers of work but what people wanted her for was the '*accessibility*' and '*populist aspect*' of her writing, rather than her serious engagement with social issues – a similar reaction, perhaps, to the way that Bobby Baker's work is often received as funny, whilst the serious point to her work is overlooked. Rebecca has turned down a lot of work for this reason – not that she feels puritanical about this, however – *'If I could try and make more money I would'*. When Elaine caught up with her post the workshop to see her new play *FUTURES* (2006), this was not in a big money-making context, but in a production at London's small, but up-and-coming new writing venue, Theatre 503. Moreover, her style of writing had shifted into something more lyrical, poetic and abstract than her 1990s work. (*FUTURES* follows three main characters – an abusive husband, his wife and the wife's dead father – who each narrate their own personal and global terrors.) This is a speculative observation on our part, but the shift in style and register might partially be due to countering the *'populist'* appeal of the 1990s repertoire. Equally, however, Rebecca would defend the right for a writer's work to evolve. Like her 'hero' Churchill, whose theatre continues to evolve in different, sometimes surprising, directions, both in terms of form and content, Rebecca's writing may be shifting in new directions. Whatever those new directions might be, what remains constant to her writing process is her instinct for language; the pleasure and the power of the word and a concern for the social 'futures' we are creating. Preoccupied with the *language* of her piece, behind the scenes of *FUTURES*, she was hard at work following her own advice to emergent writers *'to be critical of your own work'*; worrying over lines in the script, wanting to *hear* the rhythms, resonance and power of the voices she had created, and a testimony to her own acknowledgement that *'there is a real hunger for new work and new voices'*.

Notes and references

1. Rebecca's talk was given at Lancaster University on 14 October 2005. All quotations are from this talk unless otherwise stated. Her workshop continued through 15 and 16 October 2005.
2. Rebecca Prichard in David Edgar (ed.), *State of Play: Playwrights on Playwriting* (London: Faber, 1999), p. 61.
3. Explanation given in Lancaster Talk, 14 October 2005.
4. See, for instance, the various notes of discontent registered by women playwrights in the interview collection: Heidi Stephenson and Natasha Langridge (eds.), *Rage and Reason: Women Playwrights on Playwriting* (London: Methuen, 1997).
5. See David Edgar, *State of Play: Playwrights on Playwriting*, p. 27.
6. See Alex Sierz, *In-Yer-Face Theatre; British Drama Today* (London: Faber and Faber, 2001).
7. For details of this organisation see http://www.artistsagainstthewar.org.uk/aims.html.
8. *The Times*, 13 May 1998.
9. Prichard, in Edgar, *State of Play*, p. 60.

10. Prichard in David Benedict, ' "Essex Girl writes Play" Shock Horror', Features, *Independent*, 22 October 1997, p. 18.

11. For further details on this point see Dalaya Alberge, 'Charities Alarmed at Casting of Children in "Gang Rape" Play', *The Times*, 26 August 1997, p. 4.

12. For creative responses to these kinds of explorations see WWP project website, http://www.lancs.ac.uk/depts/theatre/womenwriting/, Events Archive, 'Writing for Theatre', Rebecca Prichard.

13. Rebecca explained to us how the Court's Young Writers' Festival works:
    They [the Court] *do this thing every two years – they still do as far as I know – where you can send in work and a panel of judges read it. It's to make sure that theatre draws in people who are unknown and if you get through then you get your work on at the Court. [...] They used to do it where they run workshops, like outreach workshops, so that people who see the posters or hear a radio advert or whatever, can just turn up at the Court and take part in a workshop to encourage you to start writing. You don't have to have written anything – it's open access. Then they do another series of workshops, which I think are spaced a couple of months apart and you write something and send it in and again it's open access as long as you've written something, it doesn't matter of what quality, then you have access to the next workshop. Then they begin to whittle it down and you get more support – I think I had a writer's tutor and a director's tutor.* (Lancaster Talk, October 14 2005)

14. *Essex Girls* is a two-act drama. In Act One three teenage girls discuss their lives in the girls' toilets in a comprehensive school. Act Two relocates to the council flat of a young single mother, visited by her friend.

15. Prichard, quoted in Alex Sierz, *In-Yer-Face Theatre*, p. 231.

16. Peggy Shaw talked extensively on this point in the panel presentation, 'Prison Break: Performance, Fantasy and Identity in Women's Penitentiary Systems' at Psi#12, Queen Mary, University London, June 2006. Co-panellist Carol Jacobsen, by contrast, in her presentation foregrounded the strategy of protesting against the gender injustices of the prison system.

17. Details in Rebecca Prichard, *Yard Gal* (London: Faber & Faber, 1998), production notes.

18. Ibid.

19. Prichard, *Yard Gal*, Act One, p. 1.

20. The techniques Rebecca shared were those that came originally from her community theatre studies at University, sourced principally by Boal's techniques, and Nic Fine and Fiona Macbeth's *Fireworks* (London: National Youth Agency, 1992). These she has evolved and adapted over the years of her prison theatre work, sometimes also developing these for writing exercises of the kind she introduced us to in the Lancaster workshop.

21. Rebecca explained how prison life includes the tradition of a prisoner being 'bound' to another prisoner for a period of time, during which they are obliged to do everything for them.

22. Cixous, 'The Laugh of the Medusa' in Elaine Marks and Isabelle de Courtivron (eds.), *New French Feminisms* (Brighton: The Harvester Press, 1981), pp. 245–264, p. 245.

23. See Toril Moi on this point in her chapter on Cixous in *Sexual/Textual Politics* (London: Routledge, 1985), pp. 102–126, pp. 125–6.

24. Participants can think about this by pairing up to storytell a time to their partner when they found themselves in a situation in which two social roles were in conflict. The conflicts are reported by the group, each participant reporting their partner's rather than their own story (to deflect from the story being too personal to share).

25. For film footage of the Suzanne interviews see WWP project website, http://www.lancs.ac.uk/depts/theatre/womenwriting/, Events Archive, 'Writing for Theatre', Rebecca Prichard.

8
Performance Storytelling

Vayu Naidu

Vayu Naidu. Lancaster Workshop © Women's Writing for Performance Project

Vayu Naidu originates from southern India, but came to England in the late 1980s where she now lives and works as a performance storyteller.[1] While her practice is one that clearly seems to emerge out of and to be articulated through her own personal history and identity, it is actually less obviously rooted in the autobiographical than that of some of the other practitioners in this study. In fact, in her interview with us, one of Vayu's key 'tips' for emergent women practitioners was to '*leave the personal behind*'.[2] Yet, she also acknowledged that this advice might seem contradictory in relation to some of the methods she explored with us in her workshop at Lancaster. This is because while Vayu works primarily from 'known' stories, myths, legends, folktales, epics and sacred cycles from India and other countries, she does so with a view to making connections between these stories, contemporary concerns and the immediate context(s) in which she is performing. The process by which this is achieved passes through but is not limited or confined to the personal.

Vayu describes her work as '*intracultural*' and as a performance practitioner she might easily function as a 'case study' for discussions of Diaspora subjectivity and 'cultural hybridity'. These concepts were formulated and developed by postcolonial, anti-racist and feminist theorists including Homi Bhabha, Stuart Hall, Avtar Brah, Paul Gilroy and Néstor Garcia Canclini and are evinced in the practice of an ever increasing number of practitioner/theorists, 'spearheaded' in performance studies of the 1990s by Gloria Anzaldúa, Coco Fusco and Guillermo Gómez–Pēna.

Briefly, certain types of post-colonial and/or Diaspora subjectivities are understood to potentially foreground the multiple and contradictory nature of all identity. This is because they are so markedly formed 'in between or in excess to, the sum of the parts of difference' (such as race, class, gender and national identity), 'in between or in excess to the past, present and future',[3] in between 'history, memory, fantasy narrative and myth',[4] and through 'processes of multi-locationality', across geographical, cultural and psychic boundaries.[5] As a result, postcolonial and Diaspora identities and the types of 'culturally hybrid' aesthetic production that they enable and produce, are thought to have the potential to undermine and destabilise all hegemonic identity categories (such as 'race', gender, class and national identity). As such, according to Bhabha they may contribute to the creation of 'something new and unrecognisable, a new area of meaning and representation'.[6] However, if Vayu's practice and process seems to 'embody' these ideas, her work is also 'in excess' to them, due to the quite specific differences and particular boundaries, including artistic ones, between which it has been formed.

'Cultures in between'

As a postgraduate student in India, Vayu *'studied drama as part of English as Literature'* but at this period her opportunities for formal practical study were limited. However, she occasionally performed in *'regional plays'* and became increasingly attracted to performance through the dual influences of Girish Karnad, a theatre writer and film-maker who draws on the Indian oral performance tradition, whose work was *'an inspiration for integrating folk or mythological characters in a contemporary dimension for urban Indian audiences'*[7] and through Brechtian notions of *'breaking the fourth wall through story telling'*. She also tells an anecdote of being inspired early on in her career, when, like any *'tourist'*, she took a photograph of a storyteller performing an Indian epic who instantly incorporated the resulting flash from her camera into his telling of the ancient and sacred tale.[8]

In 1988, Vayu came to study for a PhD at the Theatre Workshop at Leeds University, arriving in time to see Peter Brook's interpretation of the *Mahabharata* in Glasgow. This show has its detractors and has been severely criticised by commentators such as Rustom Bharucha for what is argued as Brook's mode of superficial cross-cultural appropriation.[9] Nevertheless, Vayu was fascinated to find herself watching a version of this Indian epic, performed in English by a multicultural cast to a largely secular and *'uninitiated'* audience. Previously she had experienced the Mahabharata *'from within a culture'*, performed at religious festivals as *'part of a rite of passage, as ritual, partly as devotional, partly celebrational [...] what I was watching was really the making of this epic from one culture have significance and meaning for an audience from another culture through the device of the storyteller.'*

This experience encouraged her to pursue research into the role and function of the storyteller, not least through her developing her own solo, storytelling performances. Her focus was on investigating the problematics and possibilities of *'transposing known stories from different Indian languages into English and performing to audiences who are not familiar with those cultural references.'* In many ways this approach was consistent with some key aspects of the classical Indian oral tradition. As Vayu indicated in the workshop, dating back to the fourth century AD, the great epics of the Mahabharata and the Ramayana have been continually 'evolving' through the process of being interpreted, performed and passed on by successive generations of storytellers. Practitioners working within this tradition *'function to ask the questions* [about the epics and their figures] *that the audience dare not ask'*. They also *'start and stop the action'* to answer hecklers and deal with audience reactions, so that as indicated by her 'camera flash' anecdote cited above, *'in the act of performance things are being shaped and changed as well as the whole epic being told'*. In pursuing this research through her own practice, Vayu quickly realised that,

> *If I had not studied English Literature in India I wouldn't have the correlatives from English literature to make sense of these Indian things* [and] *I would just be what you call a 'traditional artist' in which I have my form and that is what I will show you about my culture. So in a way I would become a museum. But having access to language – English – through English literature in India and through Indian stories in English, this really broke those fourth walls, and as it were, fifth walls.*

Even so, the challenge she had set herself became apparent when Vayu was asked to perform *at* a museum. The Cartwright Hall in Leeds was offering an exhibition of Indian miniature painting from the Moghul school based on the Ramayana. Part of the impetus for the exhibition was that the museum wanted to appeal to the large South Asian population in Leeds. As Vayu put it *'in itself you have these fascinating intercultural shifts, an Islamic influenced school of painting in India drawing on a Hindu epic, now being shown within a postcolonial ethos in England and curated by the Victoria and Albert Museum.'* In attempting to tell the stories from the Ramayana in ways that paid attention to these shifts, Vayu realised the importance of *'context'*, or rather the various 'metacontexts', informed by *'colonisation, migration, interculturalism, globalisation and other forms of interconnectivity'*,[10] within which she was operating. In Britain in the late 1980s, part of this context was the controversy surrounding Salmon Rushdie's book *The Satanic Verses* and Vayu found herself undertaking a project focussed around this issue with a multicultural group of schoolchildren. The usefulness of using 'known' stories, in this instance a Persian epic, as a means of negotiating the complex and deeply felt cross-cultural antagonisms aroused in this group by the Rushdie affair, strengthened her conviction that *'My god does storytelling work … if we know how to use it properly'*.

The story of Parvati, Shiva and Ganesha: a demonstration

We have to admit that of all the practitioners considered in this study, prior to the workshop at Lancaster, we were least familiar with Vayu's practice. It was then especially pleasurable and illuminating when she opened this event with a demonstration of her art, which indicated exactly how effective storytelling can be when *'we know how to use it properly'*. Absolutely 'core' to her art is, of course, a 'relish for language' and while she sometimes works with musicians and dancers on shows that employ costumes, props, sets, lighting and multimedia, this performance established that, for this genre of practice, all that is really required is *'a storyteller and a listener'*. Vayu did, in fact, change into a sari but otherwise worked without any theatrical devices, speaking from a standing position. The tale she performed for us was from Indian mythology and focussed on the relationship between the deities Parvati and Shiva and detailed the origins of Ganesh or Ganesha as the elephant-headed god. In the unfolding of this story Vayu's performance style moved between different tones, moods and registers. Sometimes it invoked the gestural vocabulary and imagery of Indian classical traditions in both 'serious' devotional and more popular and 'playful' modes; at other times it had something of the informality and the humour of stand-up, or again the 'presentational' style of some experimental performance. Yet, if it was sometimes 'like' these modes, it differed from them in terms of the specific relationship between Vayu as storyteller and the narrative and the characters, and between Vayu and us, her audience.

While most of us in the workshop had a general awareness of the figures in the story we were not familiar with this particular narrative and some of our pleasure in this performance came from a sense of novelty. Yet, ultimately, the impact of this demonstration depended on the way that the interpretation of this story was so obviously addressed to us, *this* audience in a manner that recalls SuAndi's remarks on the spontaneous, nature of performance poetry.[11] Vayu's mode of storytelling, however, encompasses an even greater degree of improvisation. She says

> *You may have an idea that this is the story you could be performing but once you have come into the lit space, you make eye contact with your audience, and the storyteller has to [...] be completely liberated at that moment, be a composer at the same time. So maybe in the wings I had a story in mind but I come here and there is a chemistry I engage with, and I change the story I am going to tell. I am composing the narrative on the spot.*

In this instance, woven into her telling of this ancient tale were topical references and comments that embraced the specific context of the workshop and our broader location in Britain and the Northern hemisphere.

These references were sometimes humorous but often addressed key political and philosophical questions that have arisen 'post 9/11'. These moves were achieved 'seamlessly' and allowed us an immediate sense of connection to this potentially 'distant' and 'exotic' tale. As an all-female audience, part of this 'connection' related to the way that Vayu opened up the story by focussing on the figure of Parvati, presented as a dynamic and independent figure of a type that might be found in a feminist re-working of a European fairytale. In this story Parvati takes the initiative both in terms of her relationship with Shiva and, ultimately, in causing a terrible and destructive war. While there is no doubt that Vayu 'composed' the narrative for her all-women audience, the *choice* of story for this context also exemplifies how she works across and 'in between' different cultural perspectives, in ways that encourage the audience to question their pre-existing cultural assumptions – in this case about gender. As she later explained, in contrast to gender roles in many British 'known' stories and in contradiction to assumptions that might circulate in contemporary Anglo- British culture about Indian epics, this tale demonstrates the way that, within such narratives, male gods tend to be 'neutral' and the female goddesses tend to be the ones who '*make things happen*', for good or ill.

At the same time, Vayu was careful to 'transpose' some concepts from the Hindu context, so as to avoid the sort of cross-cultural misunderstanding that supports stereotypes. So for example, instead of describing Shiva in his aspect as the 'Nataraj', through the literal English translation of 'Lord of the Dance', she defined him as the 'God of Physics', after Fritjof Capra in the *Tao of Physics*.[12] This because the literal translation can trivialise and/or create confusion as to this figure's religious and symbolic significance within Hindu culture, and simultaneously undermine some of the potential philosophical and political meanings of this story, when it is told in contemporary Britain.

'Myths' and prejudices surrounding storytelling

This illustration of practice based on ancient myth but embracing and exploring contemporary concerns, which was humorous and entertaining but addressed to us as intelligent and informed adults, prompted reflection on some of the 'myths' and prejudices surrounding storytelling in Britain. For some considerable time, as an art form, it has tended to be mainly associated either with 'pre-literary' cultures or with amateur 'fireside tales', told either in the domestic sphere or in pubs, or, in a professional context, with educational story telling for children.

This has led to an assumption *'that* [it] *worked because it was primitive and simple'*[13] and in addition that it is *'fantastical and not of political or social significance; that is not contemporary and is a reliving of the past'*.[14]

That said, when Vayu arrived in England in the late 1980s, there was a 'revival' of storytelling occurring in Britain. This was initially due to the efforts of practitioners such as Ben Haggerty and the Cric Crac club, which led to the establishing of regular 'Storytelling Festivals', events which continue to flourish all over the country.[15] One of the main aims of this movement was to re-establish the genre as a serious art form and a skilful professional practice that could be aimed at adults as well as children. This revival was later supported by the development of official polices of 'multiculturalism' at national and local governmental levels, with storytelling being promoted as a means of cultural exchange in schools and as part of community events. Vayu became part of both these types of initiative, working alongside British storytellers such as Haggerty, Sally Pomme Clayton and Hugh Lupton, and also Grace Halworth from Trinidad.

Nevertheless, Vayu began to feel constrained by the storytelling festival circuit, artistically and politically. The questions she was grappling with were ones that sought to go beyond the 'official' policies of liberal multiculturalism, which can operate on a superficial level, whereby, as bell hooks puts it, ethnicity can function simply as '"spice", seasoning that can liven up the dull dish that is mainstream white culture'.[16] Already operating within a genre defined by the mainstream as 'folksy, community – not art',[17] Vayu sometimes felt subject to a further *'minoritising impulse'* by funders and programmers, in which she was *'pigeonholed as an exotic, Indian storyteller'*. Moreover, as a part of a 'revival', the British festival circuit sometimes looked back to and celebrated the European 'bardic' and 'troubadour' traditions in ways that could be problematic in terms of gender. In these historical genres storytelling was a masculine profession, on the basis that: *'men as storytellers went travelling and could go off and tell stories about great wars and women were [...] cooking at home'* *[...] The women didn't get to tell the big stories, the women told the little stories.'*

Vayu was therefore negotiating various pressures of categorisation which collectively threatened to define her 'proper' territory as the past, the exotic, the Indian, the traditionally 'feminine' or 'little stories'. In fact, she is more than happy to play on all these things, but always beside their 'opposites', the present, the local, the intra-cultural, the masculine and the 'big stories'. For instance, she says she loved playing on the 'exotic' feminine, *'dressing up like an Indian Princess'*. However, this is again part of a strategy that plays on and 'between' different cultural expectations in relation to gender, so that she will use this guise as a deliberate counterpoint to storytelling that encompasses the immediate, the everyday and the brutal. As all of this suggests, she has a strong awareness of being gendered, even while she subverts and transgresses normative gender roles:

> *Of course I tell stories about wars, but I will have a uniquely woman's perspective on that. Not necessarily always saying women have to bear the brunt and children are the loveliest things in the world. No, there are different kinds of heroisms we can talk about and I think that's never really given space, because, like I said, conventionally the grand narratives were always the place for men to tell those tales. And I think now, with age and time and experience and indeed confidence in the system, that you feel, yes, I can tell these tales.*

Part of this confidence relates to the fact that, in contrast to some other fields where for women performers the physical appearance of youth is at a premium, in storytelling the *'lines on your forehead, the scars in your character* [...] *makes the medium'*.[18]

The programmes of more recent storytelling events suggests that since the 1980s, like many others fields, storytelling has considerably 'opened up' in terms of both ethnicity and gender. In the early 1990s, however, Vayu made a decision to take time out of the festival circuit to work at the Leicester Haymarket theatre as head of an initiative which aimed to commission and produce works designed to attract an Asian audience.[19] While her work at this venue achieved considerable success, she soon felt that: *'There were too many post-colonial hurdles in the Asian English theatre scene* [...] *I had to be true to where I was coming from and emerge with the form that was created by the chemistry of the art forms and practice I was in. Hence a contemporary, intra-cultural, performance storytelling theatre was born.'*[20] Vayu defines this as a performance practice that is *'hybrid, dynamic, mobile, accessible'* and above all, relates *'occurrences from the past to signify new meanings by integrating narratives of the imagination and externalising it to include the reality of our historic moment.'*[21]

Subsequently, Vayu founded the Vayu Naidu Company. As part of its intrinsic 'hybridity', the company undertakes a wide range of different kinds of work embracing school and community projects, festivals and radio work, as well as touring storytelling performance pieces. In addition, the work is formally as well as culturally and thematically hybrid, shaped by the rich mix of the many other performance genres she has investigated as part of her research, and the influence of the artists with whom she has collaborated. As already indicated, like many other story-tellers (traditional and contemporary), despite claiming not to have a musical bone in her body, Vayu often works with musicians and her thinking around her own technique is very much influenced by musical structures. She has frequently collaborated with composer Judith Weir and the Birmingham Contemporary Music Group (BCMG) and with the addition of Sarvar Sabri, a tabla player to this group. Works produced with the BCMG include *Psyche and Manimekalai* (2005), which cuts together an ancient Tamil story about a female monk in the Jain religion with the story of Psyche and Eros. *Nothing But the Salt* (2006) also with the BCMG, draws together stories from the Ramayana with Mahatma Gandhi's celebrated 'Salt March' and was directed by Chris Banfield with projections and photography by Tony Eva. Other Vayu Naidu Company shows include *South* (2003) made in response to 9/11 and influenced by interviews with refugees and with people from various 'South Coasts' (Cornwall, Chennai, South Africa and Greece). While this is a piece designed for studio theatre spaces, it was partly inspired by Vayu's research into 'site specific' performance. Again directed by Banfield, it was made in collaboration with jazz musician Orphy Robinson and dancers, Magdalen Gorringe and Shane Shambhu, who work in an Indian classical dance tradition, and Lia Prentaki, who works in con-temporary dance. The piece travels in time and place, within a frame-work that draws on the medieval British story of *Everyman* but also mixes together tales from ancient Greek myth, Norse legends and Indian epics, in a narrative that takes the hero from Holyhead to Heathrow, Ikea to Sainsbury's. In sum, Vayu's company's shows work between past, present and future, between 'history, memory, fantasy narrative and myth'[22] and through 'processes of "multi-locationality", across geographical, cultural and psychic boundaries'.[23]

Examining the technique

As is clear from this overview of Vayu's career history, she has also always worked 'in between' theory and practice. As part of this method-ology, and in the interests of moving beyond the 'anthropological' para-digms which then dominated the approach to the study of storytelling in Higher Education, after finishing her PhD on storytelling at Leeds, Vayu made several return research trips to India. Her intention was to explore storytelling traditions from the perspective of the contemporary practitioner. This goal was problematised by the fact that in India very few storytellers 'will let you enter their fold because there's so much sacredness involved'. Nevertheless, Vayu was able to spend some time with the Bauls of Bengal, a family whose history as professional singer/storytellers can be traced back for seven generations. Encountering these artists who started to learn their craft 'in the womb', was decisive in making Vayu reflect on the 'building blocks' of her own practice, which up until then had tended to depend very much on 'inspiration':

> That's when I started to feel okay, I must examine what is my technique because I don't want to be one of these people – we have seen her once, don't go back again, because we know her technique [...]. So I started examining what is a folk tale, what is a fairy tale, what is the Western tradition, what is the oral imagination, how do you tell an epic?

These encounters also caused her to reflect on her position as a woman in relation to a profession that in India is still overwhelmingly male-dominated. Amongst the reasons for the scarcity of female storytellers in India is that this practice often takes place as part of ritual and, 'there are certain rites of worship that you can't enter when you are menstruating, and if a performance has been scheduled then, how do you violate these things?' Nevertheless, Vayu did get to work with one of the few women practitioners, from whom she learnt an important lesson: the need to 'go with the energy within your body' even if this is the energy of a body that is tired and in pain:

> It is so important that you function by the physical moment and the energy of your body, you can't step ahead of it because it shows – you'll fumble – because you're racing ahead, you're dragging your body behind. And nobody had told me that in terms of being a storyteller, because people just think you'll come, you'll do your bit, and you'll walk off. In the theatre you have the pacing with other actors, you have a director from the outside, but in storytelling and as a woman, these were things I had to start taking into consideration.

As already indicated, Vayu defines the core characteristic of her practice as something that occurs 'in the moment', in response to a range of variables, including the 'chemistry' with the audience and the energy of her own body. Since, as a result, since she cannot actually rehearse as such, it became imperative for her to have an awareness of the 'building blocks' of her craft and a technical foundation for the work.

Finding the Rasa

In terms of these 'building blocks', it became clear in the workshop that when Vayu employs the phrase 'known story', she actually uses it with several different inflections. It refers to the practice of drawing on epics, myths, legends and folk tales for her 'core' material but also the processes whereby these stories must become 'known' for the storyteller. This means that the story is 'internalised' and owned not through memorisation of a set script, or as a set of abstract concepts but via a connection that does not reject the intellectual but is in the first instance emotional and embodied. It is this emotional, embodied connection that informs the storyteller's improvisation and allows for the creation of what Vayu terms, '*a bridge of sensibilities*' between the tale, the teller and the audience.

In the workshop, Vayu likened her storytelling performance to Jazz improvisation. In making this analogy she was once again finding intra-cultural connections for her audience, although Jazz is, of course, already a 'culturally hybrid' form par excellence. However, when it comes to key concepts in her technique, Vayu draws on Indian 'classical' music. In contrast to British notions of 'classical' music, which usually refers to works from the past, like the Indian epic, this is a tradition that is 'open' and continually evolving.[24] The performer in this tradition draws on and improvises around various '*Ragas*', which roughly speaking can be understood as various 'melodic scales', or particular groupings of notes. Different Ragas signify times of day, seasons and religious holidays and also evoke different '*Rasas*' which refer to emotional colour, feeling, mood or 'key emotional states'. As Vayu noted, in the pan-Indian aesthetic there are nine Rasas, *love, heroism, the comic, disgust, fear, anger, pathos, wonder and peace*. She describes these as '*just umbrella emotions*' and argues that, as such '*they are universally felt across all cultures*'.

In Vayu's storytelling, the 'known' story could be understood as the Raga and she borrows the concept of the Rasa to explain the concept of the '*bridge of sensibilities*'. For Vayu, the Rasa is the '*emotive intention*', the '*emotional juice*' of the story, the '*triggering of emotional resonances that suggest meaning*'. The Rasa also provides the impetus or the '*beat*' of the narrative working through the performer's body and thereby also informing gesture, expression, pace and timing. If all this seems a little 'exotic' and 'distant', we should point out that while she may not 'rehearse', Vayu does admit to '*practising*' – often on her *dog*, which of course, may not be unable to understand her words but can recognise and respond to her energy, emotional intention, or Rasa.

Vayu is insistent that the concept of Rasa must not be confused with the '*sentimental*', nor is it simply an expression of the storyteller's own individual experience and emotion. The Rasa is literally the affect, or as she puts it the '*human core*', of the story that allows the story to be 'transposed' into another culture, across boundaries of time, place and geography. However, in order for the story to become 'known' to the storyteller and for the Rasa to be discovered and performed, the storyteller does have to find a connection between the story and their own experience: '*When you have to identify with an emotion you go back into your history, through your memory. That creates a process of reflection, the reflection creates what we call your interior landscape, your internal geography, there are moods, there are colours, feelings. So it affects the tone of the telling.*'

In exploring the concept of the Rasa in the workshop, therefore, Vayu set an exercise that recalled Stanislavski's notion of 'emotion memory'. Very simply, each participant was asked to think about a time when she experienced hunger, to remember the event in some detail but to focus on recalling the embodied and emotional aspects of this incident. We were then asked to narrate this memory without ever using the words 'hunger' or 'hungry', attempting to convey to our listeners the *feeling* of hunger we had experienced through our bodies, using the expressivity of vocal tone and physical gesture. It was, Vayu explained, the physical and emotional memory of being hungry that should provide the impetus for the telling.

Like many apparently 'simple' exercises, in practice, this was more difficult to achieve than its description might suggest. While all the stories (of meals that were postponed, never arrived, or arrived too late; memories of being ill and unable to eat, etc.) were interesting in themselves, as storytellers we tended to focus on the verbal, using a very limited and rather 'illustrative' and literal indexing of the corporeal (hands on stomachs, bent over, mouths wide open). Where participants did succeed in capturing and expressing something like the 'Rasa' of their narrative, as Stanislavski might have predicted, it was often through concentrating on specific and concrete details to produce less generalised gestures. Interestingly, for some of us at least, grasping and beginning to move towards a means of performing the Rasa, was far easier in a later exercise in which we focused on 'known stories', in the sense of pre-existing narratives, underlining that the 'Rasa' is not purely a matter of the teller's *own* personal, emotional investment.

Address and character

In fact, the Stanislavski analogy made above is misleading because the role of the storyteller is not the same as an 'actor'. Not only are they not working from a set script, they are not 'playing' the 'characters'. Nor are they performing personas based on 'themselves' in the same (but various ways) as Bobby Baker, SuAndi, Jenny Eclair or Leslie Hill from Curious in *Smoking Gun* and *On the Scent*. However, a comparison with these performers is useful in so far as, like these others, aspects of Vayu's technique are reminiscent of Brecht, or rather, a 'postmodern' re-working of Brechtian ideas that are often identified with the process of foregrounding subjectivity and identity to be socially constructed or 'performative'.

Significantly, despite her comments on bringing a *'women's perspective'* to her storytelling, Vayu argues that the persona of the storyteller is *'androgynous'*. This might be understood as one of the effects of the Rasa, since *'umbrella emotions'* also cross gender boundaries. Further, as was clear in her telling of the Parvati/Shiva/Ganesha narrative discussed above, the storyteller's persona functions as an 'anchor'; as a medium *between* the story and the audience. Vayu seems then to speak from a position that moves between 'inside' and 'outside' of the narrative, and she re-presents and comments on the characters in a manner that allows the audience a degree of identification with them, regardless of gender, but at the same time firmly maintaining a distance. This is because she constantly switches perspectives between characters and keeps the main emphasis on the Rasa of the situation and events, rather than on 'individuals'. In short, all this confirms the Rasa of the story as neither a matter of the emotions of the teller, or of individual characters, but pertaining to the meaning or 'core' of the narrative as it unfolds. In any case, many of the 'characters' Vayu presents cannot be fully identified with since they are 'gods and goddesses', or symbolic or mythological figures, who may be *part* of the human but are not themselves entirely human.

Something of this sense of, and relationship to, character was evident in an exercise in the workshop that explored techniques for stimulating the imagination in creating characters. While many of the other practitioners in the workshop series approached this task through asking us to draw upon actual people we knew, it is striking that Vayu focussed on using *objects* we could find in the room. We were given a few minutes to choose the object and to think about it, were asked to describe the main 'qualities' of the object-character to the group and then to find a partner with whom to jointly invent and perform an incident in which our two 'characters' met. In these presentations a transparent plastic cup became a very nice but rather 'empty', dull man, who fell in love at first sight with an exotic nightclub dancer (a ring of keys with multi-coloured tops) in a night club. A flight of stairs provided the stimulus for the character of an energetic young woman trying to escape from her calm and warmly enveloping mother (inspired by the studio's black velvet curtains). As these descriptions suggest, many of us chose to work with a partner whose object-character was in some way 'opposite' to the one we had developed and/or we tended to stress oppositional qualities as a means of making the encounter between them more 'dynamic'. This exercise then offered a strategy for working on characters through abstract properties such as shape, textures and colour, rather than on psychology (at least initially) and in creating the encounter between them the focus was on situation, not motivation. Later, Vayu discussed this work in terms of creating the 'extra-daily from the daily', and as this might suggest, it creates a certain distance from the characters in the process of storytelling.

Interconnectivity and non-linearity

Another exercise that touched on character was based on photographs. Given photos (a clown, a woman in bridal dress walking a tight rope, a donkey and a boy and a man on a beach), we were asked, individually, to write down the stories they suggested with an emphasis on the Rasa or emotional core of the picture. We were then put into groups of three or four to 'edit together' our different interpretations, finding connections between them. Despite the fact that in Britain storytelling is often a 'solo' performance genre, this approach of starting an exercise by working on our own and later editing our ideas together in groups, was a deliberate policy throughout the workshop. Vayu explained this strategy as a means of encouraging us to find interconnections between apparently very different types and styles of stories, a technique that is core to her own practice. Within this, the finding of interconnection is not intended to ignore or foreclose differences, and the 'ensemble' editing does not necessarily aim to produce a single, linear and coherent narrative. Instead, the point is to promote the inclusion of different perspectives and viewpoints and to facilitate structures of storytelling that operate associatively, dialectally or through circularity, as is often the case in Indian and African storytelling. The effect of this approach is evinced in the (video) extracts we have seen of Vayu performing *Psyche and Manimekalai* with the BCMG and with the dancers and musicians in *South*. While in these collaborations the various performers are all clearly working with and through the same Rasa, the different contributions to the whole do not appear to function to 'illustrate', or 'mirror' each other, or to form a synthesis, but rather work 'beside' each other, sometimes associatively, sometimes dialectally.

In the workshop 'photo' exercise, in groups where individual interpretations varied widely (the clown for instance was variously seen as happy, sad and as George Bush), this process of editing together also potentially worked against an idea of characters as 'psychologically motivated' in the sense found in (Western) realism and naturalism. However, as members of this group we found ourselves trying to pull our versions together in a way that made them 'cohere'. Interestingly, the group that came closest to achieving an associative and non-linear structure and mode of performance was the one working with the photograph of the bride balancing on a tightrope. This was perhaps because the image itself was the most bizarre and open to interpretation and/or that this was the most multicultural group, including participants from England, Japan and Taiwan, who therefore, did not necessarily start from a common set of cultural assumptions.

Geography and genre

The individual-to -group working method was also used for the creation of the final presentations, which brought together most of the various themes and ideas in the workshop. This exercise was framed by two discussions on the first day of the workshop and also by a task set as 'homework'. The first discussion was concerned with the 'geography' of particular oral performance traditions and the ways in which they are shaped by environmental factors. In India, storytelling traditionally occurs outside under the shade of a tree, in a village square, or possibly on the move as part of a village festival or procession. These types of spaces allow for the development of an expansive gestural vocabulary and an extension of performance modes that might include music, puppetry and dance. There is also literally 'space' for robust participation on the part of the audience. By contrast, in the Celtic tradition storytelling has tended to be performed indoors, with the storyteller sitting in close proximity to the audience. This restricts movement, placing the focus on the head and hands, producing a far more limited visual, gestural vocabulary and an emphasis on the verbal in terms of interaction with the audience. When a storytelling tradition travels, some of these stylistic and technical characteristics may travel with it. Vayu's inability to perform sitting down (exactly the opposite of SuAndi, for instance), is a consequence she argues, of just such a geographical 'gene'. In pointing out these differences, however, Vayu was also emphasising the way that the immediacy of her contemporary storytelling technique involved a response to the 'physical' environment, in the 'in the moment' composition of the narrative.

In the second discussion, Vayu pointed up the way different forms or genres such as folktale, fairytale, myth and epic might suggest differing styles of performing. Hence the folktale, which is simple and direct, often has a local or familiar setting, frequently embraces humour and includes 'tricksters' amongst its characters. This suggests an informal, colloquial style of telling, using simple language. By contrast, the epic works on a far broader canvas and is concerned with extraordinary events and 'heroic' characters who often meet a tragic end. This clearly suggests a more formal and elevated style of delivery and a sweep of language that matches the scope of the events.

However, Vayu stressed that the contemporary practitioner has the option of either working with or playing against the genre of the story, depending on what she is setting out to achieve. As such, she was once again pointing to the possibilities of non-linear and/or dialectical structuring, of the type that she herself exploits in choosing to perform the 'exotic' feminine as a means of creating 'surprise', in ways that might encourage the audience to question their cultural assumptions about gender. Obviously, meaning shifts when performance registers counterpoint narrative: an epic tale told in the style of a folktale may serve to mock and subvert the heroic, or a fairytale performed using epic style opens up its potential for the tragic.

For some of us in the workshop, these pointers were especially useful. Those of us brought up in a mainstream Anglo culture, where in daily life (large-scale) gestural vocabularies are often limited and storytelling has been dominated by the 'fireside tradition', sometimes struggled in the workshop to find an appropriate and 'natural' feeling physical vocabulary. This exposition provided some useful, formal guidelines to play with. Most importantly when we tried them out we, could *feel* or *realise* through our bodies the way that particular types of language and gesture worked with or against each other, suggested different Rasa and produced varying dynamics in relation to the audience.

Rumplestiltskin and other stories

For the final presentation, each member of the group had been asked to choose a fairy story, epic, myth, or folktale and to consider the style in which to perform it. Rather than focussing on the whole, the instruction was to concentrate on one especially 'dramatic' moment in the tale and on the Rasa it might suggest. When we came to work on these moments, Vayu asked us to form groups of three in which, ideally, each participant was working with a different genre of story. Achieving this mix was impeded by the fact that out of twelve participants, half of us had chosen to work not just in the same genre – that of a fairy story – but on the same story – Rumplestiltskin. It is extremely tempting to speculate on this coincidence in relation to the contemporary experience of being gendered. However, this was more likely a demonstration, evident in all the workshops, of the way participants at such events 'cross infect' each other's creative thinking.

Some sort of mix of genres was achieved in most groups, so that for example one group had *Gone with the Wind* (Hollywood epic), a Taiwanese folk tale that involved an encounter with a snake (or dragon) and Rumplestilskin. Another had Rumplestilskin, Venus and Hercules from Greek myth, and a European folktale concerned with a witch who, jealous of her daughter-in-law, sets her a series of impossible tasks. The idea was that each 'dramatic moment' and its emotional resonance should be edited together in some way with the other two. Once again, the aim was to find interconnections and associations between the apparently disparate, while still preserving the play of difference in the narratives and various performance styles.

While all of these presentations were highly entertaining and/or thoughtful, some groups were more successful in achieving these aims than others. Our enthusiasm led some of us beyond the focus on single dramatic moment to trying to tell the whole, or the most part, of the stories in question. As a result, gesture and movement became imprecise and confusing and tended to stray into the purely 'illustrative' and the literal and hence into 'mime'. When these things occurred the sense of the Rasa and of attempting to create a *'bridge of sensibilities'* between the story, the teller and the listeners was lost. Nevertheless, in terms of the two groups cited above, in the first the Rasa was clearly comic and playful and the stories were edited together in a manner that, while a little confusing, genuinely revealed some unexpected intra-cultural connections through a dialectal structure. The same applied to the second which was very clearly focussed on 'moments' of being trapped and despairing in the face of impossible demands.

A storyteller and a listener: essential requirements

If we appear rather critical of the outcomes of some of the exercises in this workshop, it is not our intention to denigrate the ability or achievements of the members of this group, not least since the least 'successful' attempts were usually our own. Rather, in a British context, in which storytelling has so often been dismissed as 'primitive and simple', we wish to underline the years of research, the skill and the level of experience that informs Vayu's practice, none of which can be approached over a couple of days. The advantage of storytelling is that it can be developed and pursued outside the economic and institutional structures that pertain in most mainstream theatre and in certain areas of 'experimental' performance. In effect, '*a storyteller and a listener*' can be understood *both* as its minimum requirements and simultaneously all that is absolutely essential. As is clear from Vayu's work, and that of other serious and committed practitioners, it also has enormous potential for engaging with serious social and political issues. All the more reason, however, to recognise that '*My God does storytelling work. ... if we know how to do it properly*'. This is not something to be quickly achieved, especially if the aim is a model of intra-cultural storytelling' that seeks to avoid exploitative exoticisation and superficial multiculturalism. For some of us, this might be facilitated by starting with acknowledging and exploring the 'cultural hybridity' of our own ethnicity.

Yet, if we are aiming to underline the ways in which Vayu's practice is not 'primitive and simple', we are not suggesting that 'doing it properly' can be understood or should only be approached through 'high theory', such as that pertaining to the cultural hybridity of postcolonial and/or Diaspora subjects. As noted, Vayu herself works 'in between' theories and practice, but as with other practitioners in this study, it is noticeable that at the point of *process*, she refers to notions relating to the embodied, the experiential, the 'human' and even the 'universal', that might seem problematic within what is, after all, 'anti-essentialist' thinking. Yet in its own terms, the terms of a *specific practice* rooted in the performing arts, rather than cultural theory, like her performances, her process can be said to literally 'embody' the sorts of complex and often deeply contradictory negotiations 'in between' and in excess to differences, to which ideas of cultural hybridity actually refer. If, as Stuart Hall says, the 'Diaspora experience [...] is defined *not* by purity or essence but by the recognition of necessary heterogeneity and diversity'[25] (our italics), this 'impure' heterogeneity and diversity cannot in the theories' own terms, be limited by anti-essentialist theoretical hygiene. There are then 'other ways' of understanding Vayu's practice and process. Nevertheless, these do ultimately suggest notions of identity that, like the Indian classical music tradition and the ancient epics, are constantly evolving through interplay of difference *and* commonality or connection, the present *and* the past, history *and* myth, the modern, the postmodern *and* the 'ancient', the abstract or discursive *and* the experiential, the embodied and emotional. In her process, Vayu works between these dualisms in ways that are sometimes associative, sometimes dialectal, sometimes contradictory, sometimes circular but seldom, if ever, linear or oppositional, drawing on the 'old' and the 'known' to produce something 'new' for each particular audience.

Notes and references

1. For further information and updates on Vayu's current activities see http://www.vayunaiducompany.org.uk/.
2. We interviewed Vayu Naidu on the 31 October 2004. Unless otherwise stated quotes are taken either from this interview, or from comments she made during the workshop held at Lancaster from 29–31 October 2004. For photographs from this workshop see http://www.lancs.ac.uk/depts/theatre/womenwriting/, Events Archive, Vayu Naidu, Performance Storytelling.
3. Homi Bhahba, *The Location of Culture* (London and New York: Routledge, 1994), p. 2.
4. Stuart Hall, 'Cultural Identity and Diaspora', in Nicholas Mirzoeff (ed.), *Diaspora and Visual Culture: Representing Africans and Jews* (London and New York: Routledge, 2000), pp. 21–33, p. 24.
5. Avtar Brah, *Cartographies of Diaspora: Contesting Identities* (London and New York: Routledge, 1996), pp. 208–9.
6. Homi Bhahba, 'The Third Space', in Jonathan Rutherford (ed.), *Identity, Community, Culture, Difference* (London: Lawrence and Wishart, 1990), p. 211.
7. Vayu Naidu, 'Vayu Naidu Company's South: New Directions in Theatre of Storytelling', in Geoffrey V. Davis and Anne Fuchs (eds.), *Staging New Britain: Aspects of Black and South Asian British Theatre Practice* (Brussels: Peter Lang, 2006), pp. 141–169, p. 150.
8. Vayu told this anecdote at the 'Artists' Forum' held at the Theatre Museum, London, 11 November 2006, as part of the Women's Writing for Performance project.
9. See Rustom Bharucha 'A View from India (Peter Brook's Mahabharata)', in David Williams (ed.), *Peter Brook and the 'Mahabharata', Critical Perspectives* (London and New York: Routledge, 1991), pp. 228–52.
10. Vayu Naidu, 'Vayu Naidu Company's South', p. 142.
11. See chapter 4, 'Speaking Out: SuAndi'.
12. As her narrative made clear, Shiva's 'dance' is a cosmic one of creation and destruction which, as Capra indicated, can be compared to the movement of subatomic particles which form the Universe. See Fritjof Capra, *The Tao of Physics*, (Boston Massachusetts: Shambhala Publications, 1999).
13. Vayu Naidu, 'Vayu Naidu Company's South', p. 143.
14. Ibid, p. 144.
15. For further information see the Society for Storytelling website at sfs.org.uk/.
16. bell hooks, *Black Looks: Race and Representation* (Boston Massachusetts: South End Press, 1992), p. 21.
17. Sonia Hughes quoted in SuAndi, 'Africa Lives On in We', in Elaine Aston and Geraldine Harris (eds.), *Feminist Futures? Theatre, Performance, Theory* (Hampshire: Palgrave Macmillan, 2006), pp. 118–129, p. 124. Also see chapter 4, 'Speaking Out: SuAndi'.

18. Grace Halworth, for example, continued working into her seventies.
19. Vayu's own shows at this venue included *Playboy of the Asian World* which focused on stories of Krishna in a framework that drew on J.M Synge's *Playboy of the Western World*. This proved to be controversial with efforts being made to ban the play on the grounds that the construction of Krishna as a 'playboy' was offensive to the religious sensibilities of the local Hindu community. Vayu defended the work by pointing to Hindi and Tamil references that emphasise Krishna's 'playfulness' and the argument was mainly resolved by a change of title to *Krishna Lila: A Play of the Asian World*. These are some of the 'postcolonial hurdles' to which she refers in the main text below. See Vayu Naidu, 'Vayu Naidu Company's South', pp. 147–150.
20. Vayu Naidu, 'Vayu Naidu Company's South', p. 150.
21. Ibid, p. 142.
22. Stuart Hall, 'Cultural Identity and Diaspora', p. 24.
23. Avtar Brah, *Cartographies of Diaspora: Contesting Identities*, pp. 208–9.
24. For basic information on Indian classical music, see http://buckinghammusic. com/ or http://satrangimusic.netfirms.com/.
25. Stuart Hall, 'Cultural Identity and Diaspora', p. 31.

9
Lessons in Bad Behaviour

Jenny Eclair

Jenny Eclair © Avalon 2006

Think 'comedian' and what do you see? A man at a microphone telling jokes. Although it's not the only way of being a comedian, it's seen at the epitome. [...] Women stand-ups do not spring easily to mind.[1]

In contrast to radio (see Chapter 5), which we encountered as the most accessible medium for women to write for professionally, stand-up comedy is arguably the most challenging on account of its gender bias. Stand-up was (and to a great extent still is) the most male-dominated form of popular entertainment. As evidence of women's relatively marginal position in this profession, we cite the fact that until last year only one woman had managed to win the coveted Perrier Award (most prestigious British comedy prize): Jenny Eclair. Perrier Award winner in 1995, for the next ten years Jenny was the first and only woman to be an outright winner.[2]

Jenny Hargreaves trained at Manchester Polytechnic School of Theatre, and turned punk performance poet in the 1980s, adopting the name Eclair after (so the story goes) pretending to be French in a nightclub. '*I trained as an actress,*' Jenny explains, '*but graduated just as all the rep theatres were closing down. Lots of the pub theatres then started to have gigs and I started by doing punk poetry!*'[3] Anarchic, foul-mouthed, 'slapper superstar', Jenny's individual style of punked-up feminine has posed a seriously outrageous challenge to the 'boys own' mentality of the comedy circuit. A fan of the Lucille Balls, the '*real ball-biters with lots of badly applied orange lipstick*',[4] and of the British style of tiny but gutsy northern comediennes like Hylda Baker,[5] Jenny's own comedy brand might best be described as a lethally funny cocktail of loud-mouthed, over-glamorised femininity with a fondness for things northern.[6]

Like other practitioners in this book, Jenny's performance and writing career includes a wide range of media, not just stand-up. Her actress training is one which has served both stand-up and 'straight' comedy acting on stage and in television, where she has made numerous appearances. These include *A Packet of Three* (Channel 4, 1991), which mixed situation comedy and stand-up routines,[7] the hosting of her own series, *Jenny Eclair Squats* (Channel 5, 1995), *Jenny Eclair's Private Function* (Channel 5, 1999), and her contributions to *Comedy Network* (stand-up show, Channel 5, 1997). Jenny, like Sarah Daniels, is a huge fan of radio ('*I've got a face for radio*'), and regards BBC radio 4 as '*the last bastion of the spoken word*'.[8] She regularly hosts radio shows or writes comedy dramas or series often with her long-term collaborator, Julie Balloo. Jenny and Julie had particular radio success with *On Baby Street* that ran for three series (1996–8), a humorous look at parenting with Jenny also playing a darkly comic 'Mother Nature' figure.[9] Mothers surfaced again in her West End theatre roles when Jenny appeared in a collection of monologues, *Mum's the Word* (Alberry Theatre, London 2003, with Patsy Palmer, Imogen Stubbs and Carole Decker). She has also played the loud-mouthed, sex-obsessed, working-class Josie in Nell Dunn's *Steaming* (1997) (a revival of a proto-feminist 1980s drama about a mixed-class group of women who meet in a Turkish baths and unite in a campaign to save the baths from closure). In 2001, she appeared in Eve Ensler's *The Vagina Monologues*,[10] while her own comedy stage plays include *Mrs Nosey Parker ('another bad tempered, loud mouthed blonde, sort of hard bitten but* [...] *a lot sadder than me')*[11] and *The Andy Warhol Syndrome* (Edinburgh, 2004), a solo show which Jenny again co-wrote with Julie Balloo, and in which she played Carol Fletcher (a forty-something, working-class northerner, whose longing to get back to her former, fifteen-minutes of fame as a reality television star, drives her to commit murder). Among Jenny's many Edinburgh stand-up gigs (*'I have a very fringe mentality. I believe in writing little shows and putting them in the backs of vans and going off on the road and doing them.'*)[12] is her 1995 Perrier award-winning *Prozac and Tantrums*. This stand-up routine was filmed live and released on video as *Top Bitch*.[13] In 2000, Jenny wrote her first novel, *Camberwell Beauty* (Camberwell being where Jenny now resides in London), followed by *Having a Lovely Time* (2005). Most recently, her ability to work in mainstream theatre and television has culminated in the huge success of BBC's *Grumpy Old Women* series that has transferred from television to commercial regional and London stages (2006).[14]

Of all the artists in the project, Jenny has the most mainstream profile and is the most successful in economic terms. What makes it particularly interesting to bring her work into this study and to engage with the processes of Jenny's stand-up in the context of our project,[15] is the way in which as a solo practice Jenny's work resonates with that of others, such as Bobby Baker or SuAndi. However, it is also generically different and distinctive, and takes an oppositional gender position forward from her 'alternative' punk performance beginnings, into the commercial mainstream.

Making it in stand-up

[H]ow great a transgression it is for a woman to speak – even just open her mouth – in public. A double distress, for even if she transgresses, her words fall almost always upon the deaf male ear [...][16]

Jenny's 1980s generation of female stand-ups, comedy writers and per-formers set out to challenge the male-domination of comedy. It was a generation that, as Jenny explains, *'managed to create a small dent in the rhinoceros-hide of comedy'*.[17] Facilitating this 'small dent' was the rise of 'alternative' comedy in the 1970s and 1980s, 'alternative' in its broadest sense meaning an 'alternative' to the mainstream club circuit and its long-standing traditions of sexist and racist humour. This is what made it possible for a comedy duo such as Dawn French and Jennifer Saunders, for example, to begin to make a name for themselves, and in Jenny's case it was the mix of 'alternative' punk and stand-up that helped to get her started.[18]

However, it is important to note that this 'small [gender] dent' has not lead to a huge increase in women on the comedy circuit today. Women-in-comedy statistics do not add up, 'stand-up', to much. As a reviewer from the Edinburgh comedy fringe season in 2004 commented, there are now arguably 'fewer female comics' on the circuit than before.[19] Jenny agrees:

> *... I don't know where the thirty-somethings are. People like me, Jo Brand and Hattie Hayridge are all beyond 40. Rhona Cameron's a bit younger, but there isn't anyone else who is well known. The female comics are out there, it's just that nobody is giving them a profile.*[20]

The lack of women in stand-up is an observation that is frequently made, but generally there is little analysis of women's under-representation in this field of comedy. What little analysis there is tends to focus on the hardship for women surviving the rigours of stand-up as an artistic form (the risks and fears of the solo show where everything is down to you to make an audience laugh), coupled with the additional gender complica-tions of moving audiences beyond a tradition of laughter that has been used against rather than for women, and the necessity for women of being as 'macho' as their male counterparts in order to achieve this.[21] Sarah Kendall, emergent Australian stand-up and Perrier award nominee in 2004, has explained that in her view 'although gender did not make a big difference to performers, stand-up had a macho image that put women off': '"We think of stand-up, going into a room and facing an audience as a masculine trait."'[22] Or, as television comedy sketch artist Catherine Tate comments, the attraction of stand-up lies in its appeal to the (male) ego. If stand-up is like saying 'I'm going to play Wembley' then this is something Tate sees a lot of men aspiring to, whilst ques-tioning how many women comics want to 'play' in the same way.[23]

Part of the difficulty also lies, we would argue, with the trouble that women have convincing themselves that they can be funny. Note this observation from Dawn French:

> My best friend is the funniest woman I know in the world but she's got a proper grown-up job. She believes most women are naturally funny – something to do with being observant and sticklers for detail. They just haven't got the bottle or the desire to do it on stage.[24]

The business of stand-up requires lots of 'bottle' and an excess of 'speech': a dependence on the wit, the verbal dexterity of the artist. Yet an excess of speech is something that historically women have been punished for – as nags, scolds, or witches.[25] Mainstream, conservative comedy has tended to 'punish' women for 'speech', making garrulous women into recognisable comic types: the overbearing wife, the nagging mother, or the much-loathed (by husbands) mother-in-law. Similarly, for the more conservative audience, an excess of ('dirty') speech from a contemporary female stand-up – especially in combination with the Eclair style of 'white trash' feminine – can turn her into an object of loathing. Breaking with the tradition of an ideal, silenced, well-behaved and acceptable model of the feminine, the female stand-up risks critical condemnation for her outspoken 'unruliness', a not inconsiderable factor in accounting for why the 'rhinoceros-hide of comedy' is hard to 'dent'.

It was not that these kinds of difficulties were rehearsed in our workshop with Jenny to dissuade women from stand-up, but rather to raise our awareness of the way in which it still represents a gender challenge. With these gender considerations in mind, the processes that Jenny shared in her workshop were as much about writing tips, skills and techniques, as they were about getting a group of very different women (in terms of age, class, regionality, and sexuality) *to have confidence in their ability to be funny*. At the outset Jenny advised us that as women we have to understand that we are a lot funnier than we think we are, or have been given to believe. To persuade us into the comedy zone, Jenny interacted with the workshop group as she would with her audiences: she drew on her unabashed, sexually direct, down-to-earth, and self-deprecating mode of self-presentation. It is a manner that may shock (she was not afraid, for example, to ask women in the workshop direct questions about their sexualities), but she sets about this in a way that generates warmth and affection. You might be taken aback, but the affect is to have you wanting to be taken into her (public) confidence.

Encouraged by Jenny, one of the noticeable features of the stand-up workshop was how much more 'noise' women began to make as a group: how much 'speech' was released; how many stories were told and shared, and how much laughter spread with the growing confidence and dynamic of the group.

A comedy of words

Moving on from the masculine, macho complications of the stand-up business, and turning to the skills of the stand-up that are essential to her 'trade', Jenny began the workshop by setting tasks that encouraged us to become comic-word-aware: to understand the importance of words as comedy tools. We tried, for example, a 'five comedy words' brainstorming exercise to get us to focus on five words that we found funny. The point was not to try and block any words, nor to start worrying about whether something was funny or not. We were not allowed to be judgemental (which you cannot be, Jenny argues, until you have something to be judgemental about). With lists of words to play with we shared them out aloud. This is important in order for everyone to hear the possible sounds, stresses, intonations, and innuendoes that words have to offer. In brief, any playful way of bringing the word off the page can help to make a (comic) difference to how we hear it. Words, we noted, can be funny because of the way they sound (try saying botulism, dollop or orgasmic). Words with hard 'g' sounds seem particularly funny (or at least Jenny thinks so!). Or (very importantly) words can be funny because of the images that they conjure up (bottom, knickers, or fart).

Because the workshop attracted participants from different regions, we also became aware of the way in which accents affect comic word play. As someone who came originally from and trained in the North West of England Jenny 'plays' Northern in some of her comedy routines, and explicitly in comedy character roles, like that of Carol Fletcher in *The Andy Warhol Syndrome*. The qualities of her voice – again crucial for the stand-up – are quite gravelly: a mix of vocal training and cigarette smoking, of which until just recently when Jenny gave up, her stand-up Eclair persona was very proud.

In the workshop, as Jenny got us further into comic-word-sharing and a lot more playground humour, we also became more aware of the 'rules' between 'naughty' and 'nice': the comedy that arises when 'naughty' words get spoken as rules of social niceties get broken – and the 'nicer' the speaker and the 'naughtier' the word, the bigger the laugh. 'Naughtiness' is heavily gendered: fart jokes which are generally funny

(in the 'naughty-playground' style of body humour) may be even funnier told by women, given the idea that women are not supposed to fart
at all. Recognition of the gendered comic potential of the fart makes
Jenny an ardent fan of fart gags. Any interview she gives where there is
just the hint of a squeaking chair and she gets in the 'that's the chair, not
me' line. It is the juxtaposition of the fart and the feminine that makes
these gags work across an age range: from teenage reminiscences of farting on a date (*Prozac and Tantrums*) to the middle-aged woman who just
knows that her body massage treatment will end with her farting on the
masseuse' table (*Grumpy Old Women*).

If you go beyond the 'naughty' playground words into more in-yer-
face swearing – of which Jenny does a lot in her no-holds-barred routines –
then there is the gender shock of hearing obscenities from women. A
technique that Jenny also uses is to mix the two: swearing and play-
ground-style naughtiness in a way that disturbs and discomforts, at the
same time as it delights. The *sheer* delight (based on our audience experiences of her shows) bursts through in those moments in which she
pushes gender proprieties that bit further: the-just-when-you-thought-it
couldn't-get-any-cruder-and-then-it-does moments.

Whether working a quick five-minute slot or a full-length sixty-
minute stand-up show, the performer structures her material by means
of associative leaps – however fantastical, however strange. A stand-up
needs to be skilled at lateral rather than linear thinking, using words as
a means to get you to some place else. As a way of experiencing this,
Jenny had us playing an American board game called 'Spinergy'. We did
not play the game properly (Jenny confesses she has never worked out
how it should be played), rather she used it as a way of picking out unre-
lated words for us and then giving us a set of instructions to follow, such
as you have to speak in rhyme, or you have to speak as a particular character or be in a particular place or situation, or any combination of these
kinds of things.[26] Taking just five minutes, you have to see what lines
and stories you can come up with. The exercise was not about *trying* to
be funny, but rather about seeing how introducing a set of rules or con-
straints pushes you towards the absurd; encourages strange, wonderful,
and silly associations that might offer comic potential.

In terms of working with 'words' stand-ups vary as to how comfortable they feel improvising on the spot, or, alternatively, like Jenny, how
much they need to fully prepare and to script their act. Jenny is someone who '*like*[s] *the physical process of writing*' and has '*always written* [her]
stand-ups in Black n' Red notebooks and ink pen'.[27] She likes word games as
a way of avoiding the horror of finding herself staring at a blank white

page and she also recommends finding someone to write with: someone you can springboard ideas with, or persuade to listen and hopefully to laugh at your jokes. As our introduction suggests, Jenny and her long-term collaborator Julie Balloo have created a highly productive partnership for comedy writing. Comedy writing partnerships are, therefore, Jenny argues, very much to be encouraged.

'Female complaints': a shared experience

Moving beyond the formalistic play of words, Jenny stresses that a stand-up comic needs to think about what subjects will make for a good routine. One of the ways in which comedy works is through the laughter of recognition. An experience shared through telling a joke is funny when the joker and her audience *recognise* the comic situation or story.

A frequent complaint made against women as stand-ups concerns their foregrounding of gendered experience. Female 'body horror', jokes about vaginas, menstruation, the menopause, and so on, often attract criticism on account of the 'horror', or embarrassment factor. Yet these 'female complaints', gender specific jokes and stories, are often the ones that make women laugh because they *recognise* and *identify* with the 'body horror' comedy. Listening to the recording of *Top Bitch*, it is possible to pick out which jokes get the biggest laughs from the women in the audience as those which more often than not identify with a gender-specific topic (the jokes about 'front bottoms' that deteriorate after childbirth – 'labia like a spaniel's ears'); climbing school gym ropes for (sexual) pleasure, or standing over the pulsating water outlet at the local swimming baths. The 'comic relief' of this laughter comes from realising that we are not alone: the indignity of the female internal exam is one women suffer collectively; the period that starts at the most unexpected and inconvenient moment (we've all been there), or the hell of PMT (or in Jenny's terminology 'Premeditated Tantrum') – these are all experiences that many women can identify with and find funny. Recognising these as shared experiences provides a comic release from individualised feelings of shame and humiliation that they often provoke.

Working out of life experiences is, Jenny instructs, a good way to generate material. Life experiences are – as we found in all of the workshops – an important starting point for generating creative material for performance. You only have to think about the ways in which we make people laugh by telling family and friends about the funny things that have really happened to us (truth can be stranger, funnier than fiction). Moreover, we can probably all confess to having at some time or other exaggerated the truth to make an event seem even funnier in the telling, than it was when it actually happened. The more positive the 'audience' response, the more likely we will be encouraged to exaggerate.

An exercise that gets you to think about 'larger-than-life' comic experiences is a 'friends reunited website' task. Pretend, Jenny suggests, that you are writing an entry for 'friends reunited' (http://www.friendsreunited.co.uk/). Enter imaginatively into the person you have become since leaving school and think about what you would like to say to old classmates. This exercise works well for fictionalising life experiences into the realm of the comic and beginning to explore your 'self' as an exaggerated comic persona. Exaggerating a truth in this way mixes up reality and fantasy in the interests of the comic.[28]

Yet stand-up routines may also need more than an exaggerated autobiographical input. When inspiration from life dries up – and as Jenny argues it is best not to sit looking at a blank white page – then you need inspiration or input from other sources. Jenny's own favourites include GMTV (*'the mongers of doom'*) and holiday programmes on account of how holidays bring out the 'bitch' in women. She also enjoys women's magazines which source her topical gags on celebrities and her satirical mocking of commercial femininities. Try, for example, she suggested in the workshop, looking at the fashion pages in women's magazines as an inspiration for the female grotesque (Who would want to be seen dead in *that* dress, or *those* shoes?). Or, alternatively, another tactic is to work with newspapers and to pick on one particular story but to see how it is written up in different papers and then to exploit the comedy that comes from seeing what aspects of a story are those that get headlined or paid attention to. You can take a story straight, verbatim, but then create comedy by trying it out in different voices, intonations, accents, etc.: straight stories and funny styles produce comedy out of a collision of opposites. Or, you can scan tabloid articles for their absurd take on life. Tabloid articles often do not need any grotesquing, like the fashion or beauty material in women's magazines the material 'stands-up' on its own.

A very clear illustration of this kind of comedy sourcing and writing can be found in *Grumpy Old Women* as domestic absurdity 'climaxes' in an hilarious, pre-interval routine based on the *Lakeland* catalogue. This involves the show's grumpy trio faking sexual ecstasy over 'biscuits for one' containers ('your chocolate chip cookies, digestives and ginger nuts won't be reduced to a mass of crumbs'), a 'banana guard' ('Designed to accommodate virtually every size and shape of banana, it's especially useful for slipping in a rucksack when hiking on the fells – after all, a bit of extra energy will always be welcome.') and glow-in-the-dark coasters (exceptionally useful, Jenny jokes, for finding your alcoholic beverage in a power cut). The quotations here about the cookies and banana guard are ones taken verbatim from the Lakeland website.[29] We rest our comedy case.

As fun as all of this is, Jenny cautions that when trawling magazines, catalogues, or newspapers for topics, she has to think carefully about topics that carry a taboo factor and whether and how to reclaim these in comedy. She has to think about whether she can overcome the 'don't even think of going there' factor. In her *Top Bitch* routine, for example, Jenny compares her teenage self to Anne Frank – which is not an obvious comedy topic (though she gets laughter feedback with her punch line that points to the contrast between her 'own' teenage (sexual) exploits and Anne, the girl who didn't get out much).[30]

Blondes have more fun?

If a fading, but enduring image of stand-up has been the 'man at the microphone telling jokes' it is also the case, as we established out the outset, that women have long been the butt of his jokes. Female stereotyping is a mainstay of sexist humour and while earlier we drew attention to the garrulous female types 'punished' through comedy, there is a further comedy favourite that works through the idea of silencing: the dumb blonde. We introduce the 'blonde' here on account of the radicalised presence of the blonde in Jenny's stand-up, and as a means of furthering a more general understanding of how gender stereotyping comes into comedy.

The dumb blonde is usually thought of as a young woman who is supposed to be stereotypically beautiful, but not very bright. She is a creature much sought after by the male sex, but regarded with jealous suspicion by the female sex. Women comedians and stand-ups have looked for ways of 'objecting' to this and to other stereotypes by reworking or reclaiming them in a far more progressive or radical way. Dawn French, talking about *Girls on Top*, her successful female-centred situation comedy from Jenny's 1980s generation, for example, explains that the series had four 'girls' each of whom could be argued as a particular type, but with a 'flip side'.[31] In the case of the 'dotty blonde' character in the show, for instance, the stereotype was used as a form of masquerade for the 'blonde' to hide her cleverness. Blonde masquerades have been plentiful in alternative and mainstream women's performance from Lois Weaver's creation of the ex-country and western singer-turned-lesbian performance artist Tammy Whynot,[32] to the outrageously badly behaved Patsy in the television comedy series *Absolutely Fabulous*.[33] Turning outrageous and bad, the blonde is no longer 'dumb', but rather unleashes the repressed rage or anger of the stereotype.[34]

In Jenny's stand-up performances she uses the '*blonde by choice*' strategy to challenge dominant images of the feminine, the '*soppy*', the '*shy*', the '*fawn-like*', inviting the women ('*girls*') in her audience to agree that's not what she, or they, want to be.[35] Jenny's strategy is perhaps less that of finding a 'flip side' as one of grotesquing the blonde; 'punking the blonde' to effect an 'I'll slap on my lipstick and then kick their ass' style of performance'.[36] Playing into this image is not just the feminine, but also, given her style of 'trash' feminine, class. The general 'overdoneness' of her appearance (the heavy eye make-up, red lipstick, the dyed blond-look, the various glitter-glamour outfits) connects her to the working-class cultures of Blackpool 'glitz', which are also underlined by her northern vocal strains (see above on accents). As Jenny's stage and media career took her away from the North to London (Camberwell), the working-class 'trash' feminine, the blonde (northern) 'roots' of her persona, enable her to play 'outsider' to the London, middle-class circles she migrates to, and which come in for savage satirical treatment in her stand-up and fiction writing. Her inabilities to cook 'posh nosh', to behave properly at dinner parties, or to refrain from drinking too much, for example, are all 'achievements' that the Eclair persona is proud of.

'Comedy faces'

To reclaim the blonde stereotype as an in-yer-face style of subversive, bad girl feminine, Jenny brings her appearance and physique into play, albeit in an exaggerated way. Some physiques are a gift for comedy. At the start of the workshop, for example, Jenny looked around and commented on the number of '*comedy faces*' in the room saying, in her usual direct way, '*you know who you are*'. With blonde hair and glasses ('*I use contact lenses when I'm attempting to be sexy, but my glasses hide the ravages of time*'),[37] and pale skin ('*Without fake tan I have the skin tones of a jellyfish.*'),[38] Jenny frequently jokes about being mistaken for the television actress Su Pollard. For anyone not familiar with Pollard's image, this means (in stereotypical terms) being mistaken for the dumbest of blonds and one absolutely without glamour.[39]

Lurking in the comic anxiety of this mistaken identity is a sense of how the female stand-up often brings her own physical appearance and its 'failure' to meet a feminine ideal into play. The more she 'fails' to met the ideal, the more she can exploit this for comedy. Jo Brand, for example, uses her large body size in a number of her stand-up routines: moving behind and in front of the microphone she cracks 'now you see me, now you don't.' Jenny will regularly make jokes about her own body – her small 'tits' or having cellulite ridden thighs.

Thinking about faces and bodies as comedy tools came to us in the workshop through a very simple exercise in which Jenny asked us all to have a go at writing slogans for T-shirts. In one way this was a quick route to finding some comedy headlines, but it was also insightful for the ways in which the slogans women came up with were often saying something about their own bodies. Here is a quick selection from the group:

> If you think this shirt is bad you should see what's beneath it
> I am not carrying a bomb (to be worn in airports)
> Vacuum cleaners suck
> Down with boobs. They're dropping anyway.
> Remember me ... (front)
> ... I'm forgetting you (back)

In brief, those slogans like the 'down with boobs' gag, or the 'bad' body under the shirt, signal the comic potential of 'exploiting' the body that does not fit the feminine ideal and reclaiming the body through its comic misfit. Jenny also encouraged us to think about personality or character traits that we could 'overdo', exaggerate in the interests of exploring a stand-up personae with some comic 'bite'. Here we (Elaine and Gerry) confess to being much taken with turning menopausal experiences, bodies, moods and rages into outrageous comic possibilities. It provided an opportunity to embody and delight in the monstrous feminine, which, for us personally, became a common point of (autobiographical) reference in subsequent workshops and other of our responses to set tasks and exercises (as indeed was also the case for many other participants coming from our generation). We would argue that the attention to making the feminine monstrous through performance became a constant for us, despite the very different performance contexts which we experienced through the project, because of the way in which a dominant feminine tends to 'discipline' what it is deemed polite and acceptable to 'show and tell'.

Working the monstrous feminine into comedy is also illustrative of the way in which comedy has a darker side. Cruelty, Jenny argues, is vital to comedy. There is no point she says in starting with the virtuous: 'nasty' is what you need to be funny. So in getting us to think about the business of comic stand-up personas she was also encouraging us to think about characters and 'creatures'. In *Top Bitch* Jenny's punk blond celebrates the fact that she is the antithesis of the 'domestic goddess' and promotes herself as a *'pissed up old whore that smokes too much'*. To assume a persona or play a character that is flawed, dark, and yet funny at the same time is an important comic impulse or drive.[40]

To get a feel for the darker side of comedy that Jenny regards as important to her work, she introduced an exercise based on the idea of an 'encounter group'. For this we had to imagine ourselves in an encounter group situation. This was in the style, for example, of 'I am Jane and I am an alcoholic'. So it could be 'I am Helen and I am perimenopausal (so watch out)'. We had to put something of ourselves into this, but then exaggerate it to such an extent that whatever the (awful) problem it became something grotesquely funny. Within our diverse group of women there were any number of painful life stories ranging across acrimonious divorce or separation, 'badly behaved' bodies, or dealing with aging parents, all of which afforded darkly comic opportunities.

Jenny's cue to think about characters in an animalistic, creature-like way is also important for understanding physical comedy and clowning as a component of stand-up. Jenny's stand-up routines bear little resemblance to the stereotypical image of the male comedian at the microphone. Though she has a chair to sit down on, she is rarely seated and instead paces up and down the stage in a breathless style of electric energy. Moreover, her stories are acted out rather than simply narrated, and the acting out requires an extraordinary degree of the acrobatic. To play the female grotesque in comedy unleashes not just 'speech' (the verbal) but also the 'body' (the physical). So a smear test gag, for example, begins to look like a contortionist act: embodies the extraordinary, painfully funny 'acts' women's bodies are expected to perform in real life. This physical clowning points up the grotesquery or absurdity of the routine checking of 'female parts'. It also contributes to Jenny's larger-than-life on stage presence. Though diminutive in frame, her physical energy and manner of taking (up) the whole stage makes everything about her seem, like her hair-dos, that much bigger.[41] It also resists the way in which Jenny argues women are taught to do things *'small'*. In playground behaviour, she says, boys are expected to be tough and boisterous, dominating the playground space, while girls are encouraged to behave, to be less visible and to take up less space. That for Jenny is something to be resisted.

Age and gender

At the end of our workshop, Jenny performed her stand-up gig *Jenny Eclair Middle Aged Bimbo*,[42] and this was particularly interesting to us on account of how we could see how the punk blonde of earlier years had 'matured' into a *'middle aged bimbo'*. In Top Bitch, while Jenny focuses on playing the 'flip side' to maternal 'goodness', her comic material also anticipates her 'mature' blonde:[43] a forty-something woman who thrives on overblown glamour, glitz and guts. If, as Jenny argues, her young stage persona from her punk poetry roots needed to be hard in order to survive in male-dominated stand up, the persona of the aging blonde 'bimbo' has inherited much of that toughness. The backcombed, bleached blonde hairdo (so much hairspray she might set fire to herself, she jokes) with jeans, t-shirt and pointed-toe, glitter shoes mix up, or rather mess up, signs of femininity (the blonde) with an aging female persona that is streetwise, worldly, all-female-body-knowing, loudmouthed and foulmouthed.

If women of Jenny's generation made it into stand-up and broke the taboo on female 'body horror', starting a trend of jokes about vaginas, tampons, or periods, then one of the important topics that Jenny's 'middle aged bimbo' generation speaks to now, is the silence, fear and ignorance of the aging female body. Her jokes transgress the idea of the proper, 'classical body', described by feminist theorist Mary Russo as 'monumental, closed, static, self-contained, symmetrical and sleek'.[44] Instead, this is a badly behaved, leaking, secreting body: there are vaginas that bubble away after having soapy baths or fart during smear tests, while bladders, weakened by age, generate numerous gags about 'Tena Ladies'.

The aging female body is one, however, that is no longer considered desirable, and ought not, therefore, to be visible or talked about. Subversively, however, Eclair opts for the 'practice of risk', a comic playing of 'error'[45] as an aging woman who refuses to acknowledge the boundaries that are meant to regulate her speech, sexual appetite or alcoholic pleasures:

> *Women should lie about their age and act consequently. I'll be walking along Oxford Street like a grown-up and then all of a sudden be sucked into the basement of Topshop and I'm 15 again. But I firmly believe that it's better to look awful than 'look good for your age'.*[46]

Transgressing the 'rules' of 'grown-up', mature behaviour for middle-aged women features in one of Eclair's stand-up stories about her fortieth birthday party: a 'girls' night out in which all of her friends behave disgracefully in an evening spent boozing and cruising for sex – without being able to manage either. (*'There's nothing more scary than a bunch of 40-year-old women on the razz.'*)[47] Such excess parodies masculine pub culture and trespasses against or displaces a dominant representation of middle-aged women as respectable, well behaved and (sexually) restrained.

Through Jenny's stand-up, then, we began to understand how important age and gender are to comedy when used to challenge and upset the 'rules' governing appropriate and inappropriate behaviour. With aging the rules change and women are supposed to be less and less outrageous; less and less visible, which is why inappropriate age- and gender-related behaviour can be so very funny. In the 1990s, for instance, *Absolutely Fabulous* popularised the figure of the badly-behaved, middle-aged mother in need of lessons in good behaviour from her overwhelmingly sensible teenage daughter. More recently, Catherine Tate's foul-mouthed granny in her BBC 2 television sketch show (*The Catherine Tate Show*) is funny because women are supposed to be less and less visible and vocal as they age, and little old ladies are certainly not supposed to swear like troupers, while the *Grumpy Old Women* stage show gives itself entirely over to a riotous celebration of the miseries of aging; a refusal to play the older woman's socially 'scripted' part.

In conclusion, the fun part and the serious point to Jenny's workshop was the way it gave us licence to indulge in inappropriate gender behaviour. She encouraged participants to leave their (feminine) comfort zones, and to risk themselves in being willing to 'show and tell' the beginnings of their own comedy materials that variously worked off sexualities (gay and straight), relationships with elderly parents, or female 'body horror' experiences. With appropriate encouragement from Jenny, everybody was prepared to take that risk. As for Jenny, in her 'mature' stand-up she risks herself as an 'alternative', badly-behaved spectacle of femininity, breaking all the rules of 'appropriate' age and gender behaviour. After generations of comedy that have written women out of, or made them the butt of, laughter, her stand-up is testimony to the idea that not all women are prepared to go quietly. The workshop response to her 'lessons in bad behaviour' suggests that many more women, with appropriate levels of support and confidence, would like to make a much bigger, noisier, 'dent' in the 'rhinoceros-hide of [stand-up] comedy'.

Notes and references

1. Morwenna Banks and Amanda Swift, *The Jokes on Us: Women in Comedy from Music Hall to the Present* (London: Pandora, 1987), p. 1.
2. Jenny's ten-year record was finally broken in the summer of 2005 when Laura Solon won the Perrier Award.

3. 'The Big Interview: Jenny Eclair', http://www.officiallondontheatre.co.uk/news/biginterview/display/cm/contentId/73860, accessed 17 February 2006.
4. Jenny Eclair, 'The Secret of My Success', *Independent*, 18 April 1999, http://www.findarticles.com, accessed 20 January 2006.
5. See 'Forgotten Heroes', Jenny Eclair Interview by Charlotte Cripps, *Independent*, 13 August 2004, http://www.findarticles.com, accessed 20 January 2006.
6. For an explanation of 'things northern' and the implications (of class especially) in identifying with the British North, see Chapter 4, SuAndi, endnote 20.
7. Jenny played a kiosk attendant to Frank Skinner's stage manager at the 'Crumpsall Palladium' owned by Henry (Henry Normal). Although it was successful enough to run to a second series, 'Packing them In' (1992), Jenny does not rate it among her own successes. See 'The World According To ... Jenny Eclair' *Independent*, 19 January 2005, http://www.findarticles.com/p/articles/mi_qn4158/is_20050119/ai_n9692315, accessed 20 January 2006. Series details can be found on http://www.phill.co.uk/comedy/packet, accessed 6 February 2006.
8. 'On the Line: Jenny Eclair' with Barry Didcock, http://www.findarticles.com/p/articles/mi_qn4156/is_19990509/ai_n13937660, accessed 10 February 2006.
9. Details available on line, *http://www.angelfire.com/pq/radiohaha/ONBABYST.html*, accessed 10 February 2006.
10. In the mid-1990s, Eve Ensler wrote and starred in *The Vagina Monologues*, but over the years has had numerous Broadway or West End actresses perform the monologues, either singly or collectively. There is arguably an affinity between Ensler's vagina-centred monologues and the attention paid to the vagina in Jenny's stand-up material. Both performers indulge in an impressive range of vagina naming, though Jenny's is by far the cruder.
11. http://news.bbc.co.uk/1/hi/entertainment/edinburgh_festival/148118.stm, accessed 10 February 2006.
12. 'An Interview with Jenny Eclair', with Ruth Bloomberg, http://www.the-bloomsbury.com/extras/jennyeclair.php, accessed 6 February 2006.
13. Jenny Eclair, *Top Bitch, Live at Her Majesty's Theatre*, PNE video, 1995.
14. Jenny is co-writer of the stage show (with Judith Holder who wrote and produced the television series) and performs the show along with Dillie Keane and Linda Robson.
15. Jenny's workshop took place in Lancaster, 30–31 January 2004. Quotations and explanations by Jenny that are not assigned a referenced source are from this event.
16. Hélène Cixous, 'The Laugh of the Medusa', in Elaine Marks and Isabelle de Courtivron (eds.), *New French Feminisms* (Brighton: The Harvester Press, 1981), pp. 245–264, p. 251.
17. 'The Big Interview: Jenny Eclair'.
18. In 'Making it Funny', *Spare Rib*, June 1987, no. 179, pp. 15–21, Morwenna Banks and Amanda Swift explain:
    'Alternative' comedy grew up in and around London in the late 1970's and early 1980's, and was basically a reaction or 'alternative' to the often racist, sexist and reactionary humour of traditional stand-up comedy and light entertainment. It coincided with the Punk movement in music, and had a

similar anarchic and subversive impulse, seeking both to shock the audience out of social and political complacency, and to entertain them. (p. 17)

19. Dominic Maxwell, 'Bold Kendall willing to stand up and be counted', *The Times*, 26 August 2004, p. 24. Oliver Double's recent publication, *Getting the Joke: The Inner Workings of Stand-up Comedy* (London: Methuen 2005), also confirms this. In a 'glossary of comedians' totalling 65 only six are women.

20. 'The Big Interview: Jenny Eclair'.

21. For further discussion of this point see Stephanie Merritt, 'Outside the Box', *New Statesman*, 25 August 2003, http://www.jocaulfield.com/Interviews/FemaleComedians.php, accessed 26 February 2006.

22. Explanation quoted in 'Heard the one about the woman who makes them laugh?', Jack Malvern, *The Times*, 26 August 2004, p. 24.

23. Catherine Tate quoted in 'The Catherine Tate Show', http://www.uktv.co.uk?uktv=standarditem.index&aID=528100, accessed 17 February 2006.

24. Dawn French, interview in 'Making it Funny', Morwenna Banks and Amanda Swift, *Spare Rib*, June (1987), no.179, pp. 15–21, p. 21.

25. Stand-up Jo Brand is quoted as saying '[t]he feminist female comedian is a sort of, you know, a witch in some ways', in Oliver Double, *Getting the Joke*, p. 153.

26. Alternatively, there are lots of ways you can do this. You could get someone to pick out words at random from a dictionary, or if there is a group of you brainstorm lots of different words on bits of paper, then jumble them up, put them in a pile, and allow yourselves to pick out three without seeing what they are. Ditto the instructions. For a response to the 'Spinergy' exercise see WWP project website, http://www.lancs.ac.uk/depts/theatre/womenwriting, Events Archive, 'Women in Stand-Up', Jenny Eclair.

27. Jenny Eclair, 'Pieces of Me', *Guardian*, 27 June 2006, pp. 16–7, p. 16.

28. For a Friends Reunited example, see WWP project website, http://www.lancs.ac.uk/depts/theatre/womenwriting, Events Archive, 'Women in Stand-Up', Jenny Eclair.

29. See http://www.lakelandlimited.co.uk/product.aspx/freshcool/containers.

30. For further discussion of this point, see Oliver Double's 'Challenging the Audience', in *Getting the Joke*, pp. 139–171.

31. The four 'girls' in *Girls on Top* were the 'feminist', the 'loser', the 'American' and the 'dotty blond'. French explains about the character types and the 'flip side' strategy in *Putting Women in the Picture*, presented by Helena Kennedy, broadcast on BBC 1, 1987.

32. For a clip of Lois's Tammy in action visit clips on the WWP project website, http://www.lancs.ac.uk/depts/theatre/womenwriting/, Events Archive, International Symposium 2006.

33. Patsy is played by Joanna Lumley, co-staring with Jennifer Saunders. *Absolutely Fabulous* has been broadcast on BBC television and has run into five series since 1992.

34. For a visual encoding of the repressed rage of the 'blonde' see photographer Cindy Sherman's Untitled # 122 (1983), reproduced in (among many sources) Jo Anna Isaak's *Feminism and Contemporary Art* (London: Routledge, 1996), p. 197.

35. '*Soppy*', '*shy*' and '*fawn-like*' all take a comic hammering in *Top Bitch*.

36. This quotation comes from Lauraine Leblanc's *Pretty in Punk: Girls' Gender Resistance in a Boys' Subculture* (New Brunswick: Rutgers University Press, 2000), and is the title for chapter 5 on 'constructing femininity'. This chapter examines the difficulties for western women who are 'forced to play a no-win game of femininity' (p. 135), and the contribution 'punk girls' make to 'expand[ing] what is permissible in mainstream femininity' (p. 164). This is analogous to Jenny's 'punk girl' personae that challenges 'mainstream femininity' through stand-up comedy.

37. Jenny Eclair, 'Pieces of Me', p. 16.

38. Ibid.

39. Pollard is most famous for her role in the BBC television comedy series, *Hi de Hi!* (1979–1988) In which she played the role of holiday camp cleaner, Peggy Ollerenshaw.

40. In *The Andy Warhol Syndrome*, for example, the role of Carol Fletcher is one of the not-so glamorous forty-something woman from Yorkshire, with a failed marriage, two grown-up children and a job working in an old people's home. Although comic in style, the comedy grows darker as Carol is driven to murder Ronnie Marsden, a newly-admitted resident to the old people's home where Carol works and someone Carol knew and idolised as a young girl as variety club performer Rene Marguerite. In killing Ronnie/Rene she exits in a blaze of media publicity and attention.

41. Jenny makes jokes which draw attention to her big hair-dos which she also sees as important to her stage persona:

    My hair is very thin and very small naturally, so when I am not working I tend to put it in plaits and look like Heidi with a premature ageing disorder; then if I want to do the full-blown Eclair that requires a big hair-do.[...] I think big hair requires respect. It's a tradition that comes from Nashville, where rather insignificant women would use rhinestones and big hair. (*Independent*, 31 August 1998, http://www.findarticles.com/p/articles/mi_qn4158/is_19980831/ai_n1416 4807/print, accessed 20 January 2006.)

42. Performance in the Nuffield Theatre, Lancaster University, 31 January 2004.

43. One of the ways that stand-ups work is to evolve new shows out of routines from an existing show. For further discussion of this, see Oliver Double, *Getting the Joke*, 'The Dangers of Roll-Over', pp. 241–2.

44. Mary Russo, *The Female Grotesque: Risk, Excess, Modernity* (London: Routledge, 1994), p. 8.

45. Ibid., p. 13.

46. 'The World According To ... Jenny Eclair', *Independent*, 19 January 2005.

47. 'The World According To ... Jenny Eclair'.

10
After the Event

As the purpose of this book is to allow the different workshops with project artists to be presented 'beside' each other, and resisting the convention of pulling this work into a final 'thesis' style of statement, we propose instead to conclude our study with a more open-ended style of reflection. With this in mind, we have opened up our joint voice with individual moments of reflection: 'deleted scenes and out takes' that are more personal to one or other of us, rather than formally discursive. As a through-line, however, our aim is to draw attention to what, in the final analysis, feels important to us in respect of our post-project understanding of how the processes of making work within radical and political frameworks also offers a way of 'creating' connections between women, that potentially are productive for making change – socially, culturally, theatrically. To rehearse this point and to offer our final reflections, we focus in particular on the communities of participants in the project.

A question we found ourselves asking in the planning stage of the workshop series was to what extent would there be an interest in a project like ours? Do emergent women academics and practitioners (of all ages) working or wishing to work in the fields theatre and performance still feel the desire or need for the sort of support structures produced by feminism that were so crucial to women of our generation?

> Gerry: *After the Artists' Forum in London a young woman speaks to me. She tells me that she is just doing her first (professional) show at Battersea Arts Centre. She is working with another young woman as a director but she says how important this event has been to her. What I gather from her comments is that hearing Bobby, Vayu, Marisa, and Curious tell their stories has given her a 'context', creatively and politically,*

a sense that she is not just 'out there on her own', that she is part of something – a continuity and a community. I often feel in need of these things myself but for years I have been reading accounts by journalists who insist that 'today's young women' are now so confident and assertive that they no longer want or need the types of support structures feminism offered to my generation.

During the three-year life span of the project, close to 300 women artists and scholars participated in events.[1] We had over 300 applications to participate in one of the thirteen workshops that formed the core of the project and we were able to offer 115 of those who applied places on one of the workshops. As these figures show, for each and every workshop the demand exceeded the number of places available. The participants came from all over the UK and were from a diverse range of ages, social and ethnic backgrounds. The AHRC funding meant that we were able to offer the workshops and the London Artists' Forum for free and to heavily subsidise places at the International Symposium in Lancaster, making events open to those without institutional support and on low or no incomes. Whilst 35 per cent of the participants in the workshops were scholar-practitioners (either teaching or completing postgraduate study in performance studies at HE institutions around the country), a further 65 per cent of participants were aspiring or emerging artists drawn from the wider community. So the answer to our question of whether there was a desire and need for such a project was at the most basic level, overwhelmingly – yes.

> Elaine: *I remember two things very clearly. Firstly, the utter surprise, disbelief and sheer joy that we actually got the funding for a women's project. Secondly, that the general enthusiasm for the project once it started was brilliant and yet at times painful – for instance, when we did not have enough places for everyone and knew that we were turning women down, which was always the case for each and every workshop. There were also the moments of being overwhelmed by the enthusiasm of the participants who would ask us for even more workshops. (A lovely idea or ideal, but practically impossible for us to manage with what we were doing already). Putting these reflections together, I want to say that all of this means that there's the enthusiasm, desire and hunger still for theatre women to get together (look at the way the Magdalena Project has kept going in some shape or form all of these years) – and I would love more women to take heart from this – to go out there and make things happen.*

Of course, the hunger for 'space' in which to make work is fundamental to all practitioners, whatever their interests, whatever their practice. Yet some of the strongest and most moving responses to these events came not just from the aspiring or emerging artists, but more surprisingly (to us), from some who might be regarded as fairly or even extremely well 'established'. It was also repeatedly the case that participants were attracted to the women-centred nature of the events. The opportunity to work with and/or listen to and/or speak with the project artists and to each other, countered a general feeling of isolation and uncertainty exacerbated by the tendency towards solo work that we note in the introduction. The workshops enabled the participants to situate their work in relation to a community of creative and diverse political interests that was too often missing from their working and/or daily lives. They were enthused by the artists who time and again were viewed as important and much needed role models; practitioners who could offer them practical advice as well as creative, political, even life-changing inspiration.

> Elaine: *In another life I'd love to be a stand-up. The sheer no-limits pleasure of being so 'funny- bolshy'. Academics, female academics, or rather female academics of a certain age, are expected to behave. So I loved the bad, monstrous feminine behaviour; the licence to simply let rip through comic play. There's not enough of this in women's lives generally. We need the Jenny Eclairs of this world to give us a kick up the comic arse and remind us of what we are missing.*

Fundamental to the acquisition of knowledge and skills offered by the project artists was the way in which the workshops provided a safe space to rehearse ideas in a context that, while never simply or naively uncritical, increased rather diminished confidence. This was due in no small measure to the artists themselves: their sensitivity, generosity and skills as practitioners believing at all times and at all levels in the creativity of others. Yet it was also down to the way the participants responded to these artists – and to each other – in kind.

> Elaine: *The work that participants produced was often moving, funny, painful, surprising, disturbing. In the mix and mess of such wonderful creativity, I confess that there were moments in the workshop when I found myself wondering (just as I am now writing this conclusion) can I do this, can I really do this? It may be a cliché – and I know Sarah warned us about clichés – but I find myself resorting to one here: you*

> *don't know what you can do until you try. That's not to say those self-censoring gremlins don't keep rumbling away – troublesome little (and sometimes rather big) bug***s that they are – but you have to let them go and when you do the energy and creativity that comes with that is astonishing.*
>
> Gerry: *Can I add to this? I'm not very good at 'letting go'. I didn't always manage it in the workshop and I think the same applied to most people. Sometimes it was obvious that while the stuff we were producing might be 'good', it was clearly within the limits of what we already knew we could do, or felt 'safe' with, and/or were exploring without really taking on what was happening in that particular space and time. I'm certain of this because you could so clearly perceive (see it, hear it, feel it) when someone, or the whole group, or you yourself, did truly 'let go'. These points were exhilarating to experience whether as a spectator or a participant. While they eventually informed individual presentations, their genesis only occurred when we opened ourselves up to the process, committed to 'being in the moment' together, so that they were something that happened between us.*

It would be foolish of us to try to pretend that all the workshops were equally satisfying and successful for all participants, or that they were all totally harmonious experiences. Tensions – political, creative, personal – did arise and required constant negotiation. Yet, coming together in time and space, embodying practical experience and knowledge, involved us in the development of skills and performance ideas in a group context that affected how techniques and ideas were shaped and transformed. However distinct and different, by the end of each and every workshop, whether we were always aware of it or not, we had formed a 'temporary community'.[2] This because a key factor of the workshop environment was always a focus not just on doing but *doing with and for each other*.

Of course, in writing this, we are once again stating the blindingly obvious: doing with and for each other and a sense of 'temporary community' are intrinsic to all kinds of theatre and performance processes and practice. What was distinctive in these particular instances was the way in which this doing with and for each other was shaped through the structures provided by the workshop leaders – structures that embodied their (common and various) political interests and concerns. As we state in our introduction, in setting up the workshops we invited practitioners primarily to share their *processes* for making work, rather than to explore their own (or anyone else's) political agendas, feminist or otherwise. However, what we came to realise more fully through the *practice* were the ways in which the process and the political mapped together. In brief, and we hope this is clear from individual chapters, even though the project artists may beg, borrow or steal techniques from a wide range of sources, their processes and practices *cannot* be separated from their politics, which in turn are shaped by, but not confined to, their own 'personal'. Within the workshops, then, however much there was space for individual creativity and self expression, or an emphasis on drawing on personal material, because the processes were always informed by (to borrow from Lois) the principles of imagining, making and *changing*, they generated a 'temporary [politicised] community' amongst the participants.

After the event, once a particular workshop was over, it was possible for these 'temporary communities' to stay in touch with each other, through private email correspondence or on public electronic lists or through other project events such as the Artists' Forum in London and the International Symposium at Lancaster. The political impact of the 'temporary communities' was very much in evidence at this latter event. Attendees who had not participated in workshops remarked on the overall sense of a genuine and positive desire for exchange, understanding and dialogue, as opposed to the entrenchment of ideological divisions that can easily occur on such occasions.

Interactions at both of these events also indicated on-going performance collaborations and connections. It was inspirational to us to hear news of how some of these women were keeping in touch and developing performance pieces with the help and feedback from artists and other participants. In addition to this kind of informal contact and networking, the project was also instrumental in seeding Factory Floor, a new network of female solo performers/writers.[3]

> *Gerry:*   *Like many women (and men – feminism's tendency to be self- critical should not absolve our male colleagues of responsibility), I started my career in Higher Education with a determination that 'we' could change this institution from within. Too often nowadays I am filled with a sense that we made too many compromises and ultimately the institution changed us. Sometimes it seems that not only has there been little alteration in fundamental values but they have become increasingly conservative: we are more competitive and hierarchical, less open and cooperative. Maybe that's just my age speaking. But there were moments in the workshops and at the Symposium when we interacted with each other in ways that revived my belief that it is possible to do things*

differently in practice as well as in theory. Without the practice (social and political as well as theatrical) what is the point of the 'theory'?

As we state in our introduction, getting closer to practice through these 'temporary communities', getting close to the participants' local, embodied stories or histories – feeling, being surprised or being moved by them and, through process, becoming a part of them, did bring us back to feminism. Or rather this made us want to ask questions of feminism which was why, at a mid-point in the project, we published *Feminist Futures?: Theatre, Performance, Theory.*[4] In this collection, we invited practitioners and scholars participating in the project or having some connection to it, to debate the uncertainty that appears to hang over feminism in our contemporary moment. Mirroring our experience of the workshops, a theatre and or performance context provided the conduit for a number of different feminist views to sit 'beside' each other: a series of reflections, dialogues, questions, but without an agreed agenda or overarching thesis – our point being that feminism was no longer something we can assume or take for granted, but that we need to reflect on, question, and in particular ask what feminism is, could or should be *doing*?

Elaine: *I felt moved emotionally and politically by the talk that theatre journalist Carol Woddis gave on the Sunday morning of the Lancaster Symposium. Carol talked openly and generously about her precarious position as a theatre reviewer in a contemporary moment when professional journalism is made increasingly vulnerable by the way in which anyone and everyone can now post what they think about shows on the web, at the same time as the circulation of newspapers diminishes. She raised this general issue while also stressing the difficulty in getting women's work noticed. There may be more women reviewing today than when Carol started in the profession years ago, but less reviewing space and the pressure to 'sell' a show to arts editors (which may mean 'sexing up' a women's show) actually makes things harder. As Carol talked, the response from women artists in the room was that they very much needed reviewers like Carol who would give their work consideration – especially when performing outside the mainstream. To be 'noticing' each other's work as practitioners did in this and other of the symposium sessions, and to be understanding the personal and professional vulnerabilities of making, performing – or in Carol's case reviewing – was a powerful reminder of strengths that may come from women dialoguing, supporting and 'doing' for each other.*[5]

Given the responses of our participants to the project, then, finally, we might state that this evidences that there *is* still a need and good political reason for women to be making connections to each other, in the interests of imagining, making and changing. Creating structures of practical support, identifying communities of creative and political interests, potentially is far more empowering than working in (solo) isolation. In the apparent absence of feminism as a high-profile movement, theatre as a public, community-building forum, offers an alternative route for 'making' these kinds of contacts, connections and friendships.

> *Elaine: We could not have done the project without each other. It was hard labour really finding out how someone else works – their tempo, rhythm, interests, thoughts, views – and then finding how you can map that with your own approach to the work, and vice versa. I am not certain whether in the book, despite the textured voices, ours and those of the artists, this comes across; all the negotiating we had to do for the project generally and the book specifically.*
>
> *Gerry: Yes – as I kept gabbling after the Split Britches workshop, this project stretched our boundaries, but ultimately in a positive way. But I do wonder if we have managed to get across that although a serious project, one of the main reasons it was such a highlight for us ...*
>
> *Elaine: one that we said at the Symposium we would look back on in our dotage with affection and a real sense of achievement ...*
>
> *Gerry: was because (most of the time) it was such sheer bloody fun. There was so much humour and laughter at all the events, ranging from weeing the pants raucous and outrageous to the quietly witty and rueful. Of course this is totally the terrain of embodiment and of 'being in the moment' and so impossibly difficult to communicate retrospectively in writing. But without the laughs (to grasp for a metaphor) the work would have been like potato crisps without salt: still edible, but no where near as enjoyable.*
>
> *Elaine: Good point to end?*

Notes and references

1. Although the workshops were open to men and women, in the course of the three years only three men chose to attend the workshops and three (including two of our colleagues) attended the international symposium, despite the pre-advertised presence of a number of internationally acclaimed academics and practitioners.
2. 'Temporary communities' is a term that we are borrowing from Jill Dolan, 'Performance, Utopia, and the "Utopian Performative"' *Theatre Journal*, 53

(2001), pp. 455–479, p. 458. Dolan is talking about the 'temporary communities' that come together for a theatre event and argues the transformational possibilities that might arise from this; the ways that seeing theatre together potentially can help us to imagine and see the world differently in more hopeful, politically progressive ways. Although Dolan is discussing the experience of seeing a show, we have borrowed her idea to argue the progressive, transformational possibilities that might arise out of the 'temporary communities' that are forged in the process of making work.

3. The founding members of Factory Floor are: Louie Jenkins, Abi Lake, Emily Underwood, Clare Duffy, Lena Simic, Kerstin Bueschges. They explain:

   As a result of several conversations with numerous female artists, all of whom were taking part in at least one of the Women's Writing for Performance workshops, we, the six initiators of this network, came to realise the importance of a forum for solo practitioners. The network's intention is to meet on a regular basis, give its members a space, both an actual place for rehearsals as well as a place for discussions with each other, to explore, share and develop work both in writing and performing. The meetings will be hosted at different locations throughout the country.

4. Published by Palgrave Macmillan, 2006.

5. For further details of Carol's talk and the responses to it see the archival film footage on our website, http://www.lancs.ac.uk/depts/theatre/womenwriting/.

Index